Battery Park City

Battery Park City

The Early Years

CHARLES J. URSTADT WITH

GENE BROWN

To order additional copies of this book, contact:
Xlibris Corporation
1-888-795-4274
www.Xlibris.com
Orders@Xlibris.com
25791

CONTENTS

DEDICATION

This book is dedicated to Elinor, my dearly, beloved wife of 47 years, who was my bulwark during the twelve years I spent on Battery Park City and without whose help I could not have sustained the effort that it took. And to my children, Charlie and Cathy, who lived with this project during their early years. Unfortunately, the demands of the project on my time meant less time spent with them while they were growing up. My deepest gratitude to all three of them.

Acknowledgements

F irst and foremost, to those people who are still around and who directly or indirectly were involved in the creation of Battery Park City, my heartfelt thanks.

The real force, without whose contribution, influence and vision Battery Park City would not exist, was the late, great Governor Nelson A. Rockefeller, who took an earlier, tentative, and incomplete plan for a mixed use project on the shores of the Hudson River and gave it life. His brother David Rockefeller led the charge to revitalize downtown Manhattan by creating the Downtown Lower Manhattan Association, and lent his enthusiastic support to the Battery Park City project through its difficult early years.

Always, there was my dear long-time friend Bob Douglass, who in 1966 talked me into joining the Rockefeller team when he was the governor's Counsel, and later worked closely with, and supported us when he was Secretary to Governor Rockefeller. He was and remains my associate and confidante, whose friendship I very much treasure.

Also, to Al Marshall, the Governor's Secretary, and the late, great Perry B. Duryea, Speaker of the Assembly during our stormy birth. Many thanks to them for their help and support in overcoming numerous political obstacles.

Neither Battery Park City nor this book could have been completed without the dedicated help of Avrum Hyman, who served as Deputy Commissioner in the Division of Housing and Community Renewal and who most ably and professionally handled the public relations for the Authority after its creation. His help has been invaluable as a good friend and editor of this book.

I worked on a regular basis with Gene Brown, who is the "stem-winder" for this venture and the real "worker" of this history. Gene is a writer of enormous talent who submerged himself into this story to such a degree that he felt he was almost a part of it. My heartfelt thanks to his partnership in this venture.

Charles J. Urstadt

Introduction

"It's glorious, isn't it?" the woman said to me as I entered Governor Nelson Rockefeller Park at the northern end of Battery Park City. It was the first balmy day in early spring, and she was entranced by the glittering view of the lower harbor. Surely it must be a very special vista to prompt a New Yorker to speak to a total stranger.

Battery Park City *is* a special place, and superlatives have come easily to those who have written about it. It is one of the most significant "new towns" ever built in America, constructed by private developers on landfill with an infrastructure financed by the sale of bonds by a state-created public benefit corporation.

Its successful mix of attractive office and residential buildings was one of the major contributors to the revitalization of New York City's downtown. It's also paid off literally. The Battery Park City Authority, the public benefit corporation that was the driving force behind the entire development, is in the black and, indeed, generates more than $100 million a year in profit—altogether more than $1 billion, so far—without the city or state having a cent invested in the venture.

The development is even rich culturally. It's bookended on its south end by the Museum of Jewish Heritage, which has the most important collection memorializing the Holocaust outside of Washington D.C.'s Holocaust Museum, and on the north by the new home of Stuyvesant High School, which most years sends more graduates to Harvard than any other high school in America.

Amidst parks, sculpture, and apartments providing homes for almost ten thousand people, most of whom walk to work, stands the New York Mercantile Exchange and the imposing World

Financial Center. Within the shouting distance of young children on scooters and adolescents on skateboards are long town cars, waiting to whisk executives to their next appointment.

But if anything truly merits superlatives, it's the public amenities that grace this "city" extending out into the waters of the Hudson River from Lower Manhattan. On a summer Sunday, its long and graceful esplanade hosts thousands of bikers, hikers, and people out for a stroll along the river. The area is thronged at lunchtime. And after work on any pleasant afternoon, Battery Park City's yacht cove is ringed with workers unwinding after a busy day, and its harborside restaurants are crowded with diners enjoying the spectacular view.

The city's financial powerhouses charter yachts with names such as *Royal Princess* and *Excalibur*, anchored in the cove, for business-promoting cocktail and dinner parties. But you don't have to be rich and powerful to enjoy what the development has to offer. The indoor concerts under the high-arching crystal vault filled with palm trees and bright flowers, part of the World Financial Center just behind the cove, are free and open to the public.

Signs on the esplanade caution bikers and skaters: "Yield to Pedestrians." But one of the marvels of Battery Park City is that the whole development actually does that. Here in the heart of Lower Manhattan, on the island that the automobile long ago conquered, the public spaces have been planned for people on foot. The spaces are broad and open, the streets just wide enough to provide necessary vehicular access.

Already, although building continues on its several empty lots, Battery Park City has become one of New York City's outstanding landmarks, attracting foreign visitors as well as tourists from around America as one of Gotham's must-see sights. As with any landmark, it now seems to own the space it occupies. Despite the evident newness of everything in the development, its component parts are beginning to take on an air of inevitability.

But the truth is that there was nothing inevitable about the development of Battery Park City. Every element of it was a battleground over which politicians and planners fought. In fact, this marvelous and extremely valuable asset to America's greatest city might just as easily have remained a useless watery site dotted by abandoned piers.

That's the point of this book. There's something deceptively inevitable about land, steel, and concrete. With the passage of time it becomes harder and harder to imagine that the land wasn't always there, that the buildings could have turned out any other way than they did. They have a way of becoming part of the natural order of things. And their imposing physical reality almost requires an extraordinary act of the imagination to conceive that they might never have been built at all, that the land which these tall buildings occupy might never have existed, and that something else, such as rotting piers, could have occupied the space.

Yet between the idea for a development and its final realization, there is a world of pitfalls and possibilities. New York City is replete with unrealized plans for major projects, such as the East River's Manhattan Landing and Riverwalk. Even in a single building, the product of one developer, one architect, and one builder, there are likely to be many revisions between the original plan and the final reality. Building codes, the interplay of building site and building material, the changing real estate market, and the vagaries of personality and personal agendas among the principal participants, to mention a few factors, would make this so.

And if government is involved, as it certainly was in the Battery Park City project, politics is added to the mix. Before the idea of Battery Park City could be embodied in land and buildings, there was New York City's mayor, the Board of Estimate, City Council, Planning Commission, and the borough presidents with which to contend.

But imagine we are looking at a site that is first and foremost, under water, with only a few large, crumbling piers to disturb the fish's domain! On that site an ambitious plan calls for not one simple building, but a complex of residential and commercial buildings, parks, schools, and cultural institutions at the edge of the world's greatest financial center—a development that, if built, will be a landmark in urban planning. If it succeeds, it will do so after similarly ambitious projects involving the transformation of the waterfront, such as Manhattan Landing, have gotten nowhere.

Imagine as well that this potential project, in the eyes of some, is meant to cure or stave off a series of economic and social problems as well as turn a profit—possibly conflicting aims that could infinitely complicate the task of even getting the land created. Conjure up such a project in which the engineering difficulties begin with the fact that the "land" on which it will be built is still submerged; the financing is a huge question mark; and the political, bureaucratic, and environmental obstructions that must be navigated are enough to make a pilot boat captain's hands shake at the till.

Most of all, try to imagine guiding this mammoth undertaking through a narrow channel while subjected to a treacherous undercurrent of petty political machinations involving tortuous turf battles, the always chancy proposition of private enterprise and government effectively working together, labor-management conflict, social unrest, and personality clashes.

I don't have to imagine any of this; I've been through all. And believe me, the outcome of the plan to develop Battery Park City was for a long time far from inevitable.

For twelve years, beginning with my appointment in 1967 by Governor Nelson A. Rockefeller as a New York State Deputy Commissioner of Housing and Community Renewal, later as commissioner, and in 1968 as the first chairman and chief executive officer of the Battery Park City Authority, I was bound up in the process of turning the dream into reality. We got Battery Park City under way after a decade of countless committees, reports, and various plans for the area had produced not so much as an acre of land, a single door or window, not to mention housing and work space for thousands, and public amenities such as the magnificent esplanade that grace the site today.

Just as important, maybe even more so, but less dramatic and visible to the public, we kept the project alive during a devastating real estate recession and held off a host of politicians who would have been pleased to "deep-six" the development.

Those years of public service were a time when my family would certainly have been better off financially had I been engaged instead in the private enterprise of real estate, my primary profession.

As with many who have served the public, I have battle scars. I anticipated a certain amount of them, for surely they come with the territory. I did not enter the fray expecting an easy time of it. Nor do I need any bronze plaques to mark my accomplishments and massage my ego.

But neither did I anticipate that the rewriting of history after my term of service would make virtually a cipher of those of us whose positive role in literally remaking the geography of Manhattan—for the better, most people have concluded—calls out for recognition. Or that our achievement would be almost erased from the public record and even sometimes denigrated by people who either don't know the full story or who have an axe to grind. That I cannot accept.

The official Battery Park City Web site, where even a *New York Times* reporter went for background information for a recent page-one story, is a case in point. The site's timeline, when I began this book, gave the distinct impression that virtually nothing had happened at Battery Park City during the entire decade of the 1970s except funding of the project and completion of the landfill on which it was to be built. Those are the only two entries for the period. The Web site plays down the significance and complexity of the construction of the bulkhead and landfill, without which there would have been no buildings or parks, just water and pilings, as was the fate of New York City's proposal for "Manhattan Landing" in the East River.

In fact, although both the bulkheading and landfill were substantial and difficult accomplishments to bring off, there was a lot more going on that was essential to keeping Battery Park City viable. The creation of Battery Park City has been as much, if not more, a story of political rivalries and obstructions overcome, a social whirlwind survived, and personal interests and passions surmounted, than it is a tale of blueprints, bulldozers, and bonds. The full story is a human one, with all the interest of a good novel. The problem is that too often the official, public story has had not only the engaging quality of fiction, but its characteristic inventiveness as well.

I'm aware that many people who have participated in great enterprises, with the best of intentions, aggrandize their own role. That seems to be a basic human frailty. I am keeping that at the forefront of my consciousness as I write.

Yet given the unique perspective it was my privilege—and often my onerous burden—to have on the development of Battery Park City, I think I owe it to history as much as to myself and to those who worked so hard with me to tell this story from the inside as best as I can.

Chapter 1

DOWNTOWN

In the spring of 2001, a small barge floated off the southern end of Battery Park City near the lower tip of Manhattan. A sign on deck identified its task: "Timber Sheeting Remediation." As is the custom with such signs, it also bore the names of public officials under whose authority the work was being carried out. The third name beneath that of New York State Governor George Pataki was mine.

The story behind what that barge was doing there and why my name was where it was has as much to do with New York's economy and political culture as it does with engineering; it's as much about the clash of big egos as the erection of tall buildings. It's quite a tale, with a fascinating cast of characters, and conveniently, that barge was moored near where it all began, a long time ago.

Beginnings

New York City has always looked up, and not just up toward the tops of skyscrapers. Geographically it literally grew upward, beginning at the southern tip of Manhattan and expanding progressively to the north.

It's hard to believe from our present perspective, but even the theater district was south of city hall until the middle of the nineteenth century. Manhattan's business community, anchored by shipping and related enterprises, was also concentrated downtown in the early years of the republic. So rapid was the expansion of the shipping industry at the end of the eighteenth and beginning of the nineteenth centuries that New York had to extend its waterfront through landfill on both the Hudson and East rivers. This led to the creation of West Street on the western edge of Lower Manhattan, an entirely new thoroughfare. Fifteen wharves extended out from it by 1810, three years after Robert Fulton began the first regularly scheduled steamboat service from a point near what would be the World Trade Center.

Not far from what is now Battery Park City, between Broadway and the Hudson, wealthy merchants built four-story mansions, creating on the Lower West Side New York's most fashionable neighborhood. They lived in high style, and they could walk to work, a privilege that even the wealthiest New Yorkers whose business was downtown would not have again for another two hundred years.

Gradually, with the growth of commerce and manufacturing, people of lesser means occupied housing on the fringes of the business district—notably on Greenwich Street—in homes that ranged from modest to truly dismal. Small businesses of all kinds, many related to shipping, joined warehouses, counting houses, and coffee houses to create a busy, noisy place. The merchants who prospered from the sea trade that was this natural port's lifeblood wanted to remain close to their businesses, yet also desired a more peaceful place to live. Consequently they began to move north and established America's first suburb with their elegant brownstones just across the river in Brooklyn Heights.

Halfway through the nineteenth century, New York City was beginning to resemble the great metropolis it would become. In the 1830s the city surpassed Philadelphia as the nation's financial capital, and "Wall Street" began to take on its modern connotation.

Shipping still provided the foundation of much of the city's economy. Between 1821 and 1836 alone, the city's share of America's export trade had risen from 38 to 62 percent. On one day in 1836, an observer counted 320 vessels moored in the Hudson. Fifteen years later there were more than fifty piers on the West Side below Fourteenth Street, many of them handling transatlantic steamships. They were numbered consecutively, beginning from the Battery, a practice New York had adopted at the beginning of that century.

After the Civil War, the Lower West Side remained a beehive of commercial activity, focused on the freight that often arrived now by rail for transshipment. Cornelius Vanderbilt's freight terminal, which the Commodore erected in the area in 1868, had seen to that.

By the end of the nineteenth century, New York had become a great manufacturing city, as well as a center of commerce and finance. Skyscrapers were rising downtown while commerce, industry, and housing slowly pushed up Manhattan Island toward its geographic center. The first great apartment house had already been erected on what was to become the city's Upper Westside. But so remote did it seem at the time that it was called the "Dakota," evocative of the distant Western territory of the same name.

By 1900, city hall found itself south of much of the island's commercial development. The garment center was on Canal Street, small industries had been developed many blocks to the north, millionaires had built their mansions on the now fashionable Fifth Avenue, offices were slowly spreading uptown, and in midtown, on Forty-third Street, Adolph Ochs was building a headquarters for his newspaper that was to turn Longacre Square into Times Square. In the same neighborhood the theater district, which had paused in Herald Square on its trek north, was about to put down its permanent roots in "the Great White Way."

Subway construction in the first two decades of the new century led to the building of decent, inexpensive worker's housing in Brooklyn, the Bronx, and Queens, a phenomenon in which my grandfather participated, building and buying apartment houses in the Bronx. For laborers and the clerks and middle managers, whose importance in the city's commerce was growing rapidly, the commute by public transportation had become the norm. To the north in Westchester, west across the Hudson in New Jersey and east, in nearby Long Island, new, attractive, affluent suburbs housed those whose position higher up in the corporate hierarchy enabled them to live away from the noise and crowding of city life. Grand

Central Terminal, opened in 1871, was already handling 100,000 passengers each day.

All this growth and movement, especially after the opening of the Erie Canal in 1823, had made the buying and selling of real estate itself a major part of New York City's commerce. Property values rose in an almost unbroken line, becoming an important factor in the location of business and housing and significantly influencing the bottom line of companies whose headquarters or manufacturing facilities stood on land that had become increasingly valuable.

Yet in the midst of all this dizzying change one thing remained constant, at least through World War II: New York City was still a great seaport, its harbor crowded with ships—as late as 1914 the home port for more than 3,600 vessels—and Manhattan's shoreline continued to be broken by the piers that jutted out from it up and down the island. The streets leading to those piers were filled with wagons—later trucks—and the cheap saloons that catered to and comforted the army of laborers who loaded and unloaded the freighters, as well as the crews of those freighters themselves.

Downtown Eclipsed

By the early 1950s, when I first worked as a young lawyer on the nineteenth floor at 115 Broadway overlooking the Hudson, Downtown Manhattan had long since taken on the specialized role of the city's financial center. The New York Stock Exchange and other institutional supports for America's finance capitalism, notably major banks, occupied its tall buildings. Great insurance companies also loomed over its narrow streets.

But those buildings, with their ornate interiors, were becoming obsolete. The financial district's famous narrow canyons were hopelessly crowded. And the commute, which for most people involved at least a brief ride on the increasingly dilapidated subway, was becoming insufferable.

The financial district's chief product was mostly intangible or symbolic, represented by columns of figures and brightly colored stock and bond certificates. The now aging piers around the edges of the district increasingly had less of a connection to the businesses conducted on Wall Street and its environs. In fact, many were abandoned and deteriorating, with sections dropping into the river, serving as nothing more than flotsam and jetsam. Fires on the unused piers had become common.

Filling in the edges of the financial district was a hodgepodge of housing and retail businesses. "Radio Row," a center for small stores selling electronic equipment and parts, typical of the retail specialty areas that dotted Manhattan, prospered. And some run-down housing, mainly in the area's northern periphery, remained.

After World War II, changes in the development of midtown and new trends in the city's economy were bringing into question the economic viability of this downtown real estate mix. Midtown, a center for American corporate headquarters, the hub of the city's shopping, and the entertainment capital of the nation, was even beginning to attract some of the financial business that had been Downtown's mainstay. Staffed by workers who were now increasingly commuting to Long Island, Westchester, and New Jersey after work, firms whose demand for office space had previously bolstered real estate values below Chambers Street were now locating and relocating to the modern glass-enclosed, post-World War II skyscrapers that were so convenient to Grand Central Terminal and Penn Station.

From the Brooklyn Bridge south, things were not what they used to be, even if nothing much seemed to have changed on the surface. The Fulton Fish Market, for example, smelled as bad as it ever did. But if you held your nose and looked at it from close up, you noted a transformation that reflected the old seaport's metamorphosis. Most of the market's fish now came in by truck from elsewhere, not off local boats.

The New York Stock Exchange, the anchor and symbol of Wall Street, was looking for new headquarters, and not necessarily in the old neighborhood. The financial district, its building stock aging, its commuters from New Jersey inadequately served by the bankrupt Hudson and Manhattan railroad (popularly referred to as the Hudson Tubes), and development elsewhere draining away the businesses that had created the value of its real estate in the first place, was beginning to experience a crisis of proportions potentially huge in terms of dollars and cents. Certainly that's how David Rockefeller of the Chase Manhattan Bank saw it in the mid-1950s as he broke ground for his bank's new corporate headquarters in the midst of this disturbing flux.

Under the circumstances, One Chase Plaza, the bank's new sixty-story home, would have been a questionable undertaking had not Rockefeller been paying attention to the area's changing environment. If, as the old saying goes, location is everything, then he had to be sure that his bank was going up in a place that had a future. Guaranteeing that future would require government and private enterprise to cooperate in bringing big changes to Downtown. Fortunately there were city planning precedents on which he could draw to help effect these changes.

The Roots of Renewal

In June 1956, with the development of One Chase Plaza commencing, David Rockefeller announced the formation of the Downtown Lower Manhattan Association, of which he was the first chairman. The DLMA represented Rockefeller's hope that the heads of the greatest financial, banking, and insurance institutions in the area, acting in concert, could positively influence the neighborhood's development by proposing their own large-scale solutions to the problem of reintegrating Downtown into New York City's changing economic order. The Seaman's Bank for Savings, Morgan Guaranty Trust, Lehman Brothers, and the New York Stock Exchange were among the organizations represented in the DLMA.

The DLMA initially cast its role in broad terms, hoping for a general renewal of the downtown financial district and convenient housing for the 350,000 people who worked there. Its vision of apartments from which employees could eventually walk to work mainly encompassed the East Side, but as the *New York Times* noted, it did include "possibly some new housing *near* the Hudson River." [Italics added.]

Two years later, on October 14, 1958, the DLMA presented the city with a forty-eight-page report that filled in the blanks. Put together by Skidmore, Owings & Merrill, architects and engineers, the report boldly proposed to redevelop 564 acres of some of the world's most important real estate at a total cost of $1 billion. To facilitate this transformation, the report suggested that the city raze many of the small, older buildings that dotted the area, close streets where necessary, and relocate four thousand people then living in the area's nine hundred units of older housing. But the plan did not mention landfill.

In submitting the report to then New York City mayor Robert Wagner, DLMA Chairman Rockefeller acknowledged its audacity. "We realize that all challenges bring some hardship," he allowed. The report was also to bring in its wake a series of often competing plans for the same area from various groups and individuals, each with its own agenda, generating countless column-inches of newspaper coverage for schemes that went no further than the drawing board. The DLMA report would turn out to be the opening gambit in a decade-long struggle among politicians, planners, bureaucrats, and business people to impose their will on the gateway to America's most famous and important city.

Almost immediately, one of the players spoke out. Vincent A. G. O'Connor (some say "A. G." stood for "Almighty God"), New York City's commissioner of marine and aviation, jealously guarded his piers from even the thought that cargo shipping might be passing the city by for New Jersey. Perhaps misinterpreting the thrust of the document, he immediately endorsed the DLMA report. O'Connor expressed his belief that the plan would preserve Manhattan's Lower West Side piers, changing them only with repairs and improvements. Apparently he didn't read the text of the report. In it the DLMA had referred to "the shipping industry which may be replaced in the course of general development."

O'Connor, like King Canute, might just as well have tried to personally prevent the tide from going in and out. It is certainly clear in hindsight, and would almost surely have been evident to anyone who objectively viewed the situation by the late 1950s, that the handling of cargo freight on Manhattan's docks was becoming an increasingly smaller part of the city's economy. The numbers made the case. In 1925 Manhattan handled 51 percent of the cargo that passed through the entire port of New York. By 1964, that figure would drop to 21 percent.

The decisive reason for this decline was the kind of automation peculiar to the shipping industry: the consolidating of cargo in large containers, which replaced the smaller break-bulk crates and boxes previously used—a trend that was beginning to accelerate. These new containers were eight feet high, eight feet wide, and twenty to forty feet long, and held about twenty tons each. Huge new container ships could carry at least a thousand of them. They required many fewer longshoremen to get them aboard and take them off the giant vessels, and could be brought, fully loaded, by truck from hundreds of miles away.

The image of small crates, bundled in netting and hoisted into a cargo hold, was becoming an anachronism. Using containers, cargo could be loaded for as little as one-tenth the cost of doing the same thing piece by piece. Instead of taking a week to load, a ship could be filled with containers and on its way in two days or less. What's more the cargo was sealed, preventing wholesale inventory depletion or the accidental breakage of, say, cases of liquor—a la *On the Waterfront*.

This new shipping method required expensive oversized modern cranes at dockside to lift the containers from the flatbed trucks that could deliver them right to the side of the ship, as well as space to stack and store them. The piers themselves now had to accommodate the enormous container ships that carried their cargo stacked high on their decks as well as deep in their holds. The Port Authority of New York and New Jersey was going to put big money into container port facilities to meet these new challenges, but it would target the money for Brooklyn and the Newark-Elizabeth area on the New Jersey side of the harbor, not Manhattan, where space was at a premium in every sense of the word.

Meanwhile David Rockefeller's DLMA urban renewal plan was making some headway, helped by the support of a mayor's committee that included City Planning Commission head James Felt and Robert Moses, who had already left his substantial imprint on the face of New York. The Board of Estimate, then the city's governing body, approved the plan in principle in January 1959 but wanted to sign off on every component of it as it came up. By June, elements of the report had entered the city's Master Plan of Arterial Highways and Major Streets.

While the Rockefeller report was building, if nothing else, a paper trail, the private construction of office space downtown had picked up. Between 1947 and 1958, rentable office space grew by only 3,660,000 square feet in the area. But when 1959 began 5,861,000 square feet of space was under construction. Clearly many people still saw Downtown as filled with potential rather than as merely a played-out area. David Rockefeller, of course, was one of them, and his new Chase Manhattan headquarters contributed significantly to these figures. It would be completed in 1961.

The Port Authority Enters the Picture

When it came to Downtown Manhattan, the Port Authority definitely saw the glass as half-full. Now, with the encouragement and support of New York's governor, Nelson A. Rockefeller, David's brother, it was determined to fill that glass. Its new building project would play a major role in changing the area, and in the process, without knowing it, literally help lay a small part of the foundation for Battery Park City.

On January 26, 1960, the Port Authority announced plans for a single fifty- to seventy-story office tower on the East Side, south of the Brooklyn Bridge, near several housing projects that were already in the works. The authority included an adjoining hotel in its plans. But New Jersey withheld its necessary cooperation, holding out for a better commute for its residents, who arrived in Downtown Manhattan by rail on the Lower West

Side via the aging "Hudson Tubes." To satisfy everyone, the Port Authority moved its project westward and added a new terminal for the commuter line, which it would also take over. The development also became more ambitious. It would rise as twin towers, 110 stories each, at the edge of the Hudson River.

The agency behind this behemoth was unique when formed by New York State and New Jersey in 1921. Under pressure from the Interstate Commerce Commission to settle various disputes between themselves over issues that clearly transcended state lines and jurisdictions, the states created a bistate agency to guide the development of the entire 1,500-square-mile area. Among other things, the Port Authority's charter authorized the new body to build just about anything it deemed necessary to help it perform its duties. In time that provision would turn out to be an all-but-blank check to build the then tallest buildings in the world.

But the potential to create such a development could not have been realized without a fortunate confluence of political and economic factors. Nor would it or the adjoining Battery Park City have gotten under way without the efforts and vision of Nelson A. Rockefeller, an extraordinary political figure, whose penchant for building would so often be unfairly attacked.

It was an auspicious time for such a project. New York City's mayor Robert Wagner would be up for reelection in 1962, and he was all too aware that the city had lost about two hundred thousand jobs since 1950 as service industries replaced factories. The World Trade Center construction project would create jobs—many of them—as did several large state-sponsored housing projects in various stages of planning or development at the time, such as Rochdale Village in Queens and Co-op City in the Bronx. The mayor was a natural ally in the remaking of the Lower West Side.

The huge number of construction jobs to be generated was important as well to Harry Van Arsdale, who ruled the city's Central Labor Trades Council. Jobs were the currency with which he bought the support of his members, and the Port Authority's project figured to make him positively rich with jobs.

For Nelson Rockefeller, whose first job out of college was to work at his family's landmark Rockefeller Center development in the 1930s, building big and bold came naturally. He had allies in the Port Authority who thought just as he did, since he had already appointed several of its members. Rockefeller, too, had a political career to nurture, with his sights set on a higher goal than a governorship. Those twin towers and the construction jobs they generated earned the republican governor the support of the construction trades. To the general electorate they would be a vivid image of his commitment to the future. This project was also an opportunity to bolster and augment his brother David's plans for the broader downtown area. David had invited this support when his organization's updated plan for Downtown, revised at the beginning of 1960, specifically called for the Port Authority to consider building a world trade center as part of the renewal process.

Housing

While the retention of businesses and the jobs they provided was the prime motivation for officials in both city and state governments to advocate downtown renewal, housing also gradually came to play a role, although it was something of an afterthought when it came to the West Side. Nearby housing would attract and retain the employees that Wall Street required. Building such housing on a large scale might also create opportunities to partly solve the larger problem of coming up with decent, affordable and convenient apartments for citizens in all income groups, a long-standing goal of Rockefeller's governorship.

In the abstract, the use of downtown renewal to help solve the general housing problem might appear to have made sense. But the reality was more problematic. The question was, housing for whom? Where should these apartment units be built and under what circumstances? As always, the devil was in the details. Everyone was in favor of "more housing." But favoring housing in general was to support—not to mention actually build—no housing in particular. There was always a choice to make: middle income, low income, luxury, a mix? And if it were a mix, how would the units be allocated among income groups? How would that affect the general real estate market in the area? Would the housing be self-sustaining? If not, how would it be funded? Failure to adequately answer that last question would result in nothing being done. You could depend on it.

The federal government had first gotten involved in housing during the Depression when, understandably, the emphasis was on affordable housing for lower- and middle-income groups. After the war, pressure built for more government action as returning GIs starting families created a serious and much-publicized housing shortage. Some states and municipalities responded creatively to the crisis, making it possible, for example, for nonprofit corporations to build veteran's housing. New York City added rent-control to its mix of housing policies in 1943, a wartime approach that may have made sense at the time but would cause considerable problems of its own down the line with which I would one day be assigned to deal.

Labor unions and insurance companies were already involved in financing construction of large projects, usually with some kind of assistance from government. Metropolitan Life Insurance Co., for example, built Stuyvesant Town in New York City in the mid-1940s at a cost of $112 million after New York State passed a law making it easier for private enterprise to build on land previously occupied by tenements. The law kept real estate taxes constant and limited developer's profits. Over an area covering eighteen blocks, Metropolitan Life put up thirty-five thirteen- and fourteen-story buildings, adding almost nine thousand middle-income rental apartments to the city's housing stock. So successful was the project that by the time families began moving in in 1947, the insurance company was already involved with the building of Peter Cooper Village, just to the north, with somewhat larger apartments and slightly higher rents. In fact, my wife and I lived there for several years.

On the federal level, by the late 1940s, pressure was building for action. In response to government reports and statistics that documented the housing shortfall but left all the action to alleviate it to the cities, New York City's feisty mayor Fiorello LaGuardia snapped in 1945, "We ask for bricks and stones and plumbing, and they give us a mimeographed press release."

Relief came with the passage of the federal Housing Act of 1949, the famous "Title I" program, enacted with the notable backing of Ohio's Republican senator Robert A. Taft. Title I made federal money available for slum clearance and urban redevelopment. First the bulldozer, then the construction crane, would change the face of much of urban America, "renewing" our cities over the next several decades until disenchantment with the economic and social consequences of many of these developments put a crimp in enthusiasm for large-scale projects.

But in 1959, Title I was still very much a factor in renewal and, in fact, Robert Moses, then chairman of New York City's Slum Clearance Committee, suggested that as part of the redevelopment of Downtown, a seven-block area at the tip of Manhattan, just east of Battery Park, was primed for a Title I project. With somewhat less precision, he also alluded to plans for a future development he called Battery Park North.

If anything, housing became an even more important issue as the 1960s began. On the state level, Governor Nelson Rockefeller moved to strengthen New York's Mitchell-Lama program, named for its sponsors, State Senator MacNeil Mitchell and Assemblyman Alfred Lama. Enacted by the state legislature in 1955, Mitchell-Lama encouraged developers to build middle-income housing with state- or city-backed mortgages and twenty-year exemptions of the added value from real estate taxes. The law also limited developer's profits. Co-op City, the nation's largest apartment house development, with 15,500 units, started by my predecessor as state commissioner of housing, James W. Gaynor, and finished during my tenure as commissioner, would be built under its provisions, as would Rochdale Village, Trump Village, Starrett City, Concourse Village, and the Bridge Apartments, among many other similar developments.

In 1962, Governor Rockefeller signed legislation substantially bolstering the program, increasing the lending authorization of the State Housing Finance Agency from $500,000,000 to $1 billion. The legislation also set up a pilot program to enable low-income families to move into middle-income housing.

Increasingly for Rockefeller, housing as a political as well as economic issue was becoming tied to the embattled middle class, which felt itself squeezed out of the market for decent, affordable apartments. This issue would draw even more of the governor's attention in the decade as his presidential ambitions became clearer.

Race was also now becoming a factor in housing. In July 1963, Rockefeller formed a committee of experts to study charges of racism in the allocation of construction jobs as well as, ultimately, apartments, in state-financed housing. The building of still more housing, providing more jobs to go around, would be one way to deal with the jobs issue—although the resistance of the unions to anything approaching what we would now call affirmative action was a major problem. Also on the table were proposals to fight segregation by mixing middle- and lower-income families in state-financed projects.

Middle-class housing also loomed ever larger in New York City politics. Six months before Mayor Wagner would be up for reelection in 1962, Milton Mollen, chairman of the city's Housing and Redevelopment Board, announced that the city would diminish the role of "luxury" housing in urban renewal projects. (At issue at the time was the building of the Kips Bay Apartments, which I had worked on as a lawyer with Webb & Knapp and its leader, the legendary William Zeckendorf.) From now on the emphasis would be on apartments for the "middle class."

Although politically attractive with an election looming, this policy would have less appealing economic consequences in the long run. The city's finances were already being undermined, a condition that would not be evident to the public until the crisis of the mid-1970s. The so-called luxury housing Mollen was referring to, such as the Park West Village, Lincoln Towers, and Kips Bay Plaza projects, then being planned or built (and all of which I was involved with at Webb & Knapp), actually housed middle- and upper-middle-class residents and made the best return to the city.

A Faulty Step

David Rockefeller's DLMA spawned several visions—in some cases of excessive grandeur—of a new Downtown. A significant one was behind the Department of Marine and Aviation's study of the downtown area by consultants under the leadership of Ebasco Services. Participants in this project included Moran, Proctor, Mueser & Rutledge, engineers, and Eggers and Higgins, architects. Their three-hundred-page report was made public in April of 1963.

The urban renewal development this plan called for would continue into the twenty-first century and involve projects along the Hudson River waterfront stretching from the Battery to West Seventy-second Street, including a new convention center. Especially interesting was the proposal that the city add landfill to the area between the Battery and Chambers Street, new land that would contain eighteen apartment buildings and eight office buildings on top of shipping container port facilities. The container ships would dock parallel to the piers at one of six berths, under the buildings. The development also included a yacht basin.

The suggested use of landfill reflected an irreducible geographic fact that would have to be accounted for in any large-scale plan for housing in New York City. Appropriate, economically feasible tracts of sufficient size in the city were becoming scarce in all but its periphery, such as the north Bronx, where Co-op City would go up, or the eastern edge of Brooklyn, site of the future Starrett City. In fact the committee that Governor Rockefeller appointed in 1963 to study state-financed housing would propose that new middle-income projects be built on platforms using the "air rights" over publicly owned piers, highways, and bridge and tunnel approaches. The Bridge Apartments over the highway approaching the George Washington Bridge in Upper Manhattan is one example of this approach.

The projected cost of the downtown section of the project proposed in the Department of Marine and Aviation's report was $320,500,000. On the one hand, said Mayor Robert Wagner, the project would be "one of the most exciting and significant undertakings of its kind in the city's entire history." On the other hand, cautioned Wagner, the proposal was only "exploratory."

In fact the plan lacked a vital part: a realistic strategy for financing and executing the vast development. It would be the Battery Park City Authority that would ultimately make this vision a reality.

The Department of Marine and Aviation's plan also included an anachronism that alone was enough to sink it. Much of it was window dressing that cloaked the department's persistent attempt to preserve New York City's, and especially Manhattan's, central role in the shipping industry. Pier renovation was at the head of Marine and Aviation's agenda, but it did not reflect the direction in which the port's economy was moving: toward New Jersey and elsewhere.

By the mid-1960s, the Manhattan piers were relics of another age. Of the fifty-one piers still in existence on both rivers, only eighteen were in regular use. The rest were in various stages of decay.

Moving Closer

Meanwhile, in November of 1963, David Rockefeller updated the DLMA plan for Lower Manhattan. He revised the cost of his plan upward to $2 billion and suggested that it would need to be implemented over a period of twenty-five years. Like the Department of Marine and Aviation, he now suggested the possibility of building housing on landfill below Chambers Street. But in a telling point, his revised plan called for the demolition of the piers on the Lower Westside.

Seven months later City Planning Commission Chairman William F. Ballard echoed Rockefeller's sentiments, advocating affordable housing and parks, but not piers and commercial establishments, on the city's waterfront. Ballard had replaced James Felt in 1962 as the head of the commission. An architect who had been active in zoning reform, Ballard had actually designed some of the city's housing projects.

In September 1964, the City Planning Commission formally responded to the Department of Marine and Aviation's grand plan for renewing Lower Manhattan. It called that plan's proposal for new Hudson River piers "unworkable." It was way too costly given the value of the real estate and the inexorable technological revolution caused by containerization. Just the increased truck traffic containerization would bring meant unsustainable levels of congestion in surrounding streets. Pointedly, the commission said that the Department of Marine and Aviation should not have the responsibility for renewing the city's shoreline.

The commission also identified another factor militating against the city's commitment of funds to such a large-scale project, a factor that would have explosive repercussions a decade later: pressure on the city's capital budget mandated a minimum of new projects of this scope.

Mayor Wagner, signaling the end of an era of the city's dominance of the port, endorsed the City Planning Commission's evaluation of the Department of Marine and Aviation plan. Looking at the bright side, the mayor described the replacement of piers with parks and apartment houses as "opening windows on the waterfront."

Wagner also expressed some understandable edginess over the persistent production of words about, rather than the construction of, more new buildings in the downtown area over the years. He acknowledged, "Traditionally in New York planning of itself has been no major problem. The library shelves are filled with plans."

In fact, some of those plans were about to become reality, but not on Wagner's watch. By the summer of 1965, New Yorkers were turning their attention to the election of a new mayor. Whoever would occupy city hall over the next four years would play a major role in the configuration of the renewal of the Lower Westside, assuming such a thing would ever come to fruition at all.

Liberal Upper East Side Republican John V. Lindsay, who would capture city hall, did not initially signal interest in reconfiguring New York City through large-scale projects. He had a different approach to the economic and social imperatives of the second half of the twentieth century. During the campaign, in the spirit of certain planners of the 1960s, Lindsay seemed to be advocating that planners think small. Vest pocket, government-assisted housing in existing neighborhoods was his signature proposal, nook-and-cranny planning his forte.

But would thinking small deal adequately with the accelerating flight of the middle class to the suburbs, eroding his city's already imperiled tax base? Would thinking small allow the city to cope with an increasingly restive working class and poor population, also making its needs clear? The riots in Harlem in the summer of 1964 had punctuated the racial aspect of this burgeoning problem. These were hardly vest-pocket kinds of problems.

At the end of 1965, two weeks before he was to help precipitate a devastating transit strike on his first moments in office, the mayor-elect was presented with a federally financed report on the city's urban renewal efforts. The thrust of the report was that housing in poor neighborhoods would have to take precedence over housing for the middle class. The report, entitled "New York City's Renewal Strategy/1965," said that renewal had to be focused in "the Harlems and Bedford-Stuyvesants of the City." City officials could not ignore the report, which was likely to influence federal aid to the city.

In fact, New York City was the only major metropolis at this time carrying out a large-scale urban renewal program without an overall plan. Lindsay would have to concentrate on developing a coherent approach to urban renewal that made both social and economic sense. He finally formulated his overall approach and applied it to the area that was to become Battery Park City. I would have to deal with the consequences of his decisions down the road.

A few days before Lindsay's January 1, 1966, inaugural, with the people of New York City facing the threat of a New Year's Eve transit strike, the City Planning Commission weighed in with another variation of a downtown renaissance. The Commission's new plan called for two hundred acres of landfill sweeping down around the tip of Manhattan from both sides of the island south of Canal Street. There would be parks and luxury apartment houses on this new land, and the city would turn several streets inland into pedestrian promenades to complement the new neighborhoods.

To accommodate the landfill, the Westside Highway, which began at the Battery, and the FDR Drive, the highway's opposite number on the East Side, would have to be depressed below ground level. This proposal, too, would present me with a problem when it came time to get Battery Park City under way. And that time was fast approaching.

Chapter 2

TWIN TOWERS TIMES TWO

Eight years of plans and counter plans, visions and revisions of urban renewal projects for the Lower West Side had mostly benefited the companies making the Lucite used for scale models, and New York City's printing industry, which churned out copies of each new plan.

By the beginning of 1966, the World Trade Center was looming as a tall and solid reality in the near future—it would be completed in the '70s—but alone it would not renew the area. Big was one thing, boldness and imagination another. The city's economy was in transition, with service industries replacing manufacturing facilities. Skilled managers and professionals were increasingly finding the core of the Big Apple unappealing and were headed out to the suburbs or to other cities. Lower Manhattan was still bleeding—to other cities and other parts of town—the kind of firms that had supplied its very character. It was less accessible than Midtown, with inadequate direct transportation to the suburbs. There was a need to rethink the idea of renewal, to try something different—something at once visionary, practical, and affordable. The whole planning process needed a breath of fresh air—a sea breeze, perhaps.

The new vision would have to use all available physical and fiscal resources. It would have to have something for everyone, for politics would necessarily rear its head in any large-scale project. But it would also have to avoid the pitfall of being just another political grab bag. Furthermore, it would have to be generated in a city that had long lived beyond its means and thus, in truth, would be unable to finance it by itself, not to mention actually getting the job done even if it had the money. That was a tall order, one that no plan yet advanced for Downtown had come close to filling.

Now, in the spring of 1966, Governor Rockefeller asserted himself as a major player in the planning drama. With his brother David focusing his sights on development of the East Side, Nelson took a major step toward transforming the Lower West Side.

Over the previous eighteen months he had had the Rockefeller family architect, Wallace K. Harrison, of the firm of Harrison and Abramovitz, working out the details of a veritable new city that would rise on landfill partly adjoining the World Trade Center, the construction of which was imminent. The development would stretch fifteen blocks from the Battery to the area around Chambers Street. The plans, presented to the governor in February 1966 as "Battery Park City: New Living Space for New York," were bold and visionary, in keeping with Harrison's background. Wallace Kirkman Harrison, after all, had helped to design Rockefeller Center, was responsible for the Trylon and Perisphere that symbolized the 1939-40 World's Fair, and had designed the United Nations building on Manhattan's East Side.

His plan for a mixed-use, financially independent residential, commercial, and recreational development—a "beguiling vision," a *New York Times* editorial would call it—began with the creation of a bulkhead, or sea wall, which would contain landfill, about twenty acres of which would come from the excavation for the foundations of the World Trade Center. Developers would put light industry nearest the water, followed inland by parking space for 7,500 cars. The rest of the project would rise from a twenty-three-foot-high platform. Four sixty-story towers would contain eight million square feet of office space. There would also be 14,000 apartments, 7,500 of which would be built under the state's Mitchell-Lama program and reserved for low- and middle-income families.

The new neighborhood would feature its own marina—the number of coves would become one of many bones of contention—a museum, places of worship, a school, and a library. It would also have its own 2,200-room hotel.

One part of the plan was downplayed—so much so that when the *New York Times* reported on Governor Rockefeller's proposal, the feature apparently slipped under its radar. Battery Park City would include facilities for handling container ships. How serious anyone was about going through with this part of the plan is hard to say now. Back then it was still politically necessary to keep the longshoremen content.

The plan called for Battery Park City to rise on ninety acres of landfill—we added another nine acres to the total during its development—and cost $600 million. The state would put up $138 million toward the housing units, 20 percent of those financed by the state reserved for lower-income families. Under the Rockefeller plan, New York City would spend $42 million to provide essential services to the residents and people who would work in the office buildings that would also occupy the development. It would be a good investment for the city, because $20 million in rent from Battery Park City would replace the $300,000 it collected annually in rent from the rotting piers on the Lower West Side.

Rockefeller announced that Pittsburgh industrialist and sportsman John W. Galbreath would spearhead the new development. He would bridge the gap between government and business, getting other developers to come aboard.

The Other "Twin Towers"

Battery Park City would be built hard by the Trade Center's twin towers. But before it even got off the ground—before, indeed, that ground was even created—the development found itself in the shadow of two politically tall, imposing and very much opposing figures: Nelson A. Rockefeller and John V. Lindsay. Given their sometimes-conflicting interests, New York State's governor and New York City's mayor would naturally butt heads no matter who held the offices. In addition, these two had conflicting political ambitions—never mind Albany and city hall: each wanted to live in the White House. But these two Republicans also brought an uncomfortable personal history with each other to the table.

Some of the rancor may have been the product of bad chemistry, but there was also, according to those who knew them both, a matter of money and pride. Lindsay, a liberal Republican, had captured city hall in 1965 with the support of Republicans, many Democrats, and the Rockefeller family's $500,000 campaign contribution. It was the latter, apparently, that stuck in Lindsay's craw. He couldn't—wouldn't—acknowledge it. At least he never acknowledged it to Rockefeller's satisfaction.

Rockefeller could deal with criticism, but ingratitude was another matter. The issue would reverberate in almost every encounter the two were forced into over the next few years. Battery Park City was one of the first, and the stakes were high. Some sort of development in the area was on each man's agenda. Any project one could imagine would involve both the city and state in some capacity. And the need for bargaining was such that when it came time to hash out details and finalize decisions, personalities would also matter.

I was to observe the consequences of this mix up close in several meetings involving Battery Park City, rent control, and urban renewal in my capacity as housing commissioner. Put Rockefeller and Lindsay in a room and you could feel the tension. Rockefeller, for example, developed the habit of referring to Lindsay to his face as "Johnny Boy." This slash at the mayor's aristocratic bearing and keen sense of pride by the extrovert governor had its desired effect. Lindsay, his face white, would grip the table or the arms of his chair in anger. Imagine trying to negotiate something in that atmosphere!

This personal resentment, added to their naturally clashing interests, passed down to their subordinates. In all of our future sparring and negotiating over Battery Park City, Lindsay and his group of young urban experts and planners would give in to the governor's plans only when they had to, would undercut as well as delay, and even after a particular issue had seemingly been resolved, would fight a rearguard action to overturn what everyone thought had been a done deal. I can personally and painfully testify to that!

On May 12, 1966, at the venerable Astor Hotel in Times Square, the governor, with Mayor Lindsay at his side, made the plans for Battery Park City public. The *New York Times* put the story on its front page with a picture of Mayor Lindsay smiling at Rockefeller, who was pointing to some detail in a model of the project. The newspaper's readers could make out two long rows of buildings, bookended by two sets of twin towers, smaller versions of the World Trade Center towers that would soon push into the sky just to the east.

One could wonder about the mayor's smile. It was, after all, *his* city, but this was the governor's show. The governor's office had *informed* the mayor's office in advance of what it was up to—David Rockefeller, to his great chagrin, was being kept in the dark—but Lindsay had not been *consulted.* Moreover the City Planning Commission, as I have noted, had in hand a much more comprehensive plan, one in which the area Rockefeller designated as Battery Park City would take on a different configuration than the one the governor had just proposed. That plan only awaited the mayor's official endorsement.

Was this, then, the final word from city hall and was the mayor signing off on the specifics of the governor's proposal?

For his part, Rockefeller had not bothered to observe the little courtesies that powerful politicians usually use to signal good intentions. He had agreed to announce Battery Park City at this joint press conference with the mayor. But in his enthusiasm, Rockefeller had already broken the embargo earlier in the day, blurting out details about the project in a political faux pas while making a speech.

The *Times* story noted that Rockefeller was "clearly in charge" at the press conference. But that didn't prevent Lindsay from firing a warning shot across the governor's bow. The mayor allowed that Battery Park City was "a balanced, progressive and proper use of this part of New York City." But just to make things clear, he added, "It is entirely consistent, even identical, with the plans drafted by the City Planning Commission."

As future events would show, it was, in fact, not so consistent and hardly identical to what Lindsay had in mind. The *Times* reporter picked this up, noting that Lindsay and City Planning Commissioner Ballard "both made it plain that the city would have its own plans for the area."

In this clash of wills, the governor would maintain a distinct advantage: he could come up with the money to finance his plan. At the time, New York State had $600 million in untapped borrowing authority, while the city's sources of borrowed capital for such a project had just about run dry. In July, Standard and Poors would lower the city's bond rating, declaring, "The city faces a steadily mounting burden of expense for welfare and other services that promises to outpace the growth of revenue sources in the foreseeable future."

The governor's Battery Park City project was relatively limited in scope, at least compared to some of the other plans for Downtown that had been floated, particularly the grandiose one to which Lindsay and Ballard had referred. For the state, it was affordable and do-able. As an anonymous spokesperson for the governor confidently told a *New York Times* reporter, "We've got a good thing and we're running with it."

Almost six weeks later, on June 21, the City Planning Commission filled in the details of *its* plan, which it had first introduced the previous December. The commission proposed to house one hundred thousand on two hundred acres of landfill wrapped around the southern tip of Manhattan Island. The plan encompassed the World Trade Center, the Brooklyn Bridge Southwest urban renewal project, the renewal of the Washington Street fruit-and-produce market area, and an expanded civic center north of city hall. Much of the new area would be park land, what Lindsay called, echoing Robert Wagner's earlier remark, "windows on the water." The development would supposedly be financed through a complex web of both city and private money, one of the more ethereal aspects of the proposal.

It is of no little importance that the sweep of the project around the tip of Manhattan and the concomitant plans to run the West Side Highway below grade—a bathtub in the water—would have just about put an end to the governor's Battery Park City. So much for the governor's plans being "consistent, even identical" with the city's.

Given New York City's other priorities at the moment and its limited access to the funds it would have to put up, it's hard to believe that the city ever would have been able to bring it off. The plan envisioned *100 percent luxury housing* in the choicest areas abutting the waterfront all around, with lower—and middle-income housing farther inland in the Brooklyn Bridge and Washington Street Market renewal areas.

City Planning Commissioner Ballard called the plan "a bold guideline for the downtown renaissance," and urged that the governor modify his plan to bring it in line with what the city wanted to do. Perhaps Lindsay viewed it as a bargaining chip, seeking to exert his will over whatever configuration Battery Park City would finally take.

The *Times*'s architectural critic, Ada Louise Huxtable, although attracted to the city's plan, could not envision it ever actually embodied in real buildings and parks. She thought that "the city's traditional economic laissez faire, familiar administrative stumbling blocks and the myriad critical priorities that must be met with limited resources, present mountainous hurdles" to it. To those who might hope it would be different this time, she cautioned: "New York has a long tradition of defaulted dreams."

In hindsight, the city was edging closer to actual bankruptcy, to real default, and so while the ideas expressed in the plan might have been a nice confection for some, in reality it was $2 billion pie in the sky. A clear-eyed observer at the time could have guessed what the upshot of the matter might be—at least the part of the plan involving the landfill on the Hudson. All that was necessary was to follow the money. Was it the city or state that had access to it? Which plan was more likely to succeed within the entire economic, social, and political context of the times?

On August 3, 1966, Lindsay signed off on the building of the World Trade Center, giving permission for the street closings necessary for the project to commence. New York City would collect a payment in lieu of the taxes it would have received from private developers on that part of the Trade Center leased to private tenants. As part of the agreement, the Port Authority also agreed to turn over to the city twenty acres of landfill in the Hudson that resulted from the construction.

Meanwhile, Governor Rockefeller let it be known that he would listen to any proposal that might create a compromise between the state's plans and the city's more flamboyant visions for Lower Manhattan. But he also made it clear that he would proceed with his project. Behind the scenes, Lindsay's assistant, Donald F. Shaughnessy, director of the city's Public Development Corporation, which oversaw issues related to commercial and industrial growth, and Rockefeller's state commissioner of housing, James W. Gaynor, were meeting to try to reconcile the two plans.

Gaynor, in a letter to *New York Times* publisher Punch Sulzberger, whose paper had reported the clashes between the governor and the mayor over disposition of the site, insisted that city and state were really not far apart. His meetings with Shaughnessy were to "expedite development," not resolve serious conflict.

The City Planning Commission would have to approve any proposed action by the city before it could go ahead. In September, City Planning Commissioner Ballard said that the commission was almost ready to move on recommendations for "concrete action" on the city's plans, although a member of Ballard's staff cautioned reporters that it might take a bit longer.

By now the underwater area just off the tip of Manhattan had become a veritable field of dreams on which many visions were being imposed. On November 8, the *Times* reported that the city's Department of Marine and Aviation was floating the idea for an airplane landing strip just offshore between the Battery and Chambers street that would serve the financial district. At the same time, Robert Moses was privately discussing with Mayor

Lindsay the possibility of moving the New York Stock Exchange to the landfill created by the World Trade Center.

A year later, in June 1967, architect and planner David Wallace, who had helped draft the city's plan for Downtown, would privately propose his own addition to the mix. He would suggest that thirty acres of landfill be added to the Battery, on which would be built an enormous "space needle," 2,500 feet tall. It would contain restaurants and observation decks. A city spokesperson at the time termed it "interesting," but Robert Moses dismissed it as "not only impractical, but silly."

A few more proposals for the not-yet-created land and it would have begun to resemble Mrs. Murphy's boarding house.

Meanwhile, a vital part of whatever would be built on the West Side was coming closer to fruition. In late December 1966, the Port Authority had awarded contracts to create landfill from the Trade Center's construction that would extend Manhattan's boundaries an average seven hundred feet into the river over a six-block area opposite the future twin towers. On January 5, 1967, New York City began to demolish piers 7 through 11 to make way for the cellular steel cofferdams that were intended to contain the landfill. The $4.5 million project was scheduled to take two years

Perhaps they should have built the dams in the form of a question mark, because the new land that was created at that location may have filled in part of the picture but also created its own blank spaces in the process. The landfill would not extend out to the pierhead line, so that would have to be filled in later. The steel sheet caissons, at best, were temporary: later a rock and concrete seawall would be needed to keep the new land from slipping into the water to augment not Manhattan's real estate but rather the Hudson's riverbed. Nor was the fill itself uniform; scattered throughout were many large boulders. This latter fact would become critical when attempts to create Battery Park City's infrastructure of sewers, utilities, and the like met with physical as well as political obstructions.

But all that was in the future. More immediate was the question of how to develop the new real estate. Still on the table was David Rockefeller's grand plan for the redevelopment of Lower Manhattan, which had been around for several years; the Lindsay administration's even grander plan that would add landfill from the Brooklyn Bridge to Chambers Street, extending all of the lower tip of the island out into the river; and Governor Rockefeller's more limited proposal for Battery Park City.

If the world were rational, all concerned might have sat down, added up the pros and cons, done a little figuring on a calculator, and settled the matter. But then life would be hardly as interesting as it can often be.

Personality conflict and clashing ambitions were, if anything, coming to play increasing roles in the drama of downtown redevelopment. In fact, in a mild way, it even extended to the relationship between the Rockefeller brothers. As 1967 began the *Times* quoted David Rockefeller on how he and Nelson had been operating independently of each other with little consultation between them. "We didn't know what each other was recommending," David observed of the difference between Nelson's ninety acres of landfill containing light industry and offices as well as housing, compared to the sixty-five acres of just housing and parks that the DLMA plan would have placed in the same location.

They still disagreed on the office space. David feared that it would compete with space already available in the financial district, driving down its price and generally undercutting real estate values in the area where One Chase Plaza had become an important address.

In November 1966, Governor Rockefeller was up for reelection. Lindsay, who denied that the governor had helped him win office, pointedly withheld assistance to Rockefeller in *his* race against New York City Council President Frank D. O'Connor. Not only did Lindsay not campaign for his fellow Republican, but he also tried to maneuver the governor into supporting the

New York City Civilian Review Board that would oversee the police. It was a political hot potato that Rockefeller naturally wanted to sidestep. In fact, the governor could have reasonably deduced that Lindsay wanted him to lose. Had that happened, the mayor could then have blamed the city's problems on a Democratic governor and one of Lindsay's main roadblocks to a possible presidential nomination would have been removed from the picture.

But the governor did win, no thanks to the mayor. On election night, Lindsay did not appear at Rockefeller's victory celebration.

If the governor and mayor were operating more than ever at cross-purposes, several crucial relationships between members of Lindsay's own administration were less than cordial. This internal strife briefly hampered the city's ability to speak with one voice on what to do about the Lower West Side.

Turf wars were breaking out on several fronts. For example, as 1966 ended, Lindsay appointed Donald Elliott to succeed William Ballard, who had resigned as head of the City Planning Commission. Elliott, who had been Lindsay's counsel, took office in January and promptly refused to follow through on his predecessor's "recommendations" with respect to implementing the Lindsay administration's redevelopment plans for Downtown. He found them too vague. But then, after all, what good is taking office if all you can do with it is carry out someone else's decisions and policy? Clearly, Elliott wanted to put his own imprint on the job.

In what would ultimately be a helpful move in the ongoing negotiations between the city and the state, Lindsay announced the appointment of thirty-seven-year-old Richard Buford to head the new Office of Lower Manhattan Development. Buford had worked in city government in his native Philadelphia and had been handling anti-poverty issues for Lindsay prior to his new appointment. He would ultimately give the city that single voice it needed in negotiations over what would become Battery Park City. But that wouldn't happen before Buford had to fend off Jason Nathan, who already headed the city's Department of Housing and Development.

Nathan saw Buford's new job as a usurpation of some of *his* prerogatives and strongly objected. To complicate matters even further, Nathan was also feuding with Donald Shaughnessy, head of New York City's Public Development Corporation.

Toes were being stepped on and boundaries were being crossed. The permutations and combinations of interpersonal relations that were playing their role in impeding progress on the Battery Park City project were enough to cause vertigo.

On January 17, 1967, Lindsay formally and publicly endorsed the massive June 1966, $2 billion plan for redevelopment that included luxury housing, stores, and parks on landfill sweeping all around the tip of Manhattan. Again noting the "similarity" between his and the governor's project, the mayor hoped that talks between their representatives would yet produce satisfactory "modifications" in Rockefeller's plan.

A few days later a *Times* editorial, almost certainly written by Ada Louise Huxtable, praised the Lindsay plan as "one of the best in the country in the brilliance of its vision and the quality of its urban design." No doubt, it had its points. But then a Rolls Royce, in the realm of automobiles, also has some of these qualities. One can't help but admire it. But it doesn't necessarily follow that you can afford it.

Chapter 3

ENTER CHARLES J. URSTADT

T he *New York Times*, while enamored of Lindsay's projected vision of a new Downtown, was also wringing its hands over the devilish details that stood in its way. With respect to the landfill issue, the paper noted on January 17, 1967, "City officials have not been able to determine who would own the new land, because charters and land grants are very confused."

They needn't have worried, at least not about *that* issue. The governor was already looking into it.

Behind the scenes, away from the political tumult, there was some hardheaded work being done to bring Battery Park City into being. If it was not to become another lighter-than-air fantasy, like most of what had been proposed to date, someone would have to take care of the nitty-gritty details that could turn it into a reality.

To make Battery Park City real, the real estate where it would be located would first have to be created. At the moment, it was still under forty-five-feet of water. Even the twenty acres of landfill from the construction of the Trade Center would be problematic, since it was not yet permanently contained. In fact, given the way it was to be deposited in the Hudson, it would not be suitable as a construction site in the first place.

First things first. The city owned the on-shore part of the underwater land in the area that would be filled in, and the state owned the rest. Under what circumstances could the city-owned portion of the underwater land be leased by the state? What needed to be done?

That's when my phone rang in December 1966 at Alcoa Residences, where I was vice president and secretary-counsel. It was Bobby Douglass, Governor Rockefeller's counsel and an old friend of mine from Dartmouth College and Cornell Law School. I had been active in the New York State Republican Party and had worked on the finance committee to raise funds for the governor's reelection in 1966 but had no more than a handshake acquaintance with Nelson Rockefeller.

Douglass and I had been fraternity brothers. Bobby had been a member of the golf team at Dartmouth and was president of the student body at law school. Ultimately, he would succeed Alton G. Marshall as secretary to Governor Rockefeller.

After the usual pleasantries, Bobby got down to business. He briefly sketched in the project that the governor was proposing for the site and then asked, "What do you know about the city's right to alienate land under water?" What I knew wouldn't have filled a shot glass, but I was a real estate lawyer and I could find out with a little legwork. I told him I would get back to him with the answer.

How I Got Here

Maybe it was fate. I always had a passion for water. My mother's family had property on City Island, near the present site of Orchard Beach in the Bronx—they owned Jordan's Boathouse— and we spent summers there when I was a boy. I began to swim competitively even before I attended Bronx High School of Science, where I won three city high school championships and set some city records, and continued in the fast lane on my undergraduate swimming team at Dartmouth, where I was a two-time All-American. I'm over seventy now and I haven't stopped, competing at the championship level—and winning a world championship in 2000—in the men's senior division races. I still swim every day.

I was born at Flower Fifth Avenue Hospital in Manhattan in 1928. In the few years preceding my birth, the outer boroughs had become an increasingly appealing destination for the immigrant generation and their children. People who might have originally had to settle for whatever housing they could afford in Manhattan were becoming financially comfortable enough to give their families something better. The open space and relatively fresh air in the Bronx, Brooklyn, and eventually Queens beckoned. With tax breaks to encourage developers, those years saw a boom in the construction of six-story rental apartment buildings, many with elevators, on the city's periphery.

My father's family came to America from Zwingenberg, Germany, in 1851. A few went on to Minneapolis but the rest settled in the South Bronx. One of them remarked in a letter that I've seen that the Harlem River reminded them of the Neckar River back home.

It was my great-grandfather, who had a farm at what is now 152nd Street and Cortlandt Avenue and was also in the shoe business, who got us into real estate. He financed the construction of a building at 195th Street and Webb Avenue in the Kingsbridge area of the West Bronx and then bought it from the builder. We lived in it until I was twelve. My father, an engineer by training, managed it.

I had a typical urban childhood, except for one thing: I knew from an early age that I wanted to go into real estate when I grew up. After all, I was getting in on the ground floor (if you'll excuse the expression). As a young boy, I accompanied my father and grandfather when they made the rounds to collect the rent and check up on the properties they had bought in the '20s and '30s around the Kingsbridge Road section of the Bronx. We did this usually on Saturday mornings. Pleased with the interest I already showed in the field, my grandfather encouraged me to speak to the "supers" at each building—but never the tenants!—and learn all I could about what it took to manage and maintain the structures. We looked at the stairs, the roof, and the boiler rooms— the kind of attention to detail that can make you successful. No school could ever give me this practical, hands-on education.

I also received a practical education in real estate from another source that did not seem so benign at the time. In 1938, it looked like the new Orchard Beach would encompass the area where

Jordan's Boathouse stood and the great planner, Robert Moses, had our boathouse condemned. It had been in my mother's family since they had come to America from Ireland in the 1850s. Not surprisingly, the name of Robert Moses became anathema in our household.

The irony is that in the late 1960s, Moses and I would become good friends when he spotted an article I had written in praise of large-scale developments, such as Co-op City, Rochdale Village, and Starrett City. We thought alike on the issue at a time when the Lindsay administration was pushing vest-pocket housing and parks, opting for a casement window perspective when a more panoramic view was appropriate.

Meanwhile, my grandfather prospered. There was a huge demand in the 20s for decent housing in neighborhoods that offered all the space and conveniences that were lacking in places like the Lower East Side. His properties proved to be good investments, even through the Depression, when he and my father continued to build their real estate portfolios, adding a few stores on Kingsbridge Road to the mix. One of the keys to their success was their conservative approach to financing, sticking to a 60 percent loan-to-value mortgage from savings banks—at about 4 percent in those days. Some of those buildings are still in the family.

Early on, I determined to be a success myself, and the proof is in the headline that marked the first appearance of my name in the newspapers. It was in the *Bronx Home News*: "Wistadt (*sic*) Triple Winner at 12 and Under at Crotona Park Pool." It wouldn't be the last time that a newspaper got something wrong about me, although this time, at least, it was innocuous.

I developed a frame of mind at this early age that has helped me throughout life. It was simply this: I learned to set particular goals for myself and single-mindedly pursued them. As a result, I've been successful in achieving them. An early goal was to get into the prestigious Bronx High School of Science, where admission was through a highly competitive examination.

I made it and continued to attend Bronx Science even though we later moved to Pelham Manor. In fact, Bob Smith, the swimming coach at Bronx Science, also lived there and I rode in with him every morning. I more than paid him back for the lift, winning several Public School Athletic League City swimming championships, and setting a new New York City record for the 100-yard breaststroke in my junior and senior years. I also competed in long-distance swimming in Long Island Sound. (Now there's a great way to evaluate shorefront property!)

Previously, I had been in the rapid advance class at Creston Junior High and so was only sixteen years old when I left Bronx Science. I spent my undergraduate years at Dartmouth, where the pace was once again "rapid advance" because of World War II. We stayed in school in the summer, and so I graduated from Dartmouth at the age of nineteen. But not before I achieved Collegiate All-American status in swimming for two years.

I was an economics major at Dartmouth and had even taken the only economics course offered at Bronx Science. I also attended the business school at Dartmouth, cramming all the tax courses I could into my schedule, and even taught a few class sessions on real estate myself in one of the courses when asked to by the professor. I would love to have studied real estate, but there were no course offerings in the field. The Depression had cast a pall over real estate and there was little interest in it at the time.

At Cornell Law School I finally got to study real estate, taking all the real property courses the school offered, although they were rudimentary. Following Cornell, I did some additional tax work at NYU, working days at a Wall Street law firm that specialized in real estate and construction.

I was thinking at this time of making my first serious career move. I went to see Jack Sillcocks, a friend of my father's lawyer and a partner at Tanner, Sillcocks & Friend in the Metropolitan Life Building, about a job with his firm, and caught him just when he was going to make a serious move, himself. He was going to work at Webb & Knapp, linking up with the great William Zeckendorf Sr. He invited me to come along.

That's when military service intervened. The most important piece of real estate for me over the next few years was the flight deck of an aircraft carrier in the Pacific. I became a lieutenant in the navy and got to play a little water polo for the Armed Forces Olympic Water Polo Squad.

Out of the service in 1957, I finally took Sillcocks up on his offer and joined Bill Zeckendorf at Webb & Knapp. I stayed with Zeckendorf until 1963, when he sold his properties to Alcoa. I regard the time I spent with William Zeckendorf Sr. as an invaluable education, working for the best real estate man I've ever known.

I was at the heart of a real estate empire. We had twenty-thousand apartments, ten million square feet of office space, and several million square feet of shopping center space in prime locations. The company's holdings would probably be worth something like $20 billion today. And all of it was very highly leveraged, with a minimum of equity involved. That was fine when the economy was good, but when the stock market broke in 1962, Zeckendorf took a bath.

By the time I got to Battery Park City, I was certainly no stranger to the high-stakes world of big deals. In fact, where most people associate New Year's Eve with champagne and noisemakers, it's linked in my mind with property closings, which I had to get done before the witching hour. The only celebratory sound was that of a bank officer stamping certified checks.

That may not sound like an especially colorful way to usher in the New Year, but it could get interesting. One year in particular was truly memorable. At issue was the sub-subleasehold on the Graybar Building in Midtown Manhattan. Alex DiLorenzo and Sol Goldman were going to buy it from us for $2.5 million, but the necessary approval from Metropolitan Life was not forthcoming. This led to a very complicated New Year's Eve deal in which we took back the Graybar Building and sold it to another New York developer, Marvin Kratter, while handing over the Chrysler Building to Goldman and DiLorenzo.

Working at Webb & Knapp could be a little like playing the game of Monopoly with real buildings—a very heady experience. I even got to participate in the selling of the Twentieth Century Fox Studios in Los Angeles. Part of that assignment involved spending time in Hollywood, lunching at the studio commissary with the stars. It was hard work, but someone had to do it!

Zeckendorf sold the Webb & Knapp properties to Alcoa in 1963, and Alcoa asked me to come along and run them. The offer was appealing and I accepted, becoming vice president and secretary-counsel of Alcoa Residences, the corporation's real estate subsidiary. It put me in a position to help administer some of the most significant residential and commercial real estate in the country. We're talking about developments such as the 2,500-apartment Park West Village, the 3,800-apartment Lincoln Towers, as well as Kips Bay, and the U.N. Plaza, all in New York City, and Society Hill in Philadelphia, Hyde Park in Chicago, and Century City in Los Angeles.

A Fateful Decision

All of which explains why Bobby Douglass not only called me in December 1966 for some specific research regarding New York City's ownership of underwater property, but also might have already had in mind something bigger for me, if I was interested. In fact, although I liked the challenge that the job at Alcoa offered, and liked many of the people with whom I worked, in the end my prospects there were somewhat limited. It was a typical corporate milieu. The executives lived in Westport, Connecticut and the hierarchy was divided by country club membership. The corporate career track was not for me, nor could I see myself taking my family to Pittsburgh, where, ultimately, you had to be at Alcoa if you were setting your sights high with the company. My friends thought I was crazy not to go for the top there, but I was primed for a move.

Bobby had previously asked me to join Governor Rockefeller's Campaign Finance Committee in 1966, which I was pleased to do. I'm still active in raising funds for the New York State Republican Party, and I highly value the friendships I've made and the work I've done in raising campaign funds over four decades. And my relationship to the governor and his plans was about to deepen.

I did the legal research on the underwater land, poring over the original charters and land grants going back to colonial days, and had the results in a memo on Bobby's desk inside of a month. The city owned the underwater land for the first four hundred feet into the river. Beyond that, as far as the pierhead line nine hundred feet out, the state held title. Thus, whatever would go up on the prospective landfill would require the cooperation of city and state. But they did not have equal power in the matter. You would be literally in over your head if you stood on either piece of property. But for the city this was also figuratively true in a significant way. Any city administration was ultimately beholden to the state for legislative permission and appropriations to run its affairs. When it came to financing a project at this location, the state, with a little creative use of debt, could make it happen. Whereas, given its shaky financial condition, the city was, well, in over its head.

As it happens, that bit of legal research was a doorway that was opening into a new part of my life. I was in the right place at the right time. My experience, skills, and outlook meshed well with the governor's needs. In March of 1967, I joined his team officially and in full. Boy, was it in full. He dumped assignments in my lap that could easily have occupied two or three people full time.

I was thirty-eight when I first met with Nelson Rockefeller at his office on West Fifty-fifth Street in New York City, and he really dazzled me. He was a man who got to the point, was not afraid to devise big solutions to big problems, and had a refreshing, practical approach to governing. And yes, he could project that famous Rockefeller charm when he had to.

In the course of our meeting, I followed Rockefeller from his office through an underground connection to his townhouse on West Fifty-fourth Street. There we had lunch, sitting on nightclub-style red banquettes. It was flattering to have the governor of New York State inquire about my life, work, and interests at a private lunch. But I was perfectly aware that he was sizing me up. Fair enough.

He was blunt about what he would need from me. The 1968 presidential election was bearing down on us. "Chuck Percy's got an urban program," he reminded me, referring to one of his chief rivals for the nomination, the liberal Republican senator from Illinois. "Lyndon Johnson's got an urban program, Bobby Kennedy has one," he added. "I need an urban program." I could see what was coming.

"I want you to work up some overall urban program for me," was Rockefeller's challenge, fixing the course of my life for the next twelve years. He asked me to serve as a deputy commissioner of housing and community renewal under Jim Gaynor, then commissioner, working with him to do as much as we could with the Mitchell-Lama program to vitalize the Urban Renewal Program in New York State. Ultimately I would present the governor with the proposal for an urban development corporation, now known as the Empire State Development Corporation. Hopefully our work would create an improved picture in housing and urban planning that would make Nelson Rockefeller the man who could lead the nation out of the national urban crisis that seemed to worsen by the month.

I would also be taking a hard look at the issue of rent control, particularly as it applied to New York City. Oh, and he specifically charged me with getting Battery Park City under way, a project that would enrich the city's housing stock while relieving pressure on its mass transit system because people living there could walk to work in the financial district. Little did I know what I was getting myself into!

Governor Rockefeller graciously wrote to Jack Harper, president of Alcoa, explaining why he needed me, and asked the company to release me from my contract. He told Harper, "One of the most serious problems in our large urban centers is the lack of job-producing industries located within reasonable distances from adequate housing. If we are to preserve the viability of our large urban centers," the governor wrote, foreshadowing several of my upcoming assignments, "we must develop new methods for bringing jobs to where people live and to assist in providing decent housing within easy commuting distance of jobs. In this regard I have developed, in conjunction with private industry, a plan for a balanced community providing housing, industrial and commercial space and parks within the City of New York to be known as Battery Park City."

The company complied with his wishes, and on March 3, 1967, my appointment became official. On March 23, the *New York Times* reported that I had been appointed deputy commissioner for operations of the New York State Division of Housing and Community Renewal at a salary of $27,500 a year. The photo of me next to the story depicted a serious-looking young man, a demeanor commensurate with the heavy burden descending on my shoulders.

So powerful was the governor's influence that not only had I acquired a new title, he also changed the name by which I was known to many people. Most people who knew me called me "Jay." But by Governor Rockefeller's lights, this young Charles J. Urstadt was "Charlie." With that kind of imprimatur, it stuck, and to this day, "Charlie Urstadt" is what I often answer to.

The Urban Development Corporation

While I was brought in to innovate and reconceptualize state participation in urban development in the light of my experiences in the private sector, I was initially weighted down with housing projects already in the pipeline under previously existing urban renewal programs—Mitchell-Lama, for example. One of the projects, Co-op City, was an enormous undertaking that was going into its final stages. Others were upstate in places such as Buffalo, Rochester, and Auburn, necessitating one- and two-day inspection trips and meetings with local officials.

But increasingly my attention turned toward helping to formulate a broader and more daring approach to urban renewal in our poorest neighborhoods. There the dire need for new housing and jobs was being met with inaction, for these areas were widely perceived as economic dead-ends. The answer would be the Urban Development Corporation.

If this were an autobiography, I would be devoting considerable space to the UDC, which took at least as much of my time initially—a minimum of fifty meetings during my first year on the governor's team—as did the Battery Park City project. The UDC was the centerpiece of Governor Rockefeller's urban program, hopefully a workable response to the increasing decay of inner cities throughout New York State—and throughout the country—and the clear inability of private developers alone to stem the deterioration. But as it happens, it was also a manifestation of a new attitude toward government partnership with business that would play a significant role in Battery Park City.

We faced a volatile situation in the cities. It simply was no longer profitable for developers to build in inner-city neighborhoods. But unless these neighborhoods could be reinvigorated, and their residents' prospects for a brighter life increased, the only light cast on the situation would come from the ghetto fires and riots that were increasingly accompanying the summer months. What solution was practical and affordable?

Clearly, we needed a solution as bold as the problem, something that could stand up to the increasing despair and say, in effect, "Look, we need to break the bonds of old habits. We can do it, we can rethink the problem, recast the role of government and accomplish it all within our means with a minimum of bureaucracy and interference with private enterprise." The key was figuring out a practical way for government and business to work together. And the initial task was to identify what was holding back the developers.

My experience at Webb & Knapp and Alcoa was invaluable at this point. Even if a developer wished to build in a marginal area, getting all the necessary permits, relocating the tenants and clearing the site dragged on for so long that capital—a company's lifeblood—was effectively frozen indefinitely. Somebody had to cut the red tape and take over the preliminaries so that builders could go ahead and build.

Throughout the spring of 1967, at my staff meetings at the Division of Housing and Community Renewal and in numerous trips to the governor's New York City office on West Fifty-fifth Street, the UDC took shape. By August, Assistant Commissioner Avrum Hyman and I had a preliminary proposal to show Governor Rockefeller. At its heart, when applied to the most intractable areas, the plan was truly innovative. "For the first time in housing and industry the State would move into the development field by initiating, constructing and completing housing and industrial projects in hard-core, slum areas," the document declared. The state would do everything necessary to get things going, including acquiring the property, relocating tenants, designing the project, financing it, and even building it. Eventually the project package would be sold to a developer and the proceeds would be applied to the next project. We regarded money spent for this purpose as "preventive funds." If we didn't do something constructive, the cities would go up in smoke.

The mechanism through which we would accomplish this was a public benefit corporation. Previously, the governor had failed to get New York voters to amend the state constitution to allow government grants and loans to go directly to private developers. The UDC would circumvent this roadblock, using funds raised by selling "moral obligation" bonds, to pave the way for private investment. Stopping short of full faith and credit obligations, the moral obligation bond was the inspired idea of John Mitchell, future attorney general under President Nixon. Mitchell, at the time still in the bond business in New York City, had come up with the idea when the New York State Housing Finance Agency was created in 1962 after the electorate had turned down proposals for the sale of state-backed bonds to fund Mitchell-Lama housing mortgages. On September 29 I conferred with him at his office at 20 Broad Street to refine this mechanism by which we hoped to jump-start urban renewal throughout the state (and eventually to finance the infrastructure of Battery Park City, as well!—but more about that later).

An important part of the UDC concept, introduced by Al Marshall, the governor's secretary, would encounter serious opposition, and I must admit that I was not comfortable with it myself. As the preliminary report put it, the UDC would be "free from local controls and restrictions." In practice that meant that the state could override local zoning and other ordinances to build a project wherever it saw the need. I didn't like it, didn't want it, and knew we would have trouble getting local elected officials, concerned about home rule, to sign off on this idea. I had even removed it from the August 1967 press release announcing the program.

On November 10, I flew to the Greenbrier Hotel resort in White Sulphur Springs, West Virginia, to speak to members of the Savings Bank Association of New York State about the UDC. I played down the revolutionary aspect of our plan, positioning it as simply an innovative approach at a time when conventional responses to the urban crisis had come up short. Previously the state could facilitate the granting of mortgages and offer planning assistance to developers and other services not involving direct expenditures. But now, for the first time, state government would have all the powers of a private developer as well and could step in when even the most favorable mortgage could not entice builders from the private sector.

I knew that my audience at Greenbrier was familiar with Title I of the 1949 federal housing act, but I reminded them that although 104 projects had been devised under that law, only 40 were completed or close to it at this late date. The great insurance companies that were the potential font of capital for large projects in the 1940s and '50s had withdrawn from the housing business. We were now "long on projects but short on sponsors," I told them. I reiterated my experiences at Webb & Knapp and Alcoa: too often builders could not get beyond the stage of site preparation. They needed a partner, a role that government could play under the UDC.

I dispelled any idea they might have that such a project would involve vast government expenditures. We could get started with $50 million in seed money that, through State Housing Finance Agency mortgage loans, could eventually be translated into $1 billion in construction.

When Governor Rockefeller formally proposed the plan to the legislature in February 1968, the prospect of more urban riots ended all adjectival restraint. Rockefeller said we needed a "revolutionary" plan that might involve "drastic" government powers. It was a time for "extreme measures." Nothing less would suffice for the UDC to accomplish its goal of generating $5 in private spending for every $1 the state laid out.

By now the governor's urban program was very much a part of the political scene. Rockefeller, although not formally a candidate for president, had said he would accept a draft. When reporters covering his UDC speech asked if he saw it as a model plan for other states, he flashed that big Rockefeller grin and shot back, "I certainly would." The next day George Romney quit the contest for the Republican nomination for president and Rockefeller reaffirmed his availability for a draft.

Reaction to the UDC proposal was as expected. Developers, stymied by local laws, praised it, as did several upstate mayors, eager for help for decaying inner-city neighborhoods even if it involved surrendering some control over development in the process. But the *New York Times* criticized it as "too revolutionary," and New York City Councilman Ed Koch attacked it as a "usurpation" of the city's powers. On February 29, the Kerner Commission, in response to the urban riots, reported that America was divided into two societies along racial lines. That same day, John Lindsay, prone to find fault with almost any Rockefeller proposal, also weighed in against giving the UDC such broad power. The mayor, defending home rule, attacked the idea of allowing any higher level of government to "come into the middle of a community" and build "just for the sake of building something."

A week later, on the day our UDC proposal formerly went to the legislature, the mayor countered the governor's plan, calling for an "urban Bill of Rights." And what might that be? It appeared to be a vague mixture of direct payments and loans to, and tax breaks for, private groups to act with the state on urban programs.

The next day I joined the governor at a press conference, at which I was designated to answer Lindsay's criticism. I spoke directly to the situation in New York City. "Our power would only be used where necessary," I noted of the delicate home rule issue. "But things are at a standstill in the city and someone has to have the final say, has to break the logjam." I reminded the reporters that once local politicians got involved with objections, a developer's capital could be frozen for years. Then, in the convoluted process of project authorization in New York City, there was the matter of the Board of Estimate's approval. The board, burned by past scandals, had bureaucratized the approval process into total paralysis. Besides, as I delivered what was clearly the coup de grace, the city's counter-proposal, involving direct payments to private developers, clearly violated the state constitution.

On April 3, the governor made some minor concessions to those fearing the end of home rule, but kept the substance of his legislation. It came to the floor for a vote on April 9, grotesquely framed by a terrible moment in American history that spoke directly to the need for the UDC. Civil rights leader Martin Luther King, murdered a few days before, was being buried while the legislature deliberated. Governor Rockefeller would normally have been nearby but was this day in Atlanta for the King funeral. The Republican state senate passed it, but the assembly, controlled by the Democrats, scuttled UDC by a vote of 85-48.

The governor went to work on the telephone, coordinating a concerted campaign to reverse the vote. The assembly took a three-hour recess, during which the fears of upstate Republicans that New York City would get a disproportionate share of the funding were assuaged, and threats of reprisal and political promises were allowed to do their job. When the session reconvened, I was seated on the floor of the assembly next to Minority Leader Perry B. Duryea, feeding him information to help sway the votes. The vote was retaken and, at 2 a.m., the measure passed, 86-45.

Now New York State had one of the most innovative urban programs in the country, with the authority to issue $1 billion in self-liquidating bonds that would be paid off from the revenue generated by the rents on apartments and factories these bonds funded. The day after the vote Governor Rockefeller offered me the post of president of the UDC, but I declined. It would have meant serving under its chairman, Ed Logue, a powerful, decisive man who had made his urban renewal reputation in Boston and

New Haven. It was the only time I ever turned down the governor on anything. I simply preferred to be the skipper on a destroyer rather than serve as executive officer on a battleship.

Logue would have, at best, a mixed career running the UDC. Too often he went ahead with projects that were financially ill conceived, that were not planned carefully enough with respect to paying off the debt that funded them. As state commissioner of housing, I would have to approve his projects, some of which made one wonder what he had been thinking when he signed off on them. It isn't sensible, for example, to plan balconies on the side of a building facing Lake Erie, from which powerful storms blow in. And Logue's heavy-handed overriding of home rule would eventually create a backlash.

For the most part the successes, trials, and tribulations of the UDC program are the subject for another book, although the corporation will reenter the picture late in the story of Battery Park City. Suffice it to say that in boldly proposing the state as a partner in development with private enterprise, with New York State clearing the way for builders, doing what they could not do, and in financing its activities through moral obligation bonds, the UDC paved the way for Battery Park City.

Diving into the Fray

Although for the sake of clarity, one must deal with one subject at a time, life is never so neat. Any given day in that first year of my public service would have been typically a mix of coping with some urban renewal project or issue, perhaps of longstanding, then working on the plan for an Urban Development Corporation, followed by a meeting on Battery Park City with the Lindsay administration's Dick Buford or Jay Nathan. One day I might fly off to Syracuse, the next day meet with architect Philip Johnson, followed by a day in Albany. I didn't have to worry about what to do with my increasingly scarce spare time.

Only gradually, especially once the Urban Development Corporation was nailed down, did Battery Park City begin to surface as a central concern. But before long, it would be truly dominating my life.

Neither the state nor the city could proceed with a landfill project without the other's cooperation. But when I came aboard in the spring of 1967, the mayor and the governor were at a standstill and nothing was happening on the lower tip of Manhattan. Lindsay, it will be recalled, had a grand plan for parks and luxury housing that would sweep around the Battery and cover the waterfront on both the East and West Sides. The governor's more limited and, it seemed to me, vastly more practical plan was confined to the one hundred or so acres of potential Hudson River landfill from the Battery to Reade Street. It was more realistic in dealing with the problem of money, at that time counting on light industry and office space combined to subsidize the housing in the project. (About that light industry, I would have more to say later.)

Dick Buford was representing the city in trying to reach an accommodation with the governor on a single plan for the area. Buford and I got to know each other quite well from May 1967 through the end of the year, a period in which we held thirteen meetings as well as conferring on the phone. He was a somewhat bookish man and an urban planner with no legal background or experience with real estate. Nevertheless I found him to be an able negotiator and reasonable enough while speaking for the city's interests.

The city's architectural firm was Conklin and Rossant; ours was Harrison and Abramovitz. Although I was nominally working as deputy under Commissioner of Housing and Community Renewal Jim Gaynor in the beginning, I was actually reporting to Al Marshall, the governor's chief of staff, and Bobby Douglass, counsel to the governor.

The points of contention involved the luxury housing that Lindsay wanted versus the mix of luxury, middle-, and low-income housing that the state was proposing. The Lindsay plan did not include office space, but I felt strongly that revenues from that source were essential to support the rest of the project. I knew from my work at Zeckendorf that companies occupying that office space command land value of at least $500 a square foot.

I also knew enough about politics (and I was certainly to learn a lot more) to know that nothing but luxury housing in the political climate that then prevailed would be poison; just as building it as a 100 percent Mitchell-Lama units would make it economically unfeasible.

Given the volatile social situation, the city's attitude seemed very unwise. They were going to put all luxury housing on the river, with those wonderful views and cool summer breezes. They hoped to make enough from these units to finance construction inland, in the Washington Street Market area, of housing for people with lower incomes. In both substance and appearance, it was undemocratic at a time when we needed to restore a belief in equitable treatment for all in America. How ironic that I, a moderate conservative, had to impress this upon the consciousness of the liberal Lindsay administration!

But if a single issue, at that point, constituted the bottom line for me, it *was* the bottom line. I don't know how many statements I had been reading from people such as the *Times* architectural critic, Ada Louise Huxtable ("Critics build nothing," Robert Moses liked to say), and William Ballard, head of the City Planning Commission, which seemed to be floating like wispy clouds above the real world. They were obsessed with design when they should have first been dealing with dollars. Without a solid financial foundation, this project would never go anywhere. You don't get to the mortar and brick—and shouldn't—unless you deal adequately first with mortgages, leases, and taxes.

Speaking of wispy clouds, there were also the architects to be dealt with. Naturally, I wanted whatever we built to be attractive and interesting. But my sense of priorities put the financial and physical foundation of this project first. Not so, the gentlemen of the pens, pencils, and drawing boards, who almost immediately began to fight their own battles on the side over design.

Since the *Times* is so influential, it was perhaps good for all of us that to balance the two teams of architects we brought in the renowned Philip Johnson to serve as a third force, a mediator-arbitrator. He was Ada Louis Huxtable's favorite, and her former teacher. In her eyes, he could do no wrong and once he was involved, she was going to be enthusiastic for whatever configuration the project would take.

I can't emphasize enough how strange it was that virtually everything written and said about the ongoing negotiations at the time had to do with the project's design—its aesthetics. Everyone was obsessed with plastic models. That was the easy part! I knew that if I could get a workable mix between housing and commerce, and if I could structure the finances of the project to make it appealing to investors, the specifics of design would by and large take care of themselves.

But as luck (bad, initially) would have it, I found myself in the middle of a three-ring circus that revolved around design. We needed an architectural mediator because the two teams of architects were turning things into a team sport, with a good deal of what we would today call "trash talk" aimed at each other. Unfortunately, the addition of Philip Johnson did not help in that respect. He just became another object of vitriol and began to dish it out pretty good himself. I won't repeat the name-calling, some of it conveyed to me in post-midnight phone calls and delivered in a tone of near-hysteria.

Amazingly, in the midst of this sideshow and with the pressure of politics and the always-fractious Rockefeller-Lindsay relationship hanging over us, Buford and I made slow progress. In a sense, the city could at most play a delaying game in terms of dictating the ultimate configuration of Battery Park City. In fact, the *Times,* on January 6, had even quoted an unidentified city official as acknowledging, "The question is whether we do Nelson's plan or David's plan. We can't fight those guys down there."

By the fall of 1967, the pieces had fallen into place for a preliminary agreement on Battery Park City between us and the city, preparatory to a formal memo of understanding, which in turn would lead to a lease and master development plan and the commencement of work on the project. On October 11, Al Marshal and I met with Buford and Deputy Mayor Robert Sweet for two hours to hammer out the final details. It was at this meeting that the city finally withdrew its objections to commercial development in the project, which I felt was necessary for financing the whole thing.

A harder nut to crack was the housing ratio, really the centerpiece of the conflict so far. Initially we came up with a ratio of one luxury housing unit to every subsidized apartment. The city agreed that the state would run the entire project without any interference from the city.

Did you ever come to an agreement on something, only to wonder as time went on whether the other side was truly serious about carrying out the understanding? Ahead of us lay the memorandum of understanding, the writing of a master lease between New York City and New York State, and development of a master plan for the project. Those documents would have to pass muster with the City Planning Commission and the Board of Estimate. Anywhere along that path, there would be plenty of opportunities to delay and even block the project entirely. And the tensions between mayor and governor were about to escalate. Our done deal was very much capable of becoming undone.

Shooting the Rapids without Hitting the Rocks

I've already noted the clash between Lindsay and Rockefeller over the UDC in the spring of 1968. The deterioration in their personal relationship, the backdrop to their confrontation, would also underlie the sniping that I had to deal with as I attempted to shepherd Battery Park City through its preliminary stages.

It was the sanitation workers' strike in the early days of 1968 that really poisoned the atmosphere. The mayor felt pressure from his constituents to do something, as plastic bags full of garbage were piled high on every curb, creating levees of trash that could not contain the public's tide of anger. Lindsay, who had shown his lack of bargaining savvy by helping to precipitate a transit strike immediately upon taking office, now asked Governor Rockefeller to call out the National Guard to pick up the garbage.

Not only did the governor refuse the mayor's request, he humiliated him by finally settling the conflict himself in a marathon negotiating session at the governor's West Fifty-fifth Street office with John DeLury, head of the Sanitation Men's Union, while Lindsay napped in the next room on a couch and his deputy mayor, Bob Sweet, was fast asleep on the floor. Lindsay would later denounce the settlement as a sell-out, although it only involved a relatively small pay raise.

As the *New York Times* noted on March 10, commenting on their most recent head butting in the sanitation strike, Lindsay "has always viewed the Governor's attitude as patronizing and has reacted rebelliously." The denouement of the strike had just fueled the flames and hardly made the mayor a good negotiating partner on any issue, especially not on the governor's proposal for a huge project that would ultimately change the face of the mayor's city.

The time that I spent on Battery Park City during this period was divided between keeping the Lindsay administration from throwing a monkey wrench here and there into the process that was supposed to lead us to a lease, and working out some of the technical details of that lease. An example of the former was the news, early in the year, that the city had decided to rent out Pier 1, the distinctive pier at the end of Battery Place that demarcated the southern boundary of Battery Park City, to the Circle Line. I told Dick Buford in no uncertain terms that this latest turn of events was really throwing us a curve. It "would be a serious handicap and obstruction to the development of the entire area," I warned. This pier was in the south end of the project, the point where we intended to begin with commercial tenants who would help to underwrite the cost of the rest of the construction.

Yet, I was also absorbed in the specific details of structuring this unique development so that we could pull it off with a minimum of hitches. I had to answer questions such as, would a public benefit corporation such as Battery Park City have to pay federal taxes on any profits it might make from developing the site and leasing the space? (It would not.) That might not seem like the stuff of high drama, but this and similar details had to be resolved if the undertaking was ever to get under way. John Galbreath, the builder who in the preliminary stages of the project was responsible for bringing in private developers, appreciated what I was doing and wrote to Governor Rockefeller, praising my "practical approach" to this and similar issues.

By March 1968, the city's foot dragging was becoming more than annoying. On the twenty-eighth, I wrote a memo to Governor Rockefeller outlining where we stood. With construction expenses rising, it was probably costing us $1 million for every day we delayed. If we didn't see real progress soon toward a formal memorandum of understanding, the precursor to a lease with the city for the land on which we would build Battery Park City, I advocated taking advantage of the forthcoming power built into the Urban Development Corporation to override any city objections and to go ahead with work on the project. In a pinch, we could assign title by condemnation and begin adding the landfill and building a bulkhead, plan the rest of the project and lease space, all without consulting Lindsay. At the very least, we ought to consider this route our "trump card" to use in negotiating with the city.

Fortunately, negotiations began to move again and we were able to shelve this battle plan. On April 25, 1968 we signed a formal memorandum of understanding with the Lindsay administration in a public ceremony at the governor's office. Everything important in the struggle between city and state over just what would rise out of the Hudson River off Lower Manhattan got worked out on the governor's turf, and this significant milestone was no exception. Rockefeller was expansive, celebrating the project as exemplifying "what a creative and constructive partnership between business and government can achieve." A considerably more subdued mayor tried to save face, noting that it "fits into the master plan for developing the City."

Under the agreement, the Battery Park City Authority would become the master tenant in the project. The project would be a self-supporting, 'balanced community.' The authority would finance creation of the site and its infrastructure through the sale of tax-exempt notes and moral obligation bonds. We anticipated lining up developers and securing commercial tenants as our first task, and hoped to have much of that done within six months.

The memo looked forward toward a ninety-nine-year master lease between the Battery Park City Authority and New York City, and anticipated that market rent housing would be built in a 2:1 ratio to subsidized housing in the project—a concession to the city. At least 30 percent of the site would be devoted to open public areas. Wallace Harrison would chair a team of architects that would include Philip Johnson and William Conklin.

Having—for the moment—resolved outstanding issues concerning the nature of the project, there was nothing holding us back from giving it a legal life. Chapter 343 of the laws of the New York State legislative session of 1968 inserted a new Title XII at the end of Article 8, and with this dry bit of business, Battery Park City was on the books.

On May 31, 1968, Governor Nelson Rockefeller signed the Battery Park City Authority Act, creating a public benefit corporation called the Battery Park City Corporation Authority, and named me as its first Chairman and Chief Executive Officer. "On this site will arise a major new residential and commercial community for lower Manhattan, constituting the largest and most complex single urban real estate development ever undertaken in the country," he proudly declared.

The act provided that work on the project would commence "pursuant to the terms of a master lease" with New York City. But that would be easier said than done.

A crumbling pier on Manhattan's Lower West Side. From the depths of decay, we would seize an opportunity to remake Downtown.

The original plan for Battery Park City envisioned a big break with the past. The project that was eventually constructed would prove considerably less daring.

Governor Nelson A. Rockefeller entrusted me with several significant challenges, including the creation of an urban development corporation and the building of Battery Park City. (Bob Wands)

Viewing the Lower Manhattan of the future with members of the Downtown Lower Manhattan Association: left to right, Ed Wagner, chairman of the Seaman's Bank for Savings; David Rockefeller; and, pointing, E. Virgil Conway, president of the Seaman's Bank.

Chapter 4

UP AND RUNNING

We began work on Battery Park City on July 29, 1968. Not a spade of dirt was turned, nor did we add any new land to Manhattan. But the brand-new Battery Park City Corporation Authority did hold its first formal meeting that day.

The legislation creating the authority had specified that the three members of this body would be appointed for staggered terms of four, five, and six years. The uneven terms served the important function of assuring bondholders of continuity in the project's leadership and guidance. The legislation also specified: "Members shall continue in office until their successors have been appointed and qualified." It was a seemingly obvious and innocuous point at the time, but eleven years later, it would become the center of a personal political maelstrom for my staff and me.

I received my six-year appointment to the Battery Park City Authority on July 24—I would be chosen first chairman at our initial meeting, a formality confirming the choice Governor Rockefeller had already made—while continuing to wear my other hat as New York State deputy commissioner of housing and community renewal. The other members of the authority, good friends of mine, who were announced two days later, were Judge Samuel J. Pierce, who had been at Cornell Law School with me and was later United States secretary of housing and urban development under President Ronald Reagan, appointed for four years; and Alfred S. Mills, president of the New York Bank for Savings, on whose board of trustees I served, given a five-year term. The "fee" for their services, $100 per meeting, with a limit of

$5,000 for the year, was more of an honorarium. Such talent never comes so cheaply when you really have to pay for it.

I brought Harry Frazee over from Alcoa to be our treasurer. My assistant was Edward Levy, then assistant commissioner for special projects at the State Division of Housing and Community Renewal, and our counsel was Herman Cohen, former executive director of the New York State Joint Legislative Committee on Housing and Multiple Dwellings. We had a four-person secretarial staff, each of whom was making no more than $8,000 a year. As soon as we got some start-up money from the state, we were able to pay for about $8,000 worth of office furniture.

Taking the First Steps

At that first meeting, we created our by-laws, discussed the task of opening bank accounts, and began to consider a corporate logo. Before we could provide a new home and office space for thousands of New Yorkers, we had to provide a home for the Battery Park City Authority itself. We settled on a small space on the fifteenth floor at 393 Seventh Avenue, in the same building where the State Division of Housing and Community Renewal had its offices. Our rent was $11,040 a year. Housed there, we could tap into the rich lode of talent available in the division, which our enabling legislation had authorized.

We also realized we would have to ask the New York State Office of General Services to get us a car so we could get around. The State Division of Housing and Community Renewal was located opposite Penn Station, halfway up Manhattan Island from our construction site. The $1 billion project may have been visionary, but its beginnings were certainly mundane.

While the real estate market was favorable at the beginning, I knew that things could turn, so I wanted us to get off to a quick start. The more time that passed between creating the organizational underpinning of the project and the completion of landfill, ready for us to build on, the more construction costs would rise.

My first task was to make sure that Battery Park City remained in the public eye so that potential developers would consider building there. Avrum Hyman, a former journalist, was the man to help me with that job. I borrowed him from the State Division of Housing and Community Renewal, where he had been an assistant commissioner, to become our public information point man. On August 5, he got out our first press release to businesses, trade associations, unions, and civic groups, telling them just what we were doing. Behind the scenes, I was aggressively pressing our case with some of the most influential business people in America, including the New York and American Stock Exchanges, as possible tenants.

No sooner did word get out about our project than I got a call from developer Lewis Rudin. Huffy and puffy as he could sometimes be, Lew all but threatened to sue me if he was not given prime consideration for the role of developer for at least some of the land we had yet to create. I guess Lew turned out to be a sunshine soldier. When it came time to put down a deposit to show good intent, and with the then backdrop of a dip in construction, Lew was nowhere to be seen.

Everything we were doing cost money. By September, our architects' fees alone were running $6,246 a month. It would be a long time before we would have the proceeds from a bond sale and it would hardly do for the Battery Park City Authority, the creation of Nelson Rockefeller, to start bouncing checks. The solution was a bank loan, actually matching loans of $300,000 each from the Chase Manhattan and Morgan Guarantee Trust Co. banks. Technically, they were bond anticipation notes, payable in a year at 5.01 percent interest. But in fact, they *were* loans given to us, on my word.

In truth, I secured the money on my word and as a result of a bit of "chutzpah." I went to one bank with the story that we were already getting $300,000 from the other. Of course, by the time I went to the second bank, I had in hand a real commitment from the first, and could thus substitute the straight truth for a bit of bluff.

The authority authorized the loans on August 28 and they were issued on Friday, September 13—a Friday the thirteenth that proved lucky for us. Now solvent, for the time being, we moved into our new offices on September 20.

We were not yet in our permanent offices when a crucial piece of legislation was passed by Congress literally clearing the way for the new development. While the city and state owned the underwater land area we proposed to bulkhead and fill, it was still potentially part of the navigable Hudson River. Anyone proposing to build on landfill extending out into navigable channels has to deal with the U.S. Corps of Engineers, whose job is to make sure that nothing interferes with our nation's shipping. The Hudson River certainly qualifies as an important path of water-borne commerce. If we had just gone ahead and built, and the corps later decided that some aspect of what we had built interfered with shipping, we would have to tear down what we had put up without recompense. And with that kind of an uncertain outlook, we could never have sold bonds to finance the project.

We had to take two steps to prevent this. We took the first almost immediately when the federal government declared the part of the channel to be occupied by Battery Park City nonnavigable. On August 13, Lyndon Johnson signed the Harbor and Rivers Act, seventeen lines of which certified that status. We would still have to satisfy the Army Corps of Engineers that nothing in the construction of Battery Park City would affect the current, water temperature, silting, and other phenomenon farther out in the river, but this would come later.

At this stage, preliminary though it was, we were already considering all sorts of ways to implement the project, make it more efficient and, of course, less costly. For example, we looked at the possibility of sharing some of our infrastructure with the Washington Street Urban Renewal Project, just to our north. It was an appealing prospect, but we quickly ran up against some powerful disincentives, including the possibility that such a course might violate some federal law or regulation.

It was also not too early, or so it seemed, to begin looking at the transportation issues raised by the very presence of Battery Park City. Would existing subway lines and stations be sufficient as they were then configured, or would we need to extend some lines and rebuild one or more stations? How about within the huge project itself? We began to consider the practicality of all sorts of people movers.

A Petty Nuisance

While we were looking forward to landfill and construction, we still had to fight a few rearguard skirmishes. Although no longer commissioner of marine and aviation, Vincent A. G. O'Connor, who had launched a veritable crusade to preserve the crumbling Hudson River piers because they were at one time part of his domain, now came back to haunt us. He resurfaced as a lawyer representing New York City shipping interests and longshoremen, both of which were desperately trying to salvage what they could of the revenue and salaries that used to flow from the city's docks.

During the summer of 1968, O'Connor was busy lobbying for the pier facilities that had been originally announced as part of Battery Park City. We remained strictly noncommittal, and for a very good reason. It was clear to me that such facilities would undercut an important part of the project's core: the housing units. Those pier facilities, flush with the edge of the development, would have been in use at all hours. Imagine trying to rent apartments with the prospect of stevedores banging and clanging cargo late at night! I didn't care about the architect's fantasies of making the project everything for everybody all the time. I had residential real estate to fill.

O'Connor willfully misinterpreted our unwillingness to as yet make final our decision on the fate of the docking facilities as some kind of promise to give his client's proposals to retain them serious consideration. I guess that posture must have looked good to the people who were paying him. He tried to bully us with Governor Rockefeller's statement of sometime past that the governor was "determined" to have cargo facilities in Battery Park City, and tossed in our faces the fact that the engineering firm of Mueser, Rutledge, Wentworth & Johnson, which had worked out the design for handling ships' cargos, was now a consultant to the project.

The former New York City dock czar was also trying to go over our heads, writing directly to the governor, invoking the names of powerful labor leaders Peter Brennan and Teddy Gleason, hoping to raise fears of a potential labor vote backlash against Rockefeller. O'Connor wanted a face-to-face meeting to plead his case with Governor Rockefeller, but what he had to settle for was an October 25 meeting with me. Again, I told him that he had "misunderstood" our position—I was being polite and diplomatic—as leaning toward the cargo facilities, but I agreed to give him a week to state his case in writing. He was less than happy with that but had no choice and accepted the offer.

I was aware that there were some delicate political and economic issues involved, so I had lunch in September with Harry Van Arsdale, business manager of Local 3 of the International Brotherhood of Electrical Workers and head of the powerful Central Labor Trades, to touch base and to square us with an important labor leader, whose influence in New York City was always substantial. The upshot was that we were not going to build that cargo facility. As a compromise and sop to all concerned on the other side, we would later agree to join O'Connor's clients in advocating that equivalent space be provided for them at other locations along the city's waterfront.

Getting Attention

Although we were beginning to deal with some substantive issues involving the actual construction of Battery Park City in these first months, I cannot emphasize enough the importance to me of keeping the project in the public eye. I even found it necessary to call Manhattan Borough President Percy Sutton to complain about a private development called "One Battery Plaza" planned for a nearby site. I wanted nothing diluting our message.

I was dismayed that we were not getting the coverage from the press that the importance of Battery Park City warranted. A case in point: In late October the *New York Times* ran an editorial, "The Blockbusters," decrying the destruction of the ambience of midtown side streets to satisfy the current heavy demand for new office and commercial space. The paper had been so free with its comments about the architectural significance of this and that facet of our plans. Didn't they see its larger significance in the context of the city's economic growth? Why weren't *we* mentioned as part of the solution to this midtown problem that preoccupied *Times* writers?

I drafted a letter to the editors, reminding them of the imminent mark on the city's map we were about to make, including the office and commercial space with plenty of ambience that we would add to New York City's stock of those precious resources. I don't know why I bothered, because the editorial appeared only two days after we had staged a major publicity event, including the governor and the mayor, spotlighting Battery Park City. The *Times* was the only major publication not to cover it.

On October 22, 1968, determined that Battery Park City make a splash, in more ways than one, and intent on breaking through the tensions between the governor and the mayor that might hamper our work, I took Rockefeller, Lindsay, and numerous other city and state economic and political figures, including New York City Comptroller Mario Procaccino and labor leader Peter Brennan, on a boat ride. Had the Circle Line sightseeing boat I chartered for the forty-five-minute trip sunk, the core of New York City and State's movers and shakers would have gone down with it.

My idea was to have these eminent figures, about 125 in all, see just how decrepit the piers had become, and to inspire them with a vision of what was to replace them—given the cooperation and support we hoped to get from our guests. I was also aiming to play to the larger audience of New York's real estate and commercial developers, some of whom were aboard, making them sit up and take notice as well. Toward that end I went into my tour guide mode, pushed back my captain's hat—I never got to command a ship in the navy—and quickly filled in our guests as we pushed away from the Battery and glided up the shoreline toward pier 21, the northernmost point of the tour. Take a good look at the "moldering piers and dilapidated sheds," I urged my captive audience, regaling them with the details of what we would build in their place in a few years.

In my letter afterward to Mayor Lindsay, thanking him for attending, I wrote, "It's ironic that the world's biggest real estate development has so far been almost unnoticed by the average New Yorker, whereas in any other city it would make constant headlines." Tact and courtesy required that I thank His Honor. But I wasn't fooling myself about where our longtime opponent stood. Harry Albright, Governor Rockefeller's appointments secretary, wrote to me after the boat ride that while I was extolling the virtues of the Battery Park City to come, Lindsay "looked very much as if he needed a martini to revive his sagging spirits."

The City Drags Its Feet

Our Battery Park City Authority was certainly up and running. But legally we were standing on ground no more solid than the landfill that was as yet confined to blueprints. We had an understanding with the city, but we needed a *lease*. Mayor Lindsay, at this point, should have been our partner in ironing out the details and shepherding the project through the City Planning Commission and Board of Estimate, the bureaucratic and politically laden bodies that would have to grant their approval before we could go ahead and build. Instead, he was at best a reluctant collaborator and really more of an obstructive force.

From our end, we were constantly redrafting the proposed lease to meet the city's objections to detail after detail and to cope with new issues that continually arose. We sent each draft to the city, and then had to wait interminably for them to get back to us. There's no better way to delay such a negotiation than to find a sudden need to further "study" the document or to plead the necessity of having half a dozen commissioners and subcommissions sign off on the details. On October 31, I wrote to Dick Buford, complaining about these tactics. "One of the most crucial problems," I reminded him, was "how long the authority can sustain itself on the relatively small funds which it now has from the banks." As politely as I could, with as much tact and professional courtesy as I could muster, I urged him to move it.

It's a good thing I couldn't see into the future, for if I had I would have found it hard not to be discouraged. But we lacked a crystal ball. Samuel Brooks, our new counsel, who had replaced Herman Cohen after the latter's untimely death on November 12, gave us reason to face the New Year confidently. On December 27, he drew up a memo with a projected timetable for the various stages of approval we would need before a lease was ready for signing. He saw us agreeing to terms with the city by January 10, 1969, City Planning Commission Approval on February 5, and the Board of Estimate go-ahead on February 17, with city and state officials affixing their signatures the same day.

It's so easy to be optimistic on paper! At least this wasn't as overly cheery a view as we had mustered on October 30, when we envisioned having the document done and signed by January 24. That would have brought us close to completing the landfill by the end of 1969— let optimism reign all around—and start office building construction at the beginning of 1970. In fact, we still faced more than six months of protracted lease negotiations and delays.

The New Year of 1969 brought me a new title and more responsibilities. James Gaynor left in January and Governor Rockefeller appointed me the new state Commissioner of Housing and Community Renewal, as well as chairman of the State Housing Finance Agency.

January came and went and the beginning of February saw little forward movement on our negotiations with the Lindsay administration over Battery Park City. Besides the lease, we needed a master development plan that would serve as a planning guideline, to which prospective developers and the authority, as the primary tenant in the lease, would be bound. The master plan would set out the relationship of each part of the entire project to its other components. We hadn't made fast enough progress on this document, either, a matter I brought up with Buford at a meeting in architect Wallace Harrison's office on February 11. I used every bit of persuasion I could to get Dick to hasten matters from the city's end, reminding him that money as well as time was running out.

Ten days later, I needed to consult with Dick Buford on an important matter but couldn't locate him. I was reduced to sending him a telegram to arrange an emergency weekend meeting. This sort of thing could not go on indefinitely. We had already spent $126,000 from the two $300,000 bank loans, and had committed a further $280,000 for services that would allow us to complete the master development plan and lease. The rest of the $600,000 would drain away with the passing months to pay for basic administrative expenses—rent, salary, legal fees, and the like.

Fortunately, there was another source of income available and I drew on it now. It was common for even self-financed state projects to get a head start loan from the legislature with what is known as a first instance appropriation. This was, in effect, an advance against the revenues that would ultimately flow in from bond sales, rents, or other sources of income, depending on the project. By definition, these appropriations were supposed to be repaid. In fact, they rarely were and the state would simply continue to carry them on its books. We would receive an appropriation of $15,068,000 to help us repay the bank loans and stay afloat until we could begin to tap a revenue stream from bond sales. And we were virtually the exception among similar state bodies: we ultimately paid back our appropriation in full from the proceeds of our first bond sale.

An Onerous Issue and Another Nuisance

As negotiations plodded on, an especially contentious issue came to the fore. The lease, if we ever got one, would spell out the vital matter of the project's housing mix by income. What percentage of the units would rent at the market rate, what percentage would be subsidized? It will be recalled that the Lindsay administration originally wanted all market-rate housing—luxury rentals, exclusively. Their scheme had those rentals subsidizing middle- and lower-income units that they would build inland, away from the river with its glorious views and cool summer breezes. We had originally proposed an even split and then had compromised on a ratio of two luxury units to every one subsidized apartment in order to reach a letter of understanding with the city, the step before that elusive lease.

The issue of subsidized housing is always a potential political hot potato in New York City. Now the fires heated up from a source outside the lease negotiations, but one that could affect the approval of that document, were we ever to arrive at one to submit. It was Manhattan Borough President Percy Sutton. He had a vote on the Board of Estimate, which had to approve the lease. Because he was the chief executive of the borough in which we intended to build our project, Sutton's influence on the rest of the board loomed considerably larger than the numerical value of his actual vote. (On the Board of Estimate the mayor, comptroller and president of the city council each had two votes, while the borough presidents had but one each.)

Sutton, the highest-elected African-American in the city's government, spoke for a constituency that had little need of luxury housing, but whose requirements for subsidized units were substantial and ongoing. And he was not happy with the numbers of such apartments that the city and state were considering for Battery Park City.

In January, we heard from the borough president. Citing the "desperate need for low and moderate middle-income housing," Sutton's housing consultant, Neal Gold, suggested we finance more of it in Battery Park City by increasing the amount of office space we planned to build. He didn't say anything about the market demand for that increased office space. Then again, *he* would not have the task of finding tenants for it. I alerted Dick Buford and Jay Nathan of the City Housing Administration that there was trouble brewing.

On April 15, Sutton put a shot across our bow. He issued "A Development Plan for Battery Park City," written by Neal Gold, which declared that the current plan for Battery Park City was "irrelevant to the City's basic housing deficiencies." The document alleged that we were going to "use scarce public land resources and public powers to benefit mainly income groups and social classes fully capable of meeting their housing needs without public aid." (In fact, that land was so scarce that it wouldn't even exist unless and until we created it!)

Charging that there were no provisions in the development for the very poor, Sutton and Gold proposed that Battery Park City be used to relocate people from the slums while the substandard housing they left was rehabilitated. Much of that housing would rise over the depressed West Side Highway, using air rights. Left out of his report was that the people he was referring to had not been placed in new housing for various reasons, some of which had to do with possible antisocial behavior that would completely undermine our ability to rent the market-rate units. The attack also reiterated Sutton's proposal to add more office space to finance this bit of social engineering.

This report irked me on two counts. First, on a personal note, it made it sound as if we were merely there to serve the rich. My own work in formulating the Urban Development Corporation, administering the state's subsidized housing projects, and the governor's well-known commitment to putting subsidized housing at Battery Park City should have at least tempered the document's tone. Further, while it is not necessarily wrong to use projects such as ours to advance social goals, it has to be done with an eye to protecting the financial viability of the whole development. As I've noted, office space revenues were necessary to finance the landfill and project infrastructure. Increasing this space would throw all of the economics out of kilter and jeopardize the entire project. And making Battery Park City a way station for the very poor while urban slums would be massively renewed was pie in the sky. We wouldn't be able to get a developer to build any office space in the project under those circumstances, we wouldn't be able to float a bond issue, and the city and state would have been left to foot the bill with revenues from . . . where?

Now the *New York Times* paid attention, publicizing Sutton's reservations. On April 17, reporter David K. Shipler, noting that Sutton was calling Battery Park City "the Riviera on the Hudson," wrote that "allocations to low-income families of less than 7 percent of the project's housing threatened to throw the proposal [for Battery Park City] into new controversy." Shipler quoted me as saying that the project's housing mix was "not immutable." He also noted that the ostensibly liberal Lindsay was less flexible; His Honor, complaining of the high cost of putting any low-income housing at this location, likened it "to putting low-income housing in the middle of the East Side of Manhattan."

Neal Gold's zeal would get the best of him as this tug-of-war over housing units simmered throughout the spring. In May, Sutton's housing consultant told the Citizen's Housing and Planning Council that I had agreed to his and Sutton's version of Battery Park City's housing mix. I had to write to Roger Starr, that organization's executive director and later an editorial writer at the New York Times, informing him that Gold was incorrect.

I also complained to Gold himself about his misquoting me. He replied that Percy Sutton was now insisting that 50 percent of the residential units at Battery Park City be allocated to low-income families. It was not clear if he meant 50 percent of all housing units or 50 percent of those apartments that would receive any kind of subsidy, since middle-income families would also be subsidized. "If the Battery Park City Corporation feels that middle-income white families will not move into a development in which fifty percent of the units are for low- and moderate-income families, then I see no reason why the entire project cannot be used for relocation housing for those low- and moderate-income families," he added, restating the view he had expressed in April.

Just to make sure we were paying attention, Gold added: "This time we are not going to accept the argument that we should lower our objectives with respect to these groups to accommodate the prejudices of the white middle class. We would rather have no project at all." With the suggestion of a possible battle on the Board of Estimate, which could scuttle the whole development, we did indeed have to take notice.

During the spring, we also had to deal with another issue external to the negotiations with the city. This one was much less of a threat, although it did demand time and energy that I really needed to apply elsewhere. It was—I hoped—the longshoremen's last hurrah, as their inevitably unsuccessful efforts to keep even a few of the crumbling piers on the Lower West Side working met final defeat. Their parting shot came from Mr. Fred R. Field Jr., Local 856 (also called the "Banana Local"), general organizer, International Longshoremen's Association, known to just about everyone as "Fat Freddy." His men unloaded the banana boats on pier 3 for the United Fruit Company.

On April 16, "Fat Freddy" Field wrote to Governor Rockefeller, noting that he had just heard that the United Fruit Company, which still had been using on a month-to-month basis one of the piers in the area that we were going to fill, would be relocating to Hoboken in May. Field maintained that the company could remain in Lower Manhattan for at least another six months before we would have to demolish their pier to make way for the project. They had filed a request to do so, but Field said I had stymied their efforts to hang on.

Field, in his letter to the governor, claimed he had "reliable" information "that Mr. Urstadt does not intend to cooperate since vacant piers, even though they are unnecessarily vacant, are to Mr. Urstadt's advantage in advancing Battery Park City."

Fat Freddy was not just relying on his ability to sway minds through correspondence. The day before he had filed a lawsuit, claiming we were seeking to "destroy or seriously damage the City of New York as a commercial shipping port," and in the process "destroy the means of livelihood of many thousands of longshoremen." He asked the court to stop this by stopping us.

My move. I got labor leaders Harry van Arsdale and Peter Brennan to pressure Freddy to cease and desist. I also wrote to State Senator Paul Bookson, who was looking into the matter, that "the net result of this nuisance action by Mr. Fred Field may be to delay the start of construction which will provide 75,000 man years of work for men in the construction trades." There's nothing like the prospect of new jobs—especially true in the hard times of the 1970s, when 50 percent of the construction workers were out of work—to get a politician's attention. I was quickly learning how to play this game.

At the end of May, both sides having made some dramatic points, the talk got serious. Field came to our offices and we discussed a compromise. The gist of it was that he dropped his suit and I agreed to look favorably upon and possibly support his efforts to get the city to develop Hunts Point in the Bronx for shipping facilities rather than the housing that was being planned for the location—an approach I had already taken with Mr. Vincent O'Connor. Exit the longshoremen.

It was a relief to clear the decks of that obstruction. Not much later, on May 21, in a lesser but also pleasing development, Battery Park City's official name was squared with reality. Legally, we were the "Battery Park City Corporation Authority." That mouthful sounded too much like an animal built by a committee. What were we, corporation or authority? The public should know without having to guess. So, on May 21, at my request, the state legislature made us the Battery Park City Authority. Period.

Two Hurdles to Clear

By the spring of 1969, although we had not yet finalized the master lease, things now began to move faster. We needed a public relations push to ensure that we would enter with momentum the City Planning Commission approval process, scheduled to come up in a few months, and similarly the Board of Estimate review that would follow on its heels. Toward that end, the governor and the mayor publicly unveiled the Battery Park City Master Development Plan at the Whitehall Club on April 16. The club offered an appropriate view of the now desolate site that was to become Battery Park City.

The Lucite scale model of our project we displayed at the
press conference included the World Trade Center's twin towers,
which had not yet risen. But my attention was drawn not to those
stately architectural exclamation marks but rather to something
very strange in the model's scale. With a scale of 80 feet to the
inch, and the floors of the residential units represented by models
that showed, according to this scale, dimensions of 40 x 40 feet,
that meant each floor would cover an area of 1,600 square feet. If
one apartment contained 1,000 square feet—a reasonable
supposition—how could we economically divide the odd 600
square feet, which included space for stairs, pipes, and elevators, to
give us viable units? Had our architects been smoking something
they shouldn't?

I pulled Philip Johnson aside. He was pontificating to someone
about beauty and truth, but I wanted to talk dollars and cents. I
might as well have tried to lift the Empire State Building. Architect
Johnson seemed to have no sense of a relationship between cost
and design and continued along his merry way, extolling the
project's "complexification," whatever that was.

A little research later revealed the source of this model of
confusion. The Lucite blocks Johnson used for the model only
came in precut half-inch widths, so that's why the scale had gone
by the boards. Because of the size of the blocks that were available,
we were displaying unfeasible, economically self-defeating units.
Well, this was only costing us $250,000!

Nevertheless, we would never look so good again in the eyes of
Times architectural mandarin, Ada Louise Huxtable. She began
her review the next day with a gross exaggeration of how much we
had compromised with the city's idea of what should arise from
the riverbed, mostly in the area of enlarging the amount of space
left open, asserting that "the Governor's original Battery Park City
is barely recognizable now." John Lindsay would certainly have
disagreed with that! By his reckoning, the governor's imprint was
all over the development. It still galled him that it had not "taken
on many of the characteristics of the city's Lower Manhattan Plan,"
as Huxtable claimed it had.

But the rest of her piece was not only grist for our mill; it would supply us with some excellent sound bites for our publicity efforts. She loved the fact that the relationship of the commercial and residential space to the public spaces and amenities was written into a master plan. "Battery Park City is a progressive, sophisticated and promising development of the kind called, in professional parlance, a linear city," she rhapsodized. "It is not just housing or offices. It is a strip almost a mile long, to be built like a super seven-layer cake."

This was about planning vision and aesthetics, and Ada Louise Huxtable was in her element. "Those layers would contain the urban functions and amenities," she went on, "shops, restaurants, schools, parks, rapid transit, utilities, public and recreational facilities—that make a real community. Most important, they make it work."

Then came the piece de resistance that gave us our catch phrase: "Is this any way to plan a city? You bet it is."

In truth, I was not so concerned at this point whether we had a seven-layer cake, a croissant, or a cupcake. I knew the design elements would change as developers came aboard and various problems and issues arose as they always do in large-scale projects. But I *was* worried that if we didn't finalize a lease soon and get this project under way, we would be left with nothing but crumbs.

It was a source of satisfaction that other important publications followed Huxtable's lead in celebrating the city-to-be. *Newsweek*, for example, describing our plans as "truly impressive," called Battery Park City "the biggest single urban development in U.S. history."

Ironically, one of the features architectural critics and planners most liked about this city within a city was its isolation from the grid pattern of the rest of Manhattan. The city's streets would stop at our door, behind which would begin a different kind of urban vista in which pedestrians would hold sway over the main level, while vehicular traffic would be restricted to another. But a different set of political and economic factors would later intrude, causing the actual street pattern to work out differently.

On May 6, Paul Folwell of Milbank, Tweed, Hadley and McCoy, our master lease counsel, informed us that progress on a master lease had come virtually to a standstill. "I can't help but feel that the City is procrastinating and that a truly sincere effort is not being made to resolve major policy questions relating principally to control of the development and operation of the Project," he wrote to me. That happened to be an unfortunate, continuous part of the Battery Park City story for its first few years.

The latest obstacle was the degree of influence the city would have over the bond issue we needed to float. The city was trying to insinuate itself into the marketing of the bonds as much as possible. With time running down we compromised on this issue as much as was prudent. It was, after all, something we could bring up again when the lease would inevitably need amending to fit new circumstances. We also agreed to give the City Planning Commission the right of approval on residential construction at Battery Park City as it progressed.

As we moved into the summer of 1969, I had one eye on the calendar. We needed prompt approval by the City Planning Commission and Board of Estimate because a municipal election was looming in November. If the matter of Battery Park City was carried over until after the election and Lindsay won another term, we would be dead in the water because political pressure on him to create these construction jobs and get more new housing under way would have abated.

I also had an eye on our bank account. With Milbank, Tweed billing 630 hours for their work on the lease, which came to $46,000, the money available to us was draining away. We had just enough to make it to September 13, when the two $300,000 bank loans would come due, after which, assuming no hitches, we would begin to tap our first instance appropriation from the state.

With the arrival of hot weather, I was not sure if I would ever see the beach, even for a weekend, not to mention maybe a week's respite. I was still juggling final negotiations with Dick Buford over Battery Park City's housing mix, getting various other details of the master lease worked out, and putting the first instance appropriation request in order. Then all I would have to do would be to steer the project through the City Planning Commission and Board of Estimate, where several people with varying agendas might try to derail us. It was about as pleasing a prospect as jogging through an unchartered minefield.

The infighting and struggle to control the details of the Battery Park City development had so far been confined to government and labor officials, city planners, architects, and journalists. But one important group, the public, had not yet made its views known. We had hired for the project the prominent public relations firm of Hill and Knowlton, and they now came up with what proved to be a terrific idea.

I could speak from strength if I could go before the City Planning Commission and Board of Estimate, not to mention the developers and the possible institutional tenants for the project I would eventually need to recruit, with a show of public support. How could we get our case before the public and be able to invoke its desire that we succeed when all we could actually show them were the rotting piers? How could we line up a large, impressive group of prospective tenants for those as yet phantom apartments on imaginary land?

Well, we could draw them a picture of Battery Park City and ask them straight out, "Will you be living here in 1974?" And that's what we did in large ads in nine New York City newspapers on Thursday, June 5, 1969. We asked people who were interested to send in a coupon. The postage would be theirs, guaranteeing no more than a modest response, some of our consultants told us.

We waited and held our breath because nothing much happened on Friday, which produced just a trickle of responses. Little did we know that over the weekend the post office was accumulating a grand surprise for us. On Monday and in the days immediately following came the deluge! By the time we opened the sacks of mail we had twenty-six thousand responses from this initial surge of interest. We had to use people from the New York State Division of Housing and Community Renewal to keypunch the responses onto IBM cards—this was 1969, after all—so that we might analyze what we had received. What was worse, we had not assigned a special mailing address or post office box designation, so all of our normal business mail was mixed in among the thousands of responses in these sacks. We had to hire temporary clerical help just to find our business correspondence.

Show Time

With this huge public response, I was energized to do battle in the possibly tough days ahead. Optimistically, we proceeded as if approval by the two city bodies that lay in our path was a foregone conclusion. A week into July we announced that the firm of Dick & Merle-Smith would serve as our financial consultants. Looking down the road even further, we chose Kuhn Loeb and then later Goldman Sachs to underwrite the initial bond issue.

Our master development plan for Battery Park City, on which the City Planning Commission would pass judgment, was almost finished. In truth, some of the essential elements of the project as we then saw it were never to be, a reminder of just how much can change between the drawing board and the day the first tenants move in. These included tentative plans to put low-income housing over twenty-four acres of air rights spanning the then elevated West Side Highway, which was to be depressed at a later time when funds became available. The details would be subject to negotiations with the city. We were planning for about fifteen thousand residential units, five thousand of which would receive some subsidy from any one of several programs. In keeping with the state's Capital Grant Low Income Assistance Program, twenty percent of these units would be reserved for low-income tenants. This mix would be economically feasible.

The project's design encompassed two coves, which would separate the residential units, in towers reaching seventy or eighty stories, from the offices, which would be confined in three hexagonal towers to the south sixteen acres of the project. The coves would eat up 11.2 percent of Battery Park City. The entire project would be built on platforms and would be layered, with vehicular access on its own level, which would contain 800-1,200 parking spaces. Building heights would increase with distance from the waterfront.

A shopping mall was to run like a spine up the middle and would become a "major shopping center for Lower Manhattan." Office workers would enter their buildings through an enclosed plaza at Battery Place.

Battery Park City would not be part of the city's grid pattern of streets. It was to be, in today's terms, a gated community, with pedestrian access at several points along the length of the project. The relationship of cars to people was set out in two separate layers to secure "maximum separation of vehicular from pedestrian traffic."

In the light of the death and destruction that would one day come down from the sky next door, the overall setting of Battery Park City within its immediate environment as set forth in the preliminary master development plan takes on a poignant irony. The document stated: "The objective will be to contribute toward a pyramidal form for the skyline of Lower Manhattan and to provide a transition between the extreme heights of the World Trade Center towers and the much lower towers in the general vicinity."

On the eve of this critical period, there was a possibly good omen. Architectural critic Robert Weinberg pointed out on radio station WNYC that my last name, Urstadt, could be translated from the German as "the extended core of the old city." Maybe I was born to lead the way to Battery Park City! He likened this odd phenomenon to the naming of the Outerbridge Crossing, one of three spans that connect Staten Island and New Jersey, and the closest to the Atlantic Ocean. It would have been an appropriate descriptive name for that bridge, therefore, but it just so happens that it was named for engineer George Outerbridge, who supervised its construction.

We mustered the city's most prestigious design and planning bodies to endorse Battery Park City with enthusiasm at the initial City Planning Commission hearing on July 16, 1969. The American Institute of Architects praised our "wholly admirable urban design." And the Regional Planning Association endorsed the new-town-in-town, as we liked to call it, as "an outstanding example of inter-governmental cooperation between New York City and State."

The major stumbling point at the last minute proved to be the housing mix, where Manhattan Borough President Percy Sutton had already been making his stand in our path. Everyone was aware that a mayoral election was coming in the fall and housing for the masses was always a good rallying cry as voting day drew close. Now we really felt the pressure. The City-Wide Anti-Poverty Committee on Housing, for example, was calling for at least half of the residential units in our project to be reserved for the poor. Its chairman, Jerry Spriggs, declared, "The entire proposed plan smacks of a political scheme to appease the underprivileged . . . ." And Esther Rand of the East Side Tenants Council termed our thinking on the housing mix "wrong and socially harmful."

Dick Buford had assured me that July 16 would be the day we would really get it done, wrapping up the package with an endorsement from the City Planning Commission that would give us momentum to sail through the Board of Estimate hearings, which were up next. That's why I was furious when Donald Elliott, the commission's chairman, in the face of opposition from commission member Beverly Spatt over—what else—the housing mix, refused to hammer it through and instead let it slip out of our hands. He allowed a continuation, running the hearings into August. That, in turn, would push back our opportunity to finalize the project at the Board of Estimate. By the time we reached that body, we could be right in the political season, and odd things can happen when matters of substance clash with the call of the campaign. Worse, approval could be delayed until after the election, when pressure on the Lindsay administration to get something done would drop precipitously. That could really do us in for good.

I had to maintain a steady course through this storm, plotting the route ahead as well as keeping us on an even keel in the current rough seas. And ahead was the Board of Estimate. It was time to charm, cajole, and shore up our support on the board even before the City Planning Commission's final vote. I had at my disposal a very powerful weapon for such tasks: the in-person charisma of Nelson Rockefeller. I arranged a cocktail party on July 31 for the members of the Board of Estimate at the Radio City Music Hall studio apartment in glamorous Rockefeller Center, a good environment for getting people to think big and look to the future. The governor did what he did best, and the models and sketches of Battery Park City that I assembled presented us in our best light.

Meanwhile, behind the scenes, we turned loose several powerful allies to lobby members of the Board of Estimate privately. For instance, labor leader Peter Brennan went to work on Democratic City Comptroller Mario Procaccino, who was not only won over but who would later serve along with me on the Battery Park City Authority board. Procaccino was Lindsay's Democratic opponent in the upcoming election, with State Senator John Marchi holding down the Republican line, which had been Lindsay's the last time around. Lindsay would now run on the Liberal Party line.

The party was but a day's respite from the battle. Almost immediately afterward, we absorbed a heavy blow that blindsided us. The Lindsay administration, which had originally wanted no low-income units at Battery Park City, suddenly turned the other way. Without warning, we were informed by Donald Elliott that the mathematics of the carefully negotiated mix of 20 percent luxury, 60 percent Mitchell-Lama middle-income, and 20 percent low-income, had suddenly changed. The housing would be equally divided—one-third low-income, one-third middle-income, each of which would require subsidies, and one-third conventionally financed luxury housing. This would put a good deal of strain on our ability to successfully pay for everything with the proceeds from the office and commercial space. But it was take it or leave it.

It soon became apparent how this numbers game had been played. Although Lindsay would be running for reelection in November on the Liberal Party line, he was actually in transition to becoming a Democrat since his political future in the Republican Party was nil. He was listening to Democratic politicians and what they told him was that he needed to get religion on politically sensitive low-income housing. They cracked the whip and he jumped.

We accepted the new ratio because, as the city knew, we had to, but not without my letting Deputy Mayor Bob Sweet know what I thought of such tactics. I yelled a few things at him on the phone that I can't repeat, even these many years after, and he wasn't exactly wishing me a "good day" in return. We're on very friendly terms now because in fact, he's a very likable fellow, but the fur really flew back then. He later told me that I was the only person he ever had to hang up on—and it happened twice!

The City Planning Commission hearing continued on August 13. I testified on our behalf, accepting the one-third—one-third—one-third income ratio for Battery Park City's residential units, but not without reminding my audience that the bigger apartments for low-income families, who tended to have more children than higher-income tenants, would mean more space for their apartments and, as a consequence, fewer units overall. We were now looking at fourteen thousand apartments, not the fifteen thousand for which we had been planning.

I further reminded the plan's opponents that the rent we paid to the city could be allocated for more lower- and middle-income projects in places such as Floyd Bennett Field in Brooklyn. What's more, we would not need to relocate a single individual to create Battery Park City

A spokesperson for the mayor emphasized the social utility of upping the number of lower-income units in the project. Given the continuing opposition toward just such an approach by the Lindsay administration since the project's inception, I can think of only one printable word of reaction: "gall!"

Chairman Elliott then piled it on with what I took to be a bizarre point. Not only did he insist that the income groups be divided into even thirds to secure his support, he also specified that they be "thoroughly mixed and fully integrated." Really? My experience as housing commissioner and as a real estate professional told me that achieving integration on even general terms was hard enough. This new twist left me entirely fed up and in a moment of sarcasm, I inquired of the good chairman if his formula meant that the families would be sharing the same bathrooms. I didn't get a reply.

Finally, on August 20, by a vote of 4-1, we cleared this hurdle. The commission approved Battery Park City, noting objections to the housing mix from organizations such as the Women's City Club of New York, Operation Open City, and the East Side Tenant's Council—even after we swallowed the new ratios—but lauding the overall goal of a project that would spur economic growth and strengthen the city's tax base.

Walter McQuade, architectural critic for *Fortune* and a dissenting member of the commission, charged that the city was recklessly lending to the authority "land space" worth at least $220,000,000. Dream on! I wrote to him, explaining, if he was able to grasp the concept, "that the City is granting Battery Park City Authority permission to create land space which does not now exist and is therefore worth very little."

It's indicative of how I was viewing this whole process when I wrote to Bob Sweet the day after the vote—things had simmered down between us—that "another tooth has been pulled with one more to go." "Not so fast," a little voice should have whispered to me.

While we had the City Planning Commission's approval, and we hoped the Board of Estimate would shortly OK the Battery Park City Master Development Plan, the struggle between us and the city over the master lease proceeded on a parallel track. The issues yet to be resolved were large and small. An example of the latter: where would we send the annual rent due the city? We couldn't get them to firm up this simple matter.

A week after the City Planning Commission's vote, City Corporation Counsel J. Lee Rankin tried to drop a legal hand grenade in our laps, creating a problem where none really existed. Suddenly he seemed to "misunderstand" the terms under which we would be paying annual rent to New York City. The current draft of the lease, based on the memorandum of understanding we had achieved on April 25, 1968, stipulated that the authority would deduct from payments received from developers' money to service debt from the prospective bond issue and the costs of our administrative expenses. The latter was the sticking point for Rankin. But how else were we to finance our work? There were no other sources of income! Over more than a year of negotiations and nine drafts of the lease, nobody had questioned this fact. And I thought I had made that clear, as well, at the City Planning Commission hearings. We were going to pay 6 percent of the appraised value of the land as a rent, after subtracting debt service—the bond sale that we eagerly anticipated—and our expenses as a setoff. We were then projecting that the cash flow to the city as early as 1973 would be $3,886,000 after those deductions, rising to an annual payment of $16,270,000 by 1982—and that's all in 1969 dollars.

"I can assure you that if you persist in your position," I severely cautioned the city's corporation counsel, "you will effectively have terminated this project." I thought he was engaging in sophistry, putting a spin on my remarks to the commission that doted on mindless technicalities. Together they made for an argument specious enough to fail at impressing a high school debating society.

Just to make sure that City Planning Commission Chairperson Donald Elliott was not himself suddenly possessed of this skewed thought process as a result of something I said, I wrote to him on September 10, setting the issue in the clearest of lights. What next?

The Board of Estimate hearing was set for September 18. We needed to have all provisions of the lease straightened out by that date, but still the city dragged its heels. Now the sticking points boiled down to matters of control. The city, the Lindsay administration, to be specific, wanted to be able to sign off on aspects of the bond sale, have the power to approve fees to professional consultants, and even participate in our choice of insurance brokers. Not too many tenants would tolerate their landlord breathing down their necks to this extent. We didn't care for it either and thought much of it a petty intrusion into the running of the project, but the time element was on their side. They knew we would have to compromise.

A few days before the Board of Estimate vote, Deputy Mayor Sweet was nowhere to be found. How do you negotiate with an absent negotiating partner? I personally called him throughout the day on September 15 and again on the sixteenth but could not reach him. By the morning of the seventeenth, I was beyond this game of hide-and-seek. At 1 p.m. I sent a telegram direct to Mayor Lindsay, reminding him of the deadline closing in and its significance. I encouraged him to focus on this matter at hand, "FOR THE SAKE OF THE THOUSANDS OF PEOPLE who will be able to live and work in this worthwhile project to say nothing of the cost to the City which is incurred by delay." As I'm sure he noticed, copies of this wake-up call went out as well to eleven civic organizations.

We had been stretched on the rack this long, why not a few more days? The Board of Estimate hearing was put off from September 18 to October 9.

In the interim, we finally got our ninety-nine-year lease done— I was beginning to think it would take one hundred years to negotiate it—but even then, after the fact, there was rancor. Lindsay's Deputy Mayor Sweet accused us of not dealing in good faith because we delivered a copy of the lease to the Board of Estimate for its consideration before allowing the city to sign off on it. He kept it up like a drumbeat. We had tied up the loose ends, but now he wanted to circulate the document around, perhaps hoping for another inspired contretemps like the one that Corporate Counsel J. Lee Ranken had tried to create. Sweet advised me that the lease and associated documents should go back to the City Planning Commission, the Office of the City's Corporation Counsel, the Budget Director, and the Department of Real Estate for review. How about the guy who sweeps the lobby of the municipal building? It was like one of those horror movies where you think the bureaucratic monster had been slain, but defying all logic, he simply gets up, dusts himself off, and again runs amok.

I reminded the deputy mayor, in a hand-delivered note, that "meeting after meeting has taken place at which various elements of the Lease were reviewed and approved and revised drafts submitted only to have the City's representative insist upon new conditions." Enough. Politely as I could under the circumstances, I suggested to Sweet that at this point the project was "apparently being thwarted for some unknown reason."

We needed a little comic relief. Just when we thought we had heard the last of frustrated labor leader Freddie Field, the leader of the banana boat longshoreman, resurfaced yet again. I received a letter from him reiterating that a study had shown that a two-berth container ship facility at Battery Park City would be feasible. And *he* was playing "good cop." An accompanying note from his lawyer signaled a little New York City hardball: "The next move is yours." With three days to go to the Board of Estimate hearing, they threatened to go public. I vaguely replied that I still favored a facility in a location somewhere north of Battery Park City.

In truth, I had already bolstered my position with labor. Fearing just such a last-minute ploy, I had gotten in touch with International Longshoremen's head Thomas Gleason, reminding him of my support for new container facilities elsewhere and hinting that I would withdraw it if there were labor opposition to Battery Park City.

In spite of myself, I was becoming quite adept at this political game. You had to learn it if you wanted to get anything done in this town. I had made the right moves, and Fat Freddy soon faded into the background and with him, the lawsuit. To put the icing on the cake, I convinced Comptroller Mario Procaccino, who was challenging Lindsay for the office of mayor that fall, to endorse our position. *That* got Lindsay's attention.

The big day was October 9. I personally took our case before the Board of Estimate, reminding them of the relevant statistics about housing and construction jobs and holding before them a vision of "five million square feet of new office space—the equivalent of four Empire State buildings or three Pan Am Buildings." I contrasted the handsome returns the city would quickly reap with the measly $300,000 a year the crumbling piers had been producing.

I recited the entities that were formally behind the project, including New York City and State, the City Planning Commission, even the *New York Times* (despite their objections). But one always wants to bring such an argument down to personal terms for dramatic effect, and for that I can thank Ms. Dorothy Bianco of the Bronx, who now had a moment in the spotlight. From the total of thirty-five thousand people who had eventually responded to our ad in the newspapers, I quoted from hers. "We sit many a Sunday at Battery Park as it is," she had wistfully written to us. "What a fulfillment if living there could become a probability."

I think I gave them a peroration with punch: "We have conceived a development which is founded on hard-nosed economics, a sense of social responsibility and plain common sense. It is a development which, as they say in the trade, is 'do-able and viable.'"

We won. The board approved the lease on October 9 and the next day, I wrote to David Rockefeller, noting, "We are under way because we now have the two basic essentials for building—land and money." We even had a lease. It gave us ten years to do the job. Now all we needed was to create the land to build on, secure developers willing to put up the apartments, offices, and stores that would become an entirely new city within the city, and construct all the amenities that made up city life. Given all the things that can possibly go wrong in such a large-scale undertaking, we also needed a little bit of luck. Unfortunately, luck would have nothing to do with it.

Chapter 5

A CITY UPON A FILL

The 1970s began with a great honor for me. The Seneca Nation of upstate New York adopted me for my work as commissioner building housing and other facilities on their reservation in Salamanca in western New York State. They provided me with the appropriate headdress and named me Ha-Noh-Sonh-Nis, which means "Builder of Houses." But hundreds of miles to the south, a hard hat would have been more appropriate, because it was there I was about to preside over the building of a new city.

On November 24, 1969, in a brief ceremony, we signed the lease for the land on which we would build Battery Park City. The project was the product of the vision of two "farsighted leaders," Governor Nelson A. Rockefeller *and* Mayor John V. Lindsay, I said at the time. I managed to keep a straight face as I handed out praise to some of the very individuals who had seemed to be doing their best to keep this day from ever coming.

"All of the city officials who cooperated in making this lease a reality," I began, giving new meaning to the word "cooperated," "including Mayor Lindsay, Deputy Mayor Sweet, City Planning Commissioner Don Elliott, Corporation Counsel J. Lee Rankin, Manhattan Borough President Percy Sutton, Richard Buford, former director of the Office of Lower Manhattan Development, and his successor, Richard Weinstein, are to be commended for the favorable support they rendered and their recognition of the ability of the Battery Park City Project to supply the commercial, civic, residential, and recreational facilities needed to enable the

Lower Manhattan area to achieve its potential." Well, that was more or less true about Buford and Weinstein.

Lindsay, in particular, would remain a problem. I sometimes felt, in truth, that His Honor's "farsightedness" meant that he had us in the crosshairs, was taking dead aim, and would be delighted to blow us out of the water.

The bruising battle with Lindsay's people over the terms of the master lease already had cost us money as well as time. We had hired the law firm of Hawkins, Delafield and Wood as bond counsel, preparatory to floating a bond issue that we hoped to get done as soon as possible. They had to be aboard in the final stages of the negotiations over the lease because certain terms in that document might affect how potential buyers of those bonds viewed the project's prospects.

At a December meeting of the authority I presented my colleagues with a letter from Hawkins Delafield, explaining their fee. It read in part: "In addition to direct negotiations, we found that it was necessary to prepare a myriad of drafts of the various sections of the General Bond Resolution, as well as the provisions of the Lease relating to the financing, all of which was extremely time consuming and atypical of revenue bond financing. The files of the Authority will attest to the extensive effort devoted to the preparation of drafts, consultations and conferences with representatives of the City." Indeed, the files did and do show that.

A Sore Site for the Eyes

Physically, of course, Battery Park City was still anchored only in our vision. The 3,958,766 square feet of territory stretched almost a mile between Reade Street, then our northern boundary, to the U.S. pierhead line at Battery Park. Office workers and apartment dwellers would occupy it some day, but now it was just murky Hudson River water. The environment included the—somewhat faulty, we would discover—twenty acres of landfill from the construction of the World Trade Center and twelve decrepit, useless piers topped by crumbling sheds. These piers presented a dismal vista and our first big task would be to start tearing them down.

Even that job was not without some legal impediments, even at that late date. Now that the longshoremen and the banana boats had departed, I had to direct our counsel to spend valuable time dealing with an old legal claim on one of the docks. Developer Irving Maidman had some rights to the bulkhead, pier area, and underwater land that were to be part of the landfill area. The rights were complicated and were based partly on nineteenth-century laws governing use of the harbor. Suddenly, aware that we had to have access to the area, Maidman was contemplating some kind of development, unless, of course, he could get us to buy him off. We eventually disposed of this nuisance but it was, momentarily, a distraction.

Nor was the area defined by our lease completely free of physical impediments, aside from the piers. The city had a fireboat house on Pier A on the southern end, intruding between our property and Battery Park, and we wanted it moved out of the way. The City Planning Commission and the Fire Department agreed to move it, but to where? The appropriate place would have been a similar, no-longer-used facility at the base of Old Fulton Street in Brooklyn, near the Brooklyn Bridge. Unfortunately, the city's Housing and Development Administration already had plans for a park at that site and we were stymied.

Many individuals and groups also viewed the landfill we were going to create as fitting into their particular agenda. One of the more serious proposals came from the U.S. Department of Transportation, which for a while flirted with the idea of a temporary stolport (short takeoff and landing) facility in our front yard, serving the financial district. Federal Express, now FedEx, also looked into a similar facility geared to their needs. In fact, Fred Smith, founder of FedEx, came to my office to discuss this possibility with me. In all such cases I reminded the appropriate individuals that we would be working in the area almost continually and that having even specialized aircraft come in for pinpoint landings was not going to be practical.

Part of our landfill was already in place, in a manner of speaking. It was the twenty acres in the middle of our tract, filled with material excavated for the nearby Trade Center. The city, which had made the agreement with the Port Authority to use the excavated material for this purpose, was alerting us to their discovery that, as landfill, it did not appear to be up to par. I contacted the city's corporate counsel, J. Lee Rankin, and advised him that we might ultimately be forced to take legal action on the matter.

In the area immediately west of the Trade Center, the Port Authority's railroad tunnels—known as the Hudson Tubes—created another problem. The then nearly 70-year-old tubes nestled unprotected in the silt, which had accumulated over many decades on the river bottom. We didn't want to risk damaging them and so instead of the weighty fill that would characterize the rest of the project, we planned here to build only decks resting on piles over these tunnels and situate in this location the larger of the two coves and lighter structures that would house cultural and other public functions.

There would be a thousand and one impediments, ranging from the minor to the near catastrophic. But the time was approaching when we would have to take the bull by the horns and start the physical work. We had augmented our staff toward that end, adding Captain William T. Maley as architectural engineering coordinator. Ed Levy came over from the staff of the State Division of Housing and Community Renewal to work full time as my assistant at Battery Park City, and we also added architect Roland Middleton. Under terms of the master lease, we needed a representative on the project's Architectural Review Board, to which the city also made an appointment. Ours was going to be Wally Harrison.

On January 14, 1970, the first instance appropriation kicked in to start funding our payroll. At the same time, for a fee of $640,000, we hired Mueser, Rutledge, Wentworth & Johnson to provide us with various engineering consulting and planning services. Among these was site investigation, in which they would study the underwater locations that we would fill in, providing us with technical information we required to proceed with that task. They were also responsible for the preliminary design of the sixteen acres at the south end of the project, where we hoped to put up our first structures, the office buildings that were to help pay for the rest of Battery Park City. Mueser Rutledge was an easy decision. Besides being eminently qualified, they already had worked on the project, had inside knowledge of what we were doing, and could be instantly up to speed.

The next major step was to clear the way for our work by making sure that New York City, the Battery Park City Authority, and the Port Authority, all of which had interests in the area where we were going to build, were on the same page on all outstanding issues. We had to make sure that we didn't literally get in each other's way.

What sorts of issues might have arisen along these lines? As I've noted, the Port Authority owned the Hudson Tubes directly under our project. They and we had to be meticulous in identifying how our construction would avoid damaging them.

The level of cooperation among the three entities would never be as smooth as one might have wanted it to be. In 1976, for example, a minor problem between the Port Authority and us would almost escalate into a major one because of some carelessness on the Port Authority's part. Just before the Memorial Day weekend that year, a leak would develop in the World Trade Center air-conditioning intake line, which ran through our construction area. Our engineers ascertained that it was caused by the failure of the joint in their sixty-inch line and not by our activities. Indeed, we first spotted and reported it. The Port Authority sent out a crew with a backhoe to dig up the dirt and investigate. But they arrived without any knowledge of where the pipes involved could be found. We had to show them, lest they cause further damage. I guess you could call that cooperation.

We negotiated a tripartite agreement in April with the Port Authority and the city, and the Board of Estimate formally approved it in May. That was the last preliminary step. The agreement went into effect on June 18, 1970, the same day that our master lease became operative and we took physical possession of the site. Approximately a mile of prime New York City waterfront was now ours on which to build.

Out with the Old

Now we needed to hire one or more companies to dismantle the old piers and their superstructures so that we could begin to create the landfill. Pier 19, at the foot of Warren Street, was earmarked as the first candidate for removal. Of the twelve piers that occupied our site, it was in the worst shape, chunks of it falling with some regularity into the Hudson. The Army Corps of Engineers had already declared the 1895 structure a hazard to navigation and had told New York City's Department of Ports and Terminals to take care of it. That department, in turn, informed us, the lessee for the area in which it stood, to get going and remove it. Ironically, the wooden piles holding it up were not what were causing it to crumble, even though they had been immersed in the river for seventy-five years. Everything above the waterline, though, exposed to the elements, as well as air pollution, was rapidly becoming flotsam and jetsam on the river.

We had already paid $1,975 for a sign in front of the pier to inform the public of our intentions. We solicited bids for this demolition work and the low bidder when we opened the sealed envelopes on June 19 was the George W. Rogers Construction Corporation. They and other potential contractors had begun inspecting the site in May, before the lease took effect, preparatory to making their bids, which meant that we had to secure accident insurance even before we reached the formal starting line. We also had to put up a fence along the mile-long bulkhead for security.

We needed master architectural and engineering consultants to supervise the filling operation and the building of roads, sewers, and other parts of the project's infrastructure. These consultants would translate the general architectural plans that had been much ballyhooed in the newspapers into the specific material base of a large and complex development. For that substantial task, we secured the services of a joint venture of the thirty-year-old firm of Tippets, Abbott, McCarthy and Stratton, which had planned the huge Dallas-Fort Worth Regional Airport, and Gibbs & Hill, which had over sixty years of experience in relevant construction. This joint venture won out over five or six firms we had asked to submit proposals and we awarded them an initial contract worth $600,000.

TAMS, as we informally called them, figured to be key players in the rise of Battery Park City. Their duties would range from assessing the ecological and climatological implications of the master plan, to testing traffic patterns, drawing up preliminary plans of every vital system in the development, from sewers to playgrounds, costing out all systems, and recommending how we should build them. They would also help us to choose and supervise developers.

I was pleased to have them aboard, but New York City's arbiter of architectural taste, the *New York Times*'s Ada Louise Huxtable, was up in arms over who was *not* going to get this job. Her favorite, architect Philip Johnson, had been at the center of the preliminary planning—producing a plan that he himself admitted was little more than smoke and mirrors when viewed as a template for actual construction—so why wasn't he given the opportunity to follow through? He felt the same way and threw a tantrum. On November 22, Huxtable denigrated Nelson Rockefeller's original plan, drafted by Wallace Harrison, lauded Philip Johnson, and called our progress "a potential tragedy of errors," performed by engineers acting in place of architects. She didn't understand that now, when we were about to actually build, we needed builders, not dreamers. This thing had to work!

Starting with a Bang

The beginning of the demolition of the first pier was a great opportunity to put us in the media and give the public a sense that something very big and significant was coming on the scene downtown. I didn't have to ponder how to exploit the occasion. Let's start with a bang! The obvious thing to do would be to have Governor Rockefeller do something dramatic to signify the start of construction on what was, after all, originally his vision. What could be more graphic than an underwater charge to start pier demolition?

To set off a dynamite charge on the river, you need permission from the U.S. Army Corps of Engineers, the Coast Guard, the New York City Fire and Police Departments, and on and on. Then there was the city's bureaucracy. We got the Department of Buildings to sign off as well as the Department of Ports and Terminals, not to mention the New York City Police Department. But the final required approval from the Fire Department didn't come until a few days before the governor was to press the plunger detonating the dynamite

Speaking of explosions, Mayor Lindsay, whose relationship with Governor Rockefeller was always close to the detonation point, would as a courtesy be invited to join us on the big day, June 26, 1970. We were, after all, about to commence a project in his bailiwick. Avrum Hyman, supervising the day's activities, spoke to Hugh Morrow, the governor's press director, about that invitation and received a wry reply. Morrow mused: "Well, let's see, John is better looking, but Nelly has more money. Let's invite John." Lindsay, however, declined to attend.

George W. Rogers and Company had already been at work cleaning up the site for our ceremony on the twenty-sixth. I joined the governor early that morning for a helicopter flight down to the city from his Pocantico Hills estate. We were going to hit all five boroughs, turning the spotlight of publicity on several housing projects I was involved with as New York State commissioner of housing and community renewal, including a flyover of the huge Co-op City in the Bronx on our way south. One of our stops was on the site of what had been a batting and golf driving range in the midst of automobile junkyards in Flatlands on the outer edge of Brooklyn, near the Belt Parkway, not far from Jamaica Bay and Kennedy airport. There, I was and am proud to say, the state housing division that I headed was supervising planning and construction of a $325,000,000 Mitchell-Lama project that would become the 5,888-family Starrett City.

We almost played act two of this epic as a comedy. The governor and I were scheduled next to fly on to Floyd Bennett Field, at the southeastern tip of Brooklyn, opposite the Rockaways, where we had proposed to build more government assisted housing. At this point high technology gave way to a little legwork. We were a bit ahead of schedule and needed to alert the welcoming committee at Floyd Bennett, where we would stop for lunch, to expect us a little early. But our helicopter radio was off limits because it would interfere with military communications. No problem, I thought. I asked my deputy commissioner, Avrum Hyman, to phone ahead and—years before cell phones would be available—handed him a dime to make the call. But while the governor of New York State and his housing commissioner were preparing to fly like birds over the short distance to Floyd Bennett, poor Avrum Hyman was desperately searching on the ground for a pay phone in the most deserted part of the borough. Fortunately, he found one and I didn't have to explain to a what would have been a perplexed governor why it might have appeared that nobody was home when we landed.

That still left Avrum back in the middle of nowhere because meanwhile the helicopter had departed. My ever-resourceful public information director spotted the chartered bus that had been ordered to stand by to provide the entire entourage ground transportation to Floyd Bennett Field if the weather, which had become threatening, socked in the Starrett City site, grounding the governor and stranding him in the wilds of Brooklyn. Avrum leaped aboard the empty vehicle and in the best traditions of Hollywood, ordered the driver to "follow that helicopter!" He reached Floyd Bennett Field in time for dessert, the sole occupant of a well-equipped, fifty-passenger bus.

Ultimately, our stop at Floyd Bennett Field would prove more frustrating for me than Avrum's brief sojourn on the edge of Brooklyn had been for him. In a March 5 memo to Rockefeller, I had proposed that we create a large-scale housing development at this historic location. The city's first municipal airport in the 1930s, Floyd Bennett Field had been converted into a navy field during World War II and was later used by the naval reserve. The Department of Defense had just announced that it would phase out use of the field, and I recognized a golden opportunity for new housing. There were increasingly fewer large open areas in New York City appropriate for housing projects such as Starrett City and Co-op City. Among the few, Floyd Bennett was perhaps the jewel. If *ever* a parcel of land cried out for development, it was this one. Relatively inexpensive land, no one to evict, and a location that was close enough to public transportation to make that factor work with perhaps the extension of a subway line—what more could a state housing commissioner have asked for?

This former naval air station was my number one target site for the next large-scale development and this stop on the trip on June 26 was meant to put it on the map—eventually the City Planning Commission's map, I hoped. That's what the governor spoke to at our luncheon at the field. And if it weren't for some particularly petty politics on the mayor's part—more about that later—the city's housing stock would have been the richer for it today.

Our next stop was Staten Island. Unfortunately, the weather was rapidly deteriorating and we headed in for a landing at St. George in an almost impenetrable mist. Until we sighted the Coast Guard flares on our landing pad—not till we descended to a height of barely one hundred feet, by the way—the governor appeared visibly tense. He gazed out the window with a fixed stare, clearly uncomfortable being in an aircraft headed for . . . where?

At this stop, we viewed the site where my old boss, William Zeckendorf, was proposing to build another development. A builder who perpetually thought in terms of large-scale projects, Zeckendorf had also been discussing with U.S. Steel the possibility of putting up another mixed-use development, something like Battery Park City, only smaller, on the abandoned site of the old Staten Island Ferry Depot. After a brief ceremony at the Staten Island site, we bused to another project and finally boarded a hydrofoil for the trip across the harbor to the watery location that was to become Battery Park City.

If Governor Rockefeller was unhappy about that helicopter ride, I would have hated to have his thoughts on the hydrofoil. Driven by rear-mounted propellers, the hydrofoil traveled on skids—water skis, in effect—once it got up to speed. We had already received a proposal from one company to use this craft to provide ferry service to Battery Park City and today's ride was meant to be a demonstration of the vessel's potential. We just hadn't counted on the rain, fog, and strong winds that buffeted us once we moved out into the harbor.

At forty miles an hour on choppy water, the hydrofoil does nothing good to one's stomach. After we hit a piece of debris, the hydrofoil lost headway, dropped off its skids and came to a quick stop, nowhere near land and with virtually zero disability, I couldn't help noticing the color on the governor's face: there was none. He didn't see the NYPD launches convoying us or the NYPD helicopter hovering overhead, and it was clearly a difficult moment or two for him until the captain, using a long gaff, cleared the offending log from one of our skids, against which it had become wedged. Upon our arrival at an already soggy, rain-swept pier at our construction site, a waterlogged reporter told Governor Rockefeller, "Boy, are we glad you're here, Governor." Rockefeller replied with irony the journalist could not have appreciated, "That makes two of us!" That was the last of the hydrofoils at Battery Park City.

We had a good media turnout on the pier with, thankfully, plenty of cameras. There were politicians and other dignitaries as well as developers who hoped to be included in our plans. Now it was time. The governor would say a few words, pose at the plunger for the photographers and milking this moment in New York's history for all its publicity potential, dramatically set off an explosion. But the plunger was positioned outside in what was now an uncomfortably driving rain. It had already been a long day, Nelson Rockefeller was tired and no doubt, he had more things to come on his calendar. He strode directly to the plunger, pushed it with all the drama of opening a swinging door and walked away, oblivious to the twenty-five-foot spray he had kicked up with the blast.

Gabe Pressman, NBC TV's local news hawk, had just watched the centerpiece of his lead story for the evening dissolve in the rain. Never a shy one, Gabe quipped: "Governor, I missed that, could you do it again?"

In Search of Office Space Developers

Ever since we announced plans for Battery Park City, various businesses had been in touch with us, inquiring about supplying construction services, building retail stores, or even acting as developers for the commercial or residential structures that would go up. Chase Manhattan and Bankers Trust Company, for example, were looking at the possibility of adding Battery Park City branches, and Macy's was scouting us as a future location for one of its stores. Pace College (now Pace University) raised the possibility of a branch on our property. We had filed all of these queries as premature. Interest picked up, of course, when we finally got the approval of the City Planning Commission and the Board of Estimate and it all became official with the signing of the master lease.

In November 1969, seven months before we actually took possession of what was to be the landfill site, we had already been preparing for the task of screening prospective subleasees of the commercial sites. Our plan was to give priority to the offices and stores because, we hoped, revenues from them would subsidize residential construction and help pay for infrastructure. The developer or developers chosen would, of course, be looking at the potential market for that space.

I suppose advertising for developers to bid on the opportunity of building at Battery Park City was a little bit like placing a personals ad. We were looking for the right match. They knew what we had to offer, although we spelled it out, and we needed to tell potential developers what we would be looking for at their end. We wanted specific proposals for the space, naturally.

Developers had to have an impressive history of building major projects and had to submit financial statements to prove that they were solvent and could afford to complete their side of the deal. There's nothing like committing a lot of money to prove one's sincerity, so any developer who was approved would have to put up $500,000 as a good faith deposit. We were also looking for developers with Triple A credit ratings, a plus for us when we would enter the bond market and our own financial solidity would be scrutinized.

In the summer of 1970, just as we were about to solicit proposals from developers, an ominous economic trend began to manifest itself. At a February meeting of our board, we had briefly discussed the potential market for commercial space in our area, but it was a bit abstract and premature at the time. Now, at precisely the wrong time and with no way of predicting it, a shadow was beginning to descend on the commercial real estate market in New York City. Several developers were holding off on already announced plans to build elsewhere. Where we had expected, by this time, to see foundations poured and heavy construction equipment working around Manhattan, there remained instead the ubiquitous parking lots, placeholders until things looked up. In fact, within a few months, by the end of 1970, we would be looking at a four-million-square-foot surplus of office space downtown.

Still, we had to get some development proposals into the pipeline and we had every reason to believe that when the time came for shovels to start moving dirt on land that we had yet to create, the market would have turned. The course of previous downturns suggested that this scenario would play out as we anticipated.

At that critical moment, there were only two of us at the top to make the essential decisions about Battery Park City. Judge Samuel Pierce had resigned as a member of the Authority on June 16 to take the job of general counsel at the U.S. Treasury. It was an interim position, it would turn out, for he was on track to eventually becoming secretary of housing and urban development in the Reagan administration. Our young Battery Park City Authority also lost my assistant, Ed Levy, in August, who went on to other pursuits.

Pierce's replacement would be former New York City comptroller, Mario Procaccino. Defeated by Lindsay in the mayoral election in 1969, this Democrat and former civil court judge had backed Nelson Rockefeller for governor when he ran for reelection against Arthur Goldberg in 1970. But Procaccino would not be appointed until April 1971, and would not be ready to join us until June of that year.

So, in August 1970, with only Al Mills and myself still on board, we proceeded to solicit proposals from developers. Our ads appeared in the *New York Times* on the twelfth and in the *Wall Street Journal* on the fourteenth. We also advertised in several other relevant publications. By early September, twenty-four potential developers had responded.

We had initially set September 30 as a deadline for submissions but extended that to December 31 when several potential developers asked for more time. Among those requesting copies of the master lease with the idea of possibly bidding were such real estate giants as Helmsley-Spear, Sulzberger-Rolfe, Rudin Management, U.S. Steel, First National City Bank, Lehman Brothers, Uris Building, and Boise Cascade.

On November 20, 1970, Harry Helmsley's representative, William Lillis, called to ask about our bidding procedures. One of the factors that had made Helmsley such a significant developer in the New York market was his attention to detail, and now was no exception. Early on, he wanted to discuss the construction schedule for the buildings at our southern end. He was already envisioning what it might be like for tenants contemplating renting in the first building to be completed while the other structures, nearby, were still going up. He wanted to make sure that the half-finished office towers would not dominate the scene, affecting the rentability of the already-finished space.

By the spring, we had narrowed down the number of prospective developers to four. They were Helmsley, Sulzberger-

Rolfe, Galbreath-Ruffin, and Uris. On April 14 and 15, 1971, we interviewed each of them. Four days later I said at an authority meeting that Helmsley seemed to express the most serious interest, and at the moment seemed ready to offer a firm commitment on one of the three planned office towers with an option on the other two. Uris was still in the running and we asked for a more detailed proposal from them and Helmsley. Only Helmsley followed through and was willing to put up a cash good faith deposit, and therefore became our office developer.

At six feet three inches tall, Harry Helmsley loomed large on any stage. When it came to Manhattan real estate, he towered over everyone. He always said that the best advice he ever received was from his mother, who told him to "buy real estate." Harry was the island's largest landlord, building his empire on an astute use of leverage, formidable negotiating skills, and the careful spending of his own cash only when he had to. He and I shared a significant biographical fact: both of our grandfathers had been successful investing in New York City apartment houses.

You have to have a big, healthy ego to develop on a grand scale, and Harry Helmsley was in good health in that regard. At the end of December 1972, when Helmsley came to us for permission to put up a sign in the area he was to develop, trumpeting his intentions, he submitted a sketch of it for approval. We had to remind him that this was a joint city, state, and private development and that, therefore, the mayor's and governor's names should be printed in a larger typeface than his, and that he should refer to himself as either the "builder" or "developer," not as the "owner-builder," as his sketch had it.

By no means did we have a done deal with Harry once we had chosen him as our office space developer. There were still months of on-again, off-again discussions of details. Meanwhile, in the midst of the real estate slowdown, Helmsley began the process of lining up a prime, main tenant for one of the buildings. But throughout this process, he managed to dance away every time we pressed him to make a written commitment in the form of a letter of intent and a cash deposit.

When we finally reached agreement on a letter of intent on December 30, 1971, Helmsley had just finished building the Park Lane Hotel in Midtown, had an interest—through a syndicate—in ownership and management of the Empire State Building that his fabled wife, Leona, still holds at this writing, and was currently involved in several residential developments, including the twelve-thousand-unit Parkchester in the Bronx and the construction of more than three million square feet of office space in New York City. In short, he was more than qualified to develop the office space we were hoping would be the financial engine that would propel the rest of the Battery Park City project.

Bringing Helmsley aboard would serve us well at the beginning of 1972 as we prepared to float a $200,000,000 bond issue. Prospective bondholders could look at our prospectus and see on it the closest thing to a brand name in commercial real estate. You might say he was potentially money in the bank for Battery Park City.

We announced the Helmsley participation in Battery Park City on February 2, 1972. He was committing himself to develop five million square feet of office and three hundred thousand square feet of retail space. The office towers he would build, in accordance with the master plan, would be fifty, sixty, and seventy stories, with the first planned to be ready for occupancy in 1975.

"I am confident that the demand for large scale office space still exists in the city and that by the time we are ready to start construction in the middle of 1973 a tenant or tenants will be available to lease the Battery Park City office space," he said. And with the American Stock Exchange still a possible tenant in one building and Dun and Bradstreet also showing some interest now, his optimism seemed realistic. Meanwhile, the Helmsley organization would move ahead on plans for the buildings themselves, as our agreement specified, to be ready to start work as soon as the area where they were planned was filled.

A week later, James D. Landauer Associates, our real estate consultant for commercial space, reinforced Helmsley's optimism. They reported "that the present oversupply of downtown office space will be eliminated by early 1976 and that a resumption of new construction reflecting a renewal of demand may be anticipated in the 1974-75 period." Had it not been for OPEC turning off the oil spigot in 1973, an outcome totally unpredictable at the time, Landauer's projection would literally have been right on the money, and my story would have had an earlier and happier ending.

Helmsley would not be alone in trying to secure one or more blue-chip tenants for our office space. In the summer of 1971, Governor Rockefeller was lobbying with Gustav Levy of Goldman Sachs to use his influence to get the New York Stock Exchange to move to Battery Park City. In September, I followed up the governor's efforts. But at a presentation we made to them in February 1972, officials of the exchange made it clear that they worried that if they made a firm, long-term commitment to a New York City location, the cash-strapped city might impose a stock transfer tax once they were locked into a lease.

Still, there were many other possible quality tenants and we were optimistic of snaring at least one. We were to sublease the ten-acre construction site to Helmsley at fair market value, and he would pay us the equivalent of full taxes on the assessed value. The result, we anticipated, would be an income for the authority of more than $16 million a year. On February 12, 1972, the TV lights were shining bright and hot at Governor Rockefeller's Midtown office as Helmsley finally handed the governor a check for $250,000, required to back up the developer's letter of intent.

No such occasion can pass into history without the *New York Times* pronouncing judgment, and they handed down their opinion in an editorial that suggested the handiwork of the ever-present Ms. Huxtable. The editorial described the buildings Helmsley was to develop as "rather terrifying hexagonal towers" that were "the size of the Pan Am Building."

I personally responded in a letter to the editor, reminding the paper that these buildings were essentially the ones in the 1969 master development plan that had so pleased the *Times* back then, when Huxtable had gushed, "Is that any way to plan a city? You bet it is!" Were they now hedging their bets? I also pointed out that any changes in this plan had to pass muster with the City Planning Commission, a three-member Architectural Review Committee, and the city's Office of Lower Manhattan Development.

The editorial had cast some doubt on our viability, but more than twenty developers had put down a deposit in order to be considered for the office space, and that was dramatic proof of how *they* viewed our prospects. Finally, I suggested that the paper shouldn't think it could impose its "subjective architectural or design aesthetics upon the competent professional consultants which the Authority engages to direct its functions."

The *Times* responded in a way that is always the most effective when a paper wishes to ignore opposition: they didn't publish it.

Again, the project was being evaluated almost solely in terms of its aesthetics. Fortunately, with jobs increasingly fleeing the city, there were many people measuring the significance of Battery Park City against more mundane, but still significant, criteria: its potential value in maintaining the economic primacy of a great metropolis.

In fact, that hexagonal design was already on its way out, but not because it disturbed anyone's delicate sensibilities at our "paper of record." With the market soft, this was no time to try precedent-shaking flights of the imagination in design. We needed buildings that would make potential tenants feel comfortable.

Starting at the Bottom

From the sky above to the mud below—that's how one might describe the alpha and omega of my years at Battery Park City, dealing with the rarefied ideas and individuals at a major newspaper one moment, while in the next turning my attention to earthier matters. One could spend just so much time refuting critics: there was land to create. We had to begin finding out just what conditions prevailed under the murky waters of the Hudson, where our land would rise up from the river bottom. This initiated the parallel activities that would occupy and increasingly dominate my time for the next seven years: trying to deal with the economic and political environment in which we were creating a new-town in-town, while at the same time steering the actual construction of Battery Park City through myriad obstacles.

On October 20, 1970, I addressed the American Society of Civil Engineers. I trust that my thoughts were clear and that I conveyed them well, but my subject was muddy—literally. We faced the task of putting in a bulkhead that would contain the landfill, and that would involve dredging the silt that had accumulated on the bottom over centuries.

Riprap (a stone embankment) would surround the approximately five million cubic yards of sand dredged from the lower harbor that would form our land. Through that riprap, the contractor would sink twenty-inch square concrete piles, some as deep as seventy feet, into the bedrock below, and install a bulkhead. A concrete relieving platform would rest on these piles, and on top of that would go five feet of earth fill.

It would, in fact, be several years before we had filled our entire site, but when we finished the job we would have spent $100 million creating land that cost $25 a square foot to bring it into being. The equivalent cleared land in that area was currently renting based on at least $300 to $500 a square foot. The engineers to whom I was speaking didn't have to reach for their slide rules to recognize a good deal when they heard one. They were impressed.

We were anxious to get started that fall with test borings that would tell us what to expect when we began to drive piles into the riverbed. In keeping with the spirit of just about all of our endeavors thus far, outside forces caused a delay, although this time it was fairly brief and had nothing to do with the Lindsay administration: there was a drillers' strike.

By the beginning of 1971, however, we were back on track. Pier demolition was going according to schedule. Pier 19, as well as piers 2 and 3, were all but gone. And with the driller's strike over, we had three rigs performing underwater core boring. We could now anticipate beginning the bulkhead in the spring. Just as important, we were staying within our budget.

There's more than one way to design a bulkhead, and we had to make a choice. We could have put in concrete boxes out to the pierhead line. They would be more expensive initially, although in the long run they would have required less maintenance. Money was an object for us in the short run, so we opted for a dike formation with a pile-supported platform.

It was going to make for one heck of a sandbox and naturally, we needed to have a place from which to get the sand. On March 8, 1971, I wrote to the New York State Department of General Services and they informed us that we could take the sand from the Lower Bay, off the south shore of Staten Island, beginning four thousand feet offshore. Technically, it would come from the bottom of the bay between the shoreline and an area called Chapel Hill Channel. It would cost us $.15 a cubic yard and was just the kind of sand we needed: solid enough to support what we were going to put on it, and porous enough so that we could drive piles down through it to bedrock to support a variety of structures.

In taking and using this sand, we would be performing a public service in more ways than one. The prevailing Atlantic Ocean currents, which pick up sand from the beaches of Long Island's south shore, deposit the sand at this location at the mouth of the harbor, right in the shipping channel. The Army Corps of Engineers had to periodically dredge the channel and the sand had to go somewhere. We were prepared to give it a very good home.

For almost every bit of actual construction—or demolition, for that matter—we needed to accomplish at Battery Park City, there always seemed to have been an accompanying political or bureaucratic barrier to surmount. In the case of the bulkhead and landfill, that obstacle was the U.S. Army Corps of Engineers. We couldn't begin until they did an environmental assessment, a thorough, painstakingly long process that had us watching the calendar, once again.

Fortunately my staff was good at scheduling, and that they were all skilled enough at what they did to make it possible for me to delegate tasks without worrying, because I had enough things in the air at one time to qualify as a master juggler. I was still state commissioner of housing, which alone would have been enough to more than fill a long day. And at Battery Park City, while having to deal with building and bureaucracy simultaneously, I was also opening up another front, choosing a developer for the first residential units.

As I've noted, the commercial tenants would help to foot the bill for the rest of the project. So, our top priority was filling in and developing the south sixteen acres where the first three office buildings and retail space would go. The faster we turned on that revenue stream, the better it would be for everything else we planned. But we also had to begin the process of securing developers for the residential units, even before the landfill was completed for the office towers. And as if I didn't have enough headaches already, that would put me into a contentious relationship with the great residential developer Mr. Samuel J. LeFrak, worth his weight in politicians, bureaucrats, and ego.

Chapter 6

TIME AND TIDE AND SAMUEL J. LEFRAK

My job as chairman of the Battery Park City Authority was incredibly varied. But as any chief executive in any organization soon finds out, one of your major functions is usually to be its most visible spokesperson. I found myself giving many speeches, filling in the facts about the marvelous project that was just getting under way in the Hudson River at the southwest tip of Manhattan. I also tried to convey a vision of what Battery Park City would mean to the larger city of which it was soon to become an integral part.

One of the points I tried to get across was the sheer magnitude of our project. As I told the New York City Bar Association in April 1971, the development's "population will exceed that of White Plains, its workforce will be greater than that of Schenectady's, and its assessed valuation will surpass Syracuse." Surely, "city" was not too grand a term for it.

But immersed as I was in the specifics of Battery Park City, it was only a part of my concerns. As state housing commissioner, I had a list of projects that required some part of my attention every day. And I was constantly trying to implement my view of how our work at the Division of Housing and Community Renewal might improve the quality and availability of housing for *all* of the state's citizens.

Battery Park City was thus, initially, part of a bigger picture. In March 1970, in an article for the *New York Times*'s real estate section titled "Housing Prospect Bleak in the City," I depicted a housing stock in which "the plaster is falling, the wires are burning, the boilers are cracking, the roofs are leaking and the paint is peeling." I called for an end to the "petty politics, greed and envy" that was holding back the construction of new residential units.

I, like Robert Moses, felt that large-scale developments were the best way to go to add to our housing stock—it was this meeting of minds that had initiated our friendship. In terms of economics and efficiency, if you're going to build, you might as well build big—it takes about as much time and effort to build one thousand units as one hundred. This led not only to economies of scale but also to the possibility of creating entire new communities along with the public institutions that knit them together, such as schools and libraries, and the shopping facilities that also enhanced the quality of life.

Along with Battery Park City, I saw the possibility of doing this, as I've mentioned, at the site of the former Floyd Bennett Field. As with Battery Park City, the Floyd Bennett proposal came up against a lack of legislative will along with parochial politics that in this case were fatal. At the beginning of 1971, the proposal failed to get anywhere in the City Planning Commission, where members suggested that there were insufficient federal subsidies to help build it. But the funds *were* there for any one who cared to look hard enough. It struck me at the time that this was "planning" based on "fears, pessimism or lack of initiative."

On June 26, 1971, I testified in Washington to the Subcommittee on National Parks and Recreation of the Committee on Interior and Insular Affairs, which was examining issues related to the new Gateway Park in the metropolitan area. I proposed that the park be seen in a wider context, as part of a larger whole in which recreation and housing could be dealt with efficiently and effectively together. I said my proposal "would justify and spread the costs, both capital and operating, that housing and Gateway would require. That a portion of the potential users will be right at the doorstep of Gateway only strengthens the argument for joint development." A Floyd Bennett housing development would have used but three hundred acres, only 3.6 percent of the total Gateway area, leaving nine hundred acres at Floyd Bennett for recreation.

In truth, as I later discovered to my dismay, the project never had a chance. Mayor Lindsay stifled it and a large factor behind its demise was the objection of Brooklyn Congressman Frank Brasco, in whose district it would have been built. When it came to counting potential votes, Brasco was no dummy. The demographics of his district, heavily Italian-American, guaranteed his reelection. If the demographics of Co-op City were a model of who we could expect to live in the Floyd Bennett development, his constituents would suddenly number many more Jewish voters, who might not support him at the polls. When votes come up against vision, politicians are congenitally nearsighted. Bet on it.

Once Floyd Bennett Field was stymied, I modified the proposal to place the new development, patterned after Co-op City, at the edge of Marine Park, which was adjacent to the Gateway Park. But this, too, failed to catch on.

I continued to advocate this approach to new housing right up through early 1973, when I left my state position to concentrate entirely on Battery Park City. At the end of 1972, for example, Governor Rockefeller asked me for a position paper on housing goals for New York State and the nation. I told him that we ought to be using Battery Park City as a model for new construction. "State-created and State-funded public authorities should be responsible for undertaking revitalization of existing communities through development of new-towns in-town and for development of entirely new towns or even new counties outside of existing communities," I wrote. Had it been politically possible at the time, I would have advocated some form of a national urban development corporation, with the proviso that it not be allowed to override home rule.

The Army Corps of Engineers

Fortunately, I was in a position to directly carry out the spirit of this proposal, at least at one site. In October 1971, speaking to the State Assembly Standing Committee on Corporations, Authorities and Commissions, I said that "families will be living in Battery Park City in four years." Acknowledging the complexities of the development, I pointed out that we were overcoming delays and were pretty much on track to meet our schedules. Battery Park City "has gained production momentum, and has developed an operating rhythm that makes meeting these schedules not only possible but predictably probable."

But all the cheerleading in the world cannot move the tides. In fact, it was the tides and other nautical phenomena that now held us up.

By early September 1970, half of pier 19 was gone and we had put up a sign on what was left of the pier's head house announcing our project. It was clearly visible to drivers on the West Side Highway. By the end of the month, similar signs greeted drivers emerging from the Brooklyn Battery Tunnel into Manhattan, where piers 1 and 2 were about to be demolished. Things were looking up for us as the remnants of Manhattan's once dominant shipping business came tumbling down.

Tearing down was one thing. But what we wanted to put up was about to receive intense scrutiny. The beginning of our building process in the Hudson faced mandatory environmental review by a gaggle of government agencies. By the time we could proceed with the landfill, we would have already *had* our fill of forms and procedures, bureaucrats and delays. And the worst was yet to come.

Given the way our project could potentially affect shipping on the Hudson and the very flow of the river that sustained it, the federal government was going to hold us up to a high environmental standard. We needed the approval of the Council on Environmental Quality before we could actually proceed with building the bulkhead and pouring the sand for the landfill, and that group's approval was contingent on a favorable report from the Army Corps of Engineers.

By the spring of 1971, our test borings had allowed us to map out the geology of our building site and we were anxious to get under way with the actual bulkhead and filling of the south sixteen acres so we could get those revenue-producing office buildings up and renting. On May 21, we authorized the Corps of Engineers to build a scale model of our project at their facilities at the U.S. Waterways Experiment Station in Vicksburg, Mississippi, for the purpose of testing the way our construction was likely to influence our surroundings. The process would cost us $25,000.

Among the issues that concerned the Army Corps of Engineers was whether our landfill might redirect river currents in such a way as to increase sediment in the shipping channel, making it necessary for them to do more dredging. They were also looking at our potential effect on tides, river salinity, water temperature, and the like.

The initial tests went well and we asked the corps to expedite the rest. But on June 21, our engineering coordinator, William Maley, reported to me that the council's review process would also require twenty-four divisions of various government agencies to certify that the test results caused no problem for *them* and whatever segment of our lives *they* watched over. "Uh-oh," I thought to myself. Maley optimistically suggested that the whole process could be completed in thirty days. We had just let the contract for the initial bulkhead and filling to the George W. Rogers Company and we were anxious to begin the process of land creation.

On June 28, we announced that Rogers would be filling the area stretching from pier A at our southern tip, northward to just south of Rector Street. We expected that the contractor would be able to get under way in about a month and would be finished with this section of landfill in fifteen months. At this point, the state's first instance appropriation would still be paying for the work.

It was important to maintain the public's sense of our momentum, especially with our bond issue looming not too far in the future. On July 15, we held a "waterbreaking," in lieu of a groundbreaking, beginning the final demolition of the piers in the sixteen-acre area we were going to fill first. Governor Rockefeller, always enamored of heavy construction equipment, was on hand to man the controls of the machine that pulled the first pile from pier 2.

The Corps of Engineers reported to us in September 1971 on the tests at Vicksburg. They showed that the effect of our building on shoaling, salinity, and tidal heights was going to be marginal. We represented no threat to navigation. About the only thing they had to advise us about was that we keep our coves shallow to avoid a build-up of silt in them. Striped bass copulation was not the problem it is today, and environmental paralysis with respect to development had not yet set in.

But by now, there were many cooks looking for an opportunity to stir the stew. New York City Park's Commissioner August Heckscher, for example, was worried. What about? Well, he was concerned that our digging up sand from just offshore at Staten Island might somehow affect park land nearby in that borough. He was also afraid that Battery Park City might not dispose of its solid wastes to his satisfaction. But our withdrawals from the offshore sand bank were not going to hurt his park land one bit. In fact, it's hard to imagine how they could. As for waste disposal, we were about to come to an agreement with the city in which they would accept the sewage from Battery Park City for treatment at their proposed West Side treatment plant south of the George Washington Bridge, making it unnecessary for us to build our own treatment plant. Heckscher also fretted that his department, stretched thin as it was, could not administer the open land on our project site, something that our lease specified was *our* responsibility in the first place.

The Army Corps of Engineers wanted to know if we would disrupt local transportation. William J. Ronan, chairman of the Metropolitan Transit Authority, assured them that much of the new residential population we would add to Lower Manhattan would walk to work. Those who didn't could be accommodated with relatively minor changes in train and bus service.

The strangest response to the corps' solicitation of views as to our effect on our environment came from the acting regional director of the Bureau of Sport Fisheries and Wildlife in Boston, who carped at our plans for reasons known only to him. He wrote, "The Applicant has failed to establish a definite need for creation of new land as opposed to restoration or renovation of existing blighted areas within the City. Such lands presumably do exist in close proximity to the project site." What did that have to do with fish or game?

Now that was a real fishing expedition, looking for an opportunity to apply bureaucratic muscle where it didn't belong. The essence of our project had already run the gauntlet of approval by several city bodies with regard to its economic appropriateness and social utility and had passed. And what blighted areas could he possibly have had in mind "nearby"? America's financial center on Wall Street? Sitting in Boston he clearly had no conception whatsoever of what we were building or where we were going to build it and why. Instead of running on like this, he might more profitably have spent his time on a coffee break, contemplating the environmental effect of the lint in his navel. In fact, it took four months, a trip to Washington, and political help to override him.

By November 1971, we had completed all the necessary borings and testing preliminary to beginning construction of the bulkhead and the storm sewer outfall relocation that would also be necessary in the south sixteen acres. Mueser, Rutledge had finished its overall design for the bulkhead and was ready to attack the upgrading of the problem-loaded twenty acres of fill we had inherited from the excavation for the World Trade Center. On the nineteenth, they reported success in their pile-load tests. In these tests, they had used seventy-five-foot-long piles and stressed them with a load of three hundred tons as they drove them into bedrock. That would be more than twice the load needed for bulkhead construction in the south sixteen acres.

A few months before, in consultation with our engineers, we had decided on how we would dredge the landfill area. We could have opted for digging out all the silt, right down to bedrock, but settled instead for removing soft material from the bottom to the point where its thickness was uniform. This less costly approach would be just as effective for our purposes and involved less dredging, allowing the fill to settle on the remaining silt evenly, without any slippage.

But still we waited for final approval from the federal government. We would be literally dead in the water until we received it and further delays were going to cost us money. On December 27, 1971, I wrote directly to Russell E. Train, chairman of the President's Council on Environmental Quality. I told him we needed clearance prior to our upcoming bond sale. We couldn't go to market with the environmental issue in doubt. Who would buy bonds backed by a project that could be dismantled by an unfavorable decision from a government agency? I told Train that without that permission to build, "work on this eight and one-half million dollar contract is now being delayed and the Authority is faced with the prospect of major delay claims from the contractor." I asked him to expedite approval once he received a favorable report from the Corps of Engineers. At issue was the additional thirty days that was usually tacked on for public comment once the corps' report was in. We hoped to bypass that extra month of forced inactivity.

The fact of the matter was that we had to cool our heels. On January 25, 1972, the corps finally gave us its approval, 184 days after they had begun to consider our application. An additional delay, till February 7, when the New York City Department of Ports and Terminals gave us *their* required approval, seemed almost brief in comparison. I have to admit after all of this that I was sorely tempted to ask out loud, "Anybody else here object?"

Walk to Work

Land would soon be rising from the river at our location and a big chunk of it was earmarked for housing. With that land on the horizon, and about to settle on a developer for the project's office buildings and begin the selection process to choose a developer for the apartment units, we needed a property manager. In May 1971, I hired Ralph Peterson, who had been with United States Lines, managing their waterfront property and office building.

The year 1971 was significant in many ways. In April, we advertised for developers to sublet land on our site and erect slightly more than three thousand apartment units in the first two neighborhoods of Battery Park City, along with almost four

hundred thousand square feet of shopping space. This was the
area that would ultimately become Gateway Plaza, in the heart of
the project west of the World Trade Center. The deadline for
applications was July 1. The stores would be of two types.
Department stores and specialty shops would cater to residents
and nearby workers as well as outside visitors, while convenience
stores such as groceries and drug stores would be geared primarily
toward residents.

Eventually we would include a hotel in the mix. We had
contracted with the firm of Harris, Kerr, Forster & Company,
specialists in hotel accounting, to direct a study of the feasibility
of one on our site. In March they had reported that although
visitors to New York City—even those with business downtown—
currently preferred to stay in Midtown to take advantage of that
areas' shopping and entertainment possibilities, a residential hotel
with luxury apartments and hotel services at Battery Park City
would have good prospects because of the nearby financial center.
Since we anticipated more shopping in the area by the time we
were through, we felt even better about it.

In our advertisement for residential developers, we specified
that applicants would have to be willing to put up a good faith
deposit, the amount or amounts to be determined by us. The ad
attracted responses from twenty-three developers, none of whom
we could rule out immediately. That "good faith deposit" would
help us immeasurably in the task of winnowing down the list,
because we were going to keep upping the ante into the millions
to make sure we were left with developers who were *really* serious.
We set the bar initially at $500,000 and ultimately raised it to $1
million. Suddenly, fifteen of the twenty-three discovered that their
interest had flagged and they dropped out.

On October 5, we met with one of the survivors, Samuel J.
LeFrak, his son Richard, and his architect, Moshe Safdie, who had
designed Habitat at the Montreal Expo in 1967. Sam LeFrak,
whose net worth was then $100 million, was his usual expansive
self. Battery Park City was "forever," Sam effused. Let's leave
"forever" to the ages, I thought, and concentrate on the here and

now. I cautioned him that it would be two years before we were ready to build and that the infrastructure was going to be complicated. In fact, I emphasized, "This may be the most complicated project that anybody has ever undertaken." That wouldn't stop him. It just spurred him on. "We will put our money where our mouth is," he assured us. "We want this job so bad we can taste it."

Perhaps I should have read this as a hint of oral aggression, because there would be times in the next few years when Samuel J. LeFrak would give the impression that he would like to swallow us whole.

How about a $2 million good faith deposit? Five more developers couldn't clear the bar and left the field. Finally, by mid-1972, after increasing the good faith deposit a few more notches, only two remained: Fisher Brothers and LeFrak.

Over the next year or so of discussions, we refined exactly what we wanted from the developers in this initial stage. It would be 660 market-rate apartments and 1,400 state-subsidized Mitchell-Lama units in the first phase, known as Pod III; a 1,000-room hotel; and 700,000 square feet of shopping space.

One day I bumped into Larry Fisher, one of the Fisher Brothers, at "21," and with the final determination of a residential developer still pending, I suggested on the spur of the moment that Fisher Brothers and LeFrak do it together as a joint venture. Larry took me up on the proposal, the strong-willed developer deciding to work with a man whose ego was even bigger than his. Fisher also brought the Sulzberger-Rolfe organization in to serve as renting agents.

Fisher Brothers had more than fifty years of experience building offices and residential space, including middle-income housing developments. They had put up thirty apartment buildings in the city's outer boroughs and luxury high-rises in Manhattan, as well as the Frontenac Hotel in Miami Beach. Three brothers ran the business, but it would be Lester Fisher who headed its Battery Park City work.

There was no doubt, though, about who the senior partner of this joint venture was going to be. Harry Lefrak (note the lowercase *f)* had founded the Lefrak organization in 1905. Headed by his son, Samuel J. LeFrak, since 1948, it had built three hundred thousand apartment units over the years and currently owned one hundred thousand. These apartments housed one of every sixteen New Yorkers. They had also constructed 3,000,000 square feet of office space. (And somewhere along the line, Samuel also constructed a capital *F* in the middle of his last name.)

Perhaps even more to the point, given our requirements, Lefrak had been the sponsor-developer of five Mitchell-Lama projects, including the first in 1957. Their Lefrak City project abutting the Long Island Expressway in Queens consisted of twenty eighteen-story towers, along with office space, a post office, restaurants, and other amenities and was the first "satellite city" built by a private company. If ever a developer was up to the task, it was Lefrak, which our real estate consultant, James Felt & Company, one of the most respected in the field, called "the largest single successful developer of housing in the City."

Sam J. LeFrak himself was a piece of work. True, he was a noted philanthropist and served on many civic bodies. He was also known for minimizing his expenses—often at someone else's expense—and being a difficult person to deal with. Perhaps it's in his life history. He originally intended to be a dentist and was on the wrestling team at the University of Maryland. Dealing with Sam was like trying to pull teeth from someone who has you in a headlock.

LeFrak was certainly up to the task of getting the best possible deal for himself, and it took a year of negotiating before we had something on paper. Finally, by the summer of 1973, we arrived at the terms of a letter of intent with the Lefrak/Fisher joint venture. A letter of intent, of course, is just that. It expresses intent. It's not a lease but rather a statement that we have agreed in principle and would be working out the details of an actual agreement to formally designate Lefrak/Fisher as developers of apartment units at Battery Park City. Even at the time, I knew that this was going to be "the world's most complicated and longest handshake."

But for the moment, at least, they were aboard, and on August 7, 1973, we announced that the joint venture would develop the first 5,800 units, a hotel, a shopping center, and other amenities. The letter of intent ran forty-four pages and required them to put down an initial deposit of $1 million. We also handed them a list of ten thousand families who had already expressed an interest, in writing, in living in Battery Park City.

The Lefrak/Fisher joint venture would be able to begin work thirty days after the City Planning Commission approved our housing plans in a revised master development plan and after the Board of Estimate had approved a special zoning district for Battery Park City that would incorporate the updated plan. We anticipated that the units they were to build would include some seven hundred market-rate apartments renting for about $135 a room per month and 1,600 units subsidized under the Mitchell-Lama program for which tenants would pay $40-$90 a room, depending on their income. Lefrak would use Harrison & Abramovitz as consulting architects to coordinate their design with the rest of the project.

We announced the agreement at our offices, where Sam LeFrak, this time, hit the right note in his statement. "As a builder and a New Yorker I have never subscribed to the bulldozer-and-wrecking-ball method of development," he said. "I believe in the use of our creative energies to recycle land, to create new land and in turn to build in order to meet the needs of the people. Battery Park City epitomizes this humane and creative approach."

Bonded

Money was an issue that always lurked in the background, and now it was to step front and center. The first instance appropriation was never meant to take us too far into the project, just get us started. And we were supposed to repay the $5 million we had drawn down. To pay for finishing the landfill and building the infrastructure of Battery Park City, we had always intended to rely on the proceeds of a bond issue.

As far back as 1969, *Eliot Sharp's Tax Exempt Newsletter* had carried an item about prospective bond financing for our project. Premature in its timing and understandably off on its facts at that early date, it read, "Battery Park City Auth. N. Y. expects to issue up to $155,000,000 in tax exempt bonds to finance development of a 118-acre commercial, residential and recreational project along the Hudson River in lower Manhattan."

On April 8, 1971, in a memo to Governor Rockefeller updating him on our project, I reported that I anticipated the first instance appropriation being "fully committed by the summer for bulkhead and fill in the south sixteen acres, now scheduled to be finished in early 1972." (We were all brimming with optimism in those days.) As a backstop to any delays in securing outside financing, we had also applied for an additional $17 million in first instance funds, which would be earmarked for upgrading the landfill made up of debris excavated for the construction of the World Trade Center.

I made it clear that I much preferred to have this money come from an expedited bond sale. I knew that full faith and credit debt issued by the state would not be available to us, and I urged the governor to use his influence to get for us from the legislature bond authorization containing a "moral make-up." This approach, to which I have referred earlier, would mean that the state could not legally bind all future legislatures to make good on our debt should we default. But it was almost as good, stating that the government of New York State was morally committed to guaranteeing that investors would be paid back, but each new session of the legislature would have to confirm this by vote, if necessary. The Urban Development Corporation was already using this type of debt. But they were issuing bonds backed by their general revenue flow, while ours were to be paid back by the returns on a specific project. For the Urban Development Corporation, as we shall see, this difference turned out to be fatal.

I reminded the governor that without the sale of these bonds we would have to depend on rents from the office space to carry the heavy burden of financing virtually our whole project. With the authorization and the sale of bonds, the office rents instead would go toward paying the debt service. A week later, I followed up the memo with a direct appeal for action to the governor's secretary, Bobby Douglass. I urged him to get the bond legislation "into print so that I can do whatever possible to assure its passage."

April 1971 was one of those critical moments in the development of our project, when preventing misperceptions about Battery Park City was as important as signing contracts, hiring personnel, and putting in landfill. We were about to advertise for residential developers as we geared up for what we hoped would be a successful bond sale. Legislative support was crucial. We needed that enabling legislation. Yet just then I began to pick up scuttlebutt that our lease with the city was way too favorable to the Lindsay administration and that it would substantially impede our ability to create an economically viable Battery Park City. This canard could make extremely difficult the task of getting state legislators to sign off on a bond sale.

I wrote to Governor Rockefeller to give him the ammunition he needed to make our case. Addressing the issues I had heard being tossed around, I reminded him that, in general, strategy during the lease negotiations had required that we let the city feel as if it had been getting more than it did. As for the financial commitments that we had to city hall, I pointed out that no rent was actually due the city until 1983 and that inflation in the interim would reduce its actual value when the time came to pay. Bondholders would legally come before the city in any claims to our assets, decreasing the chances that the state would ever have to pay up on the moral make-up clause.

I had also heard rumblings of dissatisfaction about the housing mix that had been such a contentious issue in our lease negotiations. But I emphasized that when the time came to actually allocate apartments by income, the market would play a bigger role than we had previously allowed. Some informal conversations we had recently had with members of Lindsay's administration indicated that they knew the score and would not be rigid on the mix if it proved to be a hindrance to renting the market-rate units—as ultimately proved to be the case. A meeting with Dick Buford and Percy Sutton helped to clear the air on the matter. The housing mix, by the way, was an issue we were determined to avoid in public until the bonds had been sold.

We were able to quiet the fears and the legislation sailed through, authorizing the Battery Park City Authority to sell up to $300 million in moral obligation bonds. Governor Rockefeller signed the authorization into law on June 3, 1971.

As 1971 ended, we were preparing the prospectus that would entice investors to lend us their money. And once we secured the formal approval of the Army Corps of Engineers early in the New Year, we were ready to plan the actual sale.

Those early months of 1972 were heady times for us. The old piers were coming down and we were anticipating the beginning of our landfill operation. We were about to drive the first piles for the bulkhead. Our project engineers were taking the studies we had commissioned by our real estate consultants, James Felt & Company for residential real estate and James Landauer Associates for commercial space, and projecting how and when we would spend the proceeds from the bond sale on construction. Our efforts to secure developers for the apartments, offices, and stores were proceeding apace. All in all, our vision of the future of this prime bit of Manhattan's Lower West Side was beginning to crystallize before our eyes.

True, the economy was—momentarily, the experts assured us— sounding a sour note, but there was as yet no indication that anything prolonged might be in the offing. Nevertheless, regulations required that we be scrupulous in our prospectus to point out all the possible pitfalls investors could face. Thus, the document contained an evaluation by James D. Landauer Associates that acknowledged the slump. "The Manhattan office market is currently in an oversupplied condition," it read, "arising both from a significant contraction in demand and a sharp increase in the supply of new office space." But it was Midtown that was then most seriously affected.

On May 5, 1972, we went to market. The $200 million in 40-year Series A bonds we elected to sell of the possible $300 million the state had authorized went at 6.35 percent and drew an "A" rating from Moody's and Standard and Poor's. Thomas E. Dewey Jr., a principal in Kuhn, Loeb & Company, one of the bond issue's underwriters, and the son of a former New York State governor, helped immeasurably with the road show that helped to put it over. At the last minute Comptroller Arthur Levitt had suggested that we limit the sale to $50 million, a sum that was unrealistically low, and I ignored him.

May 22 was perhaps an even nicer occasion. We received the proceeds of the bond sale from the underwriters, less their commission, at a ceremony at Governor Rockefeller's Midtown Manhattan office. It feels nothing but good to be handed a check for $197,425,016! Just as satisfying was the next transaction. I turned to the governor and handed *him* a check for $5,075,464.54, the full amount we had drawn from the original 1969 first instance appropriation of $15 million. Such a total reimbursement was a rare occasion in state history.

We anticipated that the proceeds from the bond sale, less our repayment of the first instance appropriation, would allow us to bulkhead and fill the entire ninety-one acres currently still underwater, put in the infrastructure for the office space and Battery Park City's first two residential neighborhoods, and complete plans for the remaining two neighborhoods.

Room for a Little Fun

There's a footnote to this bit of New York State and City history. On June 19, the *New York Times* ran a story reporting State Comptroller Arthur Levitt's complaint that only about 15 percent of public authorities ever paid back their first instance appropriations. The remainder just continued to carry the debt on their books. When the reporter who wrote the story contacted me, I proudly told him how we had bucked that trend, and I handed him a press release about the incident with a picture of Governor Rockefeller receiving the repayment check from me. The *Times*, of course, didn't use it.

When the story ran about Levitt's complaint, I had a little fun with the comptroller. On the same page, the *Times* had also reported about a Westchester County collection agency that had harassed debtors with official-looking documents that threatened to attach their wages.

I sent the clipping to Levitt at the "Levitt Collection Agency, A Levitt, Proprietor." I noted the check for more than $5 million that we had turned over in May for our "alleged debt." Then I threatened, "If you do not desist from such harassment we will get the people's lawyer after you." In truth, I don't think he feared a midnight knock on the door from then New York State attorney general Louis Lefkowitz, but I trust Arthur Levitt had a good laugh.

Chapter 7

ONE IF BY LAND, TWO IF BY SEA

B y the middle of 1972, thanks to our demolition contractors, the old piers were beginning to fall like duckpins. On May 18, I wrote to Richard Weinstein, Dick Buford's successor at the city's Office of Lower Manhattan Development, that we were ready to demolish piers 14 and 15, part of 13, and the old Delaware, Lackawanna, and Western Railroad Ferry Terminal at the foot of Barclay Street. (Ironically, after destruction of the World Trade Center and the terminal for the Port Authority Trans-Hudson (PATH) connection to New Jersey beneath the Twin Towers, ferry service across the Hudson would be resumed from the Battery Park City pierhead immediately west of Barclay Street on our landfill.)

The project was also beginning to become something of a presence to New Yorkers, even though there was yet nothing much there to catch their eye. In the spring of 1971 we had made our formal public relations debut, taking out a half-page ad in a special World Trade Center supplement that ran in the Sunday *Daily News*. Avrum Hyman, our director of public information, was getting us mentioned in a variety of publications with increasing frequency.

My name was also getting into the papers, although not always in connection with Battery Park City. Following his landslide reelection in November 1972, President Nixon was planning to make some changes in his cabinet. On November 22, the *New York Times* reported on a meeting that the president had held with Governor Rockefeller the previous day at Camp David. Although the meeting scotched rumors that Rockefeller would take a position in the second Nixon administration, it did raise a new one about me. The *Times* speculated that Rockefeller might be pushing for me to replace the departing George Romney as secretary of housing and urban development. But nothing came of it.

Meanwhile, on the Hudson, external events were often putting us on the defensive, taking up time and energy that we needed for advancing our project through the formation of landfill and the beginning of actual construction. In the midst of this turmoil, in April 1972, Jerome L. Sindler took over as the Battery Park City counsel. We were going to keep Jerry very busy.

In 1972 and 1973, we would face two significant hazards. One came from a potentially competing development across town that could have kept us from fully renting our apartments. It was John Lindsay's pet project, and was called Manhattan Landing. The other hazard arose from the replacement of the crumbling West Side Highway. The exact route that the replacement road would take was yet to be determined. The farther inland it stayed, the less we had to be concerned with it. But there were some people who thought it would be best to put it out over the water at the southern tip of Manhattan, creating the possibility that it could drive right through part of our site, like a stake through the heart.

Finally, that perennial issue, our housing mix, made one last appearance on the scene, roiling the waters. Again, we were forced to change the income ratio. But at least this time we had a good reason to do so and the change produced a more realistic combination.

Manhattan Landing

Mayor Lindsay and his coterie of urban planners had not forgotten their grand design of a redevelopment project that would sweep around the southern tip of Manhattan. But now they were concentrating on the East Side, since we had spoken, and acted, for the area on the Hudson.

The Lindsay administration announced Manhattan Landing, their project's new incarnation, just before our bond sale, which fortunately was not negatively impacted by the news. But the new development was already casting a shadow over our plans. For example, I was almost constantly on a chase to get the New York and American Stock Exchanges to tie their future physical presence to our space. Might Manhattan Landing offer them a better deal?

Lindsay, along with David Rockefeller, had unveiled the new 113-acre East Side development on April 12, 1972. It was to stretch for a mile, south from the Manhattan Bridge, expanding on the already existing Brooklyn Bridge Southwest Urban Renewal Project and encompassing the South Street Seaport. It was to include nine thousand luxury apartments and six million square feet of commercial space, as well as public amenities such as parks. Much of it would be built on pilings out over the river.

Among its aims was to secure "the full utilization for community development of the land and land under water between the project's main bulkhead and pierhead lines in the East River which is now characterized by decay and nonuse." Well, that sounded familiar.

The plan gained quick approval from Lindsay's City Planning Commission on May 17. In truth, more than civic-mindedness was at work. Some very big banks were cheering the project on. They held debt from the organization running the South Street Seaport, which was not in good financial shape. Manhattan Landing could offer a comprehensive cure for their problem by making the air rights over the seaport extremely valuable.

According to the seaport's May 1972 newsletter, "About 20 lending institutions, half a dozen major real estate developers, [and] a dozen elements of city, state, and federal government" were among the Manhattan Landing's participants. The seaport also cautioned, "There are countless things that can go wrong." I'll say! One very big thing would be that nothing would come of it. But before that denouement would play out, their pie-in-the-sky proposal was going to create a mess for us.

The city knew since 1968 that our project's viability depended on our ability to sublease valuable office and commercial space to support the rest of Battery Park City. Yet, now, with that market weak, Lindsay was planning to sponsor several new office buildings directly across Manhattan's narrow southern end from us.

Further, as our residential real estate consultant, James Felt & Co, had noted just prior to our bond sale, we assumed that we could successfully market in stages a total of 4,700 luxury apartments, "provided no significant competitive facilities are also brought to market in simultaneous stages" in the area. Manhattan Landing would present us with those competitive facilities.

Bobby Douglass, at Governor Rockefeller's office, was keeping his eye on this new development and was already raising some pointed questions with Lindsay in a memo to the mayor on May 11, 1972. Given the large number of luxury apartments projected for Manhattan Landing, how could Battery Park City make a go of it, since we were now at a comparative disadvantage in renting our market-rate units because, at the city's insistence, they were going to be mixed in with middle- and lower-income apartments? Our lease with the city dictated that housing mix. Only someone totally divorced from reality—or equally cynical—would not conclude that people able to pay the higher rents were much more likely to opt for the more exclusive community to our east.

Douglass also brought up the possible use of the civic facilities, such as schools, that Battery Park City was mandated to build as infrastructure for our project. Might people moving to Manhattan Landing—not far away, after all—be able to make use of them at no expense to the Lindsay project? He also asked that the city not consider placing any office space on the market before 1980 to ensure that they did not directly compete with Battery Park City in *that* area. And he pointed out that our soon-to-be-revised lease should contain nothing more restrictive in terms of design than that which the city intended for its East Side development. Without that provision, we could easily become less competitive with the new project.

In fact, at a meeting in the city comptroller's office four days later concerning revisions in our lease, the Lindsay administration specifically refused to be limited as to when they could market office space in Manhattan Landing.

We suggested that the housing mix at Battery Park City should be approximately duplicated at Manhattan Landing to keep that development from draining away our potential tenants for the higher-priced apartments. The city rejected this, protesting that the federal Section 236 housing subsidy funds they would need to finance the apartments for lower-income families were already committed to slum areas.

It was with some satisfaction that I watched the politicians go after Lindsay's folly. Bronx Borough 'President Robert Abrams who, with his borough's welfare in mind, had initial misgivings about Battery Park City but was now a supporter, blasted Manhattan Landing in a reply to a TV editorial that supported it, protesting that the project would divert money needed for housing in all the boroughs. He pointed out that—unlike our project—city money would be used to build the Manhattan Landing infrastructure. All in all, he concluded, it was "the wrong project, in the wrong place, at the wrong time."

We finally did negotiate some concessions from the city that would protect us from potential damage caused by Manhattan Landing. In the bargaining over our lease revisions, we managed to secure from the city a commitment to make our master development plan at least as flexible as the one it had developed for its East Side project.

But Manhattan Landing remained on the drawing boards and it even affected the terminology we had to use with the city's Office of Lower Manhattan Development as we worked on an updating of our lease. That office was working on both projects simultaneously and began to insist that we use the same terminology that surfaced in the plans for the other development. For example, they were referring to a pedestrian mall in Manhattan Landing—and it *was* pedestrian in more ways than one—as a "waterfront esplanade." They decided they wanted us to use the same specific phrase in any reference to our esplanade. What if we should decide to call it a "promenade"? That decision was taken out of our hands.

There were times that we almost seemed to be in a tug-of-war with the city over our respective developments. In fact, on May 10, Richard Weinstein of the city's Office of Lower Manhattan Development put it to us directly. Frustrated that we were intent on limiting Manhattan Landing as much as we could, he threatened not to meet with any of *our* developers unless he got more cooperation from the state on the city's project.

By the end of 1973, elements of Manhattan Landing had worked their way to the Board of Estimate and had received that body's approval. But by then the whole project was beginning to smell as badly as the nearby Fulton Fish Market. On November 28 I wrote to the board, protesting that the proposed housing that was part of Manhattan Landing would involve "a blatant give-away of more than $70 million in public monies to provide unprecedented windfalls for developers and outrageous subsidies for tenants of unlimited incomes." What we were really looking at was "a 'sweetheart' deal with developers" that bypassed less costly bond financing and the use of less expensive landfill in favor of platforms built on piling. To top it off, TAL, the joint venture involved in this fishy deal, would not owe ground rent to the city for a mind-boggling thirty-three years, the equivalent of being given free land. At Battery Park City, developers were going to pay tax equivalencies besides fair market ground rents. It was not only a blatant giveaway, it violated the New York State Constitution, with the city's credit being used to finance a private corporation. The bottom line for us was that this shady arrangement would enable the developers at Manhattan Landing to price their apartments much lower than their market-rate counterparts at Battery Park City.

I also continued to feel that in pushing his Manhattan Landing development, John Lindsay remained obsessed with overshadowing the project that Nelson Rockefeller had initiated. Otherwise, how else can one explain that on the very morning of August 7, 1973, when we had told the city that we were going to announce at a press conference the Lefrak/Fisher letter of intent to develop our first residential units, the Lindsay administration scheduled a bus and walking tour of *its* downtown development plans?

At one point, it seemed to me that the only way to undercut the threat to Battery Park City from Manhattan Landing would be to co-opt it. With that in mind I wrote to Governor Rockefeller, suggesting that with city comptroller Abraham Beame looking like a good bet to win the mayoralty in the fall of 1973, the chance might be there to have Battery Park City itself eventually take over the development of Manhattan Landing, which was "floundering without a single strong agency to coordinate its various developers."

When Manhattan Landing came up for a vote in the Board of Estimate in December 1973, Manhattan Borough President Percy Sutton voted for it. Shortly afterward, I wrote to him, chiding him for his hypocrisy. I reminded him that he had voted against Battery Park City at one time in protest over our housing mix, which fell short of the number of low-income units he thought we should have. But here he was approving a project that had *no* low-income apartments whatsoever. Nor, for that matter, was it going to have any middle-income units either.

To dwell much longer on Manhattan Landing would be to give it more than its due. For a while, it seemed to pose a very real threat to us. But it literally never got off the ground—or the water. The city had given insufficient thought to how it would finance the whole thing and the plans were way too grandiose and diffuse. To this day a gussied-up South Street Seaport is all there is to show of Manhattan Landing. As a total project, it exists only in its plans, gathering dust somewhere in the city's archives.

No Way!

As far back as March 29, 1971, we had begun to be concerned about the reconstruction of the West Side Highway. At an authority meeting that day, Bill Maley, our engineering coordinator, first addressed the issue. He warned that we should push for the road to be routed as far east of our bulkhead as we could get it.

The Julius Miller Elevated Highway, as it was officially called, stretched from the Battery north to Seventy-second Street. By the early 1970s, neglect had left it in terrible shape and repairs would have been prohibitive. While the debate over its future dragged on in those years, part of it would collapse, necessitating closing it to cars and leaving the city with an eyesore that served as a scenic but extremely expensive bicycle path.

With a budget that was already setting off red danger lights, the city was in no position to rebuild it with its own funds. What to do? Whom to turn to? New York State and Uncle Sam, naturally. The West Side Highway could be rebuilt as part of the interstate highway system, bringing in substantial federal funding. The state's Urban Development Corporation would sponsor the project. There were, of course, some big strings attached. The biggest was the requirement that the new road be sufficiently wide to handle interstate truck traffic. That meant eight lanes in a right-of-way often simply not wide enough to accommodate them.

On July 7, 1971, I met with a seven-man task force from the Urban Development Corporation, headed by Samuel Ratensky, a former New York City housing official, charged with redesigning the West Side Highway. Ratensky was working with the UDC's head, Ed Logue, whose letterhead should have consisted simply of a wrecking ball and a bulldozer. In our case, I feared, they could be knocking down something that hadn't yet even gone up: Battery Park City.

Sure enough now, in the summer of 1971, after eight months of study, they were angling to move the highway to the west, out over the water and parallel to the pierhead line, thus putting it right through what was to be part of our landfill. This would completely overturn a provision of our carefully negotiated lease with the city, which had anticipated keeping the road in the right-of-way on West Street and, if the funds were available, depressing the road below grade.

The next day I called Bobby Douglass at the governor's office to discuss the matter. I pointed out to him that *New York* magazine had already mentioned this possible water route and we had to stop it before it gained any more public momentum.

But the juggernaut was picking up steam. By now, the plan had evolved into something called Water Edge, and on July 19, 1971, Logue brought it to Governor Rockefeller. The UDC head must have known that Rockefeller would be receptive to any plan involving the expenditure of large amounts of money on construction, and the governor initially endorsed it.

With so much at stake, I would have to become a traffic cop. The new highway could take two routes. The ideal configuration for us would be to have it curve eastward and slightly inland as it passed us and do the same thing between Forty-second and Fiftieth streets, at the time the area designated for construction of a new convention center.

The nightmare possibility was that the other route would be chosen. That would have taken it along the outer edge of our project, over the water, slashing right through our residential section. It would force our buildings into a narrow, north-south vertical strip hugging the shoreline. Our esplanade would have been moved ninety feet back from the pierhead line and would have been substantially elevated above the water level instead of remaining just seven feet up, as it is today. All told, Battery Park City would lose 5,640 apartments and slightly more than 21 acres, about equivalent to the amount provided by the landfill from the World Trade Center.

With this version of the plan, Ratensky and Logue were going to include along with the road a new subway line. There's *more*. To meet protests from people along the right-of-way that this new road was going to heighten pollution, our intrepid builders were going to deck over the highway and build housing on top of it. All in all, it was beginning to sound like Manhattan Landing goes on the road.

As chairman of the Battery Park City Authority, I was an ex officio member of the Hudson River Edge Development Corporation, the committee formally constituted, along with other city and state officials, to consider these plans. I left no doubt in the minds of my colleagues where I stood on the issue.

In a memo to Nelson Rockefeller on October 7, 1971, I attacked the version of the plan that would have taken the road over the water. Should that version be adapted, I reminded him, Battery Park City would most likely be delayed by as much as three and a half years, wasting millions of dollars and the three years of work we had already put into it.

We had put together a report on the West Side Highway analyzing how it might affect our project, and eight days after filling in the governor on the possibly dire consequences, I sent it out to Donald Elliott of the City Planning Commission, Austin Tobin, head of the Port Authority, David Rockefeller, and other officials and interested parties.

And so with the sword of Damocles poised to slice right through us, we carried on with our work. I continued to advocate for our needs and in June 1972, I thought I had us in the clear. Lowell K. Bridwell, director of the Water Edge project, offered me an informal commitment that the road would not be built through our development. But by the fall, they were pointing it at us again. At this point, we had even more incentive to fight it off because it could possibly hamper our ability to meet debt payments on our bonds.

In February 1973, I again protested to the governor that we still had no assurance that "they do not intend to ram this highway through the middle of our project." A month later our consulting architects and engineers issued a report along similar veins, warning that the choice of the water route for the West Side Highway "would have serious adverse and, in some instances, fatal impact on the accomplishment of Battery Park City."

Finally, on September 18, 1973, we signed a letter of understanding with Lowell Bridwell in which we agreed to defer until April 1, 1975, any construction along a sizeable part of our eastern border near the Trade Center, the stretch of landfill nearest to the then current right-of-way of the highway. Bridwell, in turn, agreed to "expedite" development of proposals that might include an "inboard" option, the one we preferred.

Ultimately they did turn to the inland option. The project's name was changed to Westway, and its configuration would undergo many changes over the years. At this writing, a quarter of a century later, Battery Park City is there and thriving, and they *still* haven't started Westway.

Again the Housing Mix

All things being equal, I could have lived with the housing mix divided by thirds that had been suddenly forced on us without warning or time to protest and negotiate during the City Planning Commission hearings on Battery Park City's lease. But I certainly would have preferred the division we had originally agreed to before the sneak attack—20 percent low-income, 60 percent middle-income, and 20 percent luxury. However, the changing economy since that time, the nature of the housing market in general, and the potential threat from Manhattan Landing in particular forced our hand. To have stayed with the city-imposed equal mixture by thirds would have been economic suicide. In its own way, it posed as much of a threat as Westway had through its possible over-the-water route.

In 1971, in a real estate study for the Downtown Lower Manhattan Association, James Felt & Company projected a growing demand for housing in the area. But they suggested that this demand was contingent on keeping "an aura of a dominant middle to upper middle atmosphere." Upper-income people were likely to wait till the character of the growing residential community became more established.

We took this study very seriously as we contemplated the economic bind that holding to the city-generated mix would create for us. We sounded out the city on the possibility of decreasing the percentage of low-income units at Battery Park City and they were amenable to *some* revision of the figures.

By May 1972, Sam LeFrak was letting it be known that while he favored mixed housing, mandatory division by thirds was pushing the envelope farther than it would go in the real world—

especially with the prospect of competing with Manhattan Landing and possibly the large project on Staten Island that William Zeckendorf was planning. Lefrak/Fisher advocated 20 percent luxury, 30 percent middle income, 30 percent moderate income, and no more than 20 percent low income. The latter figure rested on a familiar fact in the real estate business. Approximately 20 percent low income was the "tipping point" in most neighborhoods or projects. If the percentage of lower-income families moved much beyond that, the other families would move out or not move in, in the first place.

One must remember that this was the early 1970s. Every June brought fears of a "long hot summer" of urban rioting. "Crime in the streets" was still a phrase heard in every political campaign. People weren't just nervous about riots. In truth, they were downright frightened.

Reasonable or not, fair or not, personal safety was a paramount issue. The fact that there would be limited access to Battery Park City, since it was surrounded on three sides by water and abutted a highway to the east, with only two points of access from the wide and busy thoroughfare, spoke to this concern. But opinion surveys also made it clear that middle- and upper-income people— the bulk of our potential market—felt threatened when the number of poor people around them exceeded 20 percent. That was the hard reality that was staring us in the face and we would have a fiduciary responsibility to our bondholders to do all we reasonably could to make the project an economic success. We needed to rent those apartments—all of them—to produce the revenues we needed. That was the bottom line.

We and the city knew when we signed our original lease that it would require periodic revising as conditions warranted. The housing mix was to be high on our agenda for changes, but we also wanted to take this opportunity to unburden ourselves of the power the city had to unnecessarily interfere with our operations in a variety of ways. For example, the city had veto power over whom we chose to sell us insurance. This provision was written into the original lease for nuisance purposes, with no function other than to permit the Lindsay administration to flex its muscle where it had no business being.

Negotiations over the lease revisions heated up in the spring of 1972 and initially we made little progress. Finally, the logjam broke in a meeting I had on June 7 at the Downtown Lower Manhattan Association offices with the city's Richard Weinstein, Bobby Douglass from the governor's office, and a few other officials. We hammered out the basic points of the revisions and I was pleased with the results. I got the housing mix upped to 30 percent luxury, no more than 20 percent lower income, and the balance middle income. I also had them remove Donald Elliot's onerous business about the housing being "thoroughly mixed." In truth, given the complicated nature of subsidies and mortgages, we could not have mixed the luxury apartments in with the low-income units any way—not to mention the virtual impossibility of marketing such a mix.

What's more, I decreased the city's power to unnecessarily interfere with our operations. We no longer had to consult them on a future bond issue to the extent we did on the first one, and we had the minimum rent we would ultimately owe them reduced from $14 million a year to $12 million. I also managed to push our project boundary north to pier 21, increasing our land by almost nine acres, for a total of approximately one hundred—a payoff for dropping opposition to Manhattan Landing. And now we were assured that Battery Park City would have to build infrastructure and community facilities only to serve its own residents.

I knew it wasn't going to be that easy, particularly when it came to the housing mix. By the end of June, as the details of the revision became known, a familiar voice was raised in protest. Manhattan Borough President Percy Sutton went on the attack. He called our new numbers an "outrageous attempt" to create a city of the rich downtown. He contended that even the apartments we had allocated for middle-income tenants would be priced too high and would be another contributing cause of a middle class exodus to suburbia.

Sutton's June 30 press release called our changes "a reneging on a promise to the community," a betrayal that would produce "a new city of the rich, by the rich, and for the rich." Our attitude, he charged, was "taxpayer-be-damned." On July 6, he and Bronx Borough President Robert Abrams held a press conference to attack both our lease revision, pending at the City Planning Commission, and the Manhattan Landing project, then before the Board of Estimate.

In mid-July, local radio station WMCA also called for us to maintain the equal ratio of upper- to middle- to lower-income apartments. I replied, reminding them "that middle-income families, whether they belong to a minority group or not, will object and are reluctant to live in a building which, in their opinion, has too high a proportion of lower-income residents.

"On the other hand," I explained, "we have found from several years' experience with the state low rent subsidy program, where 2,300 low-income families are spread throughout 15,000 middle-income apartments in over fifty projects, that 20 percent is a good working limit." Upping this percentage resulted in more segregated housing as middle-income families looked elsewhere for shelter.

On July 12, 1972, I appeared before the City Planning Commission to testify in support of our revised lease and the accompanying changes in the Battery Park City Master Plan. I reminded the commission that the tripartite 1:1:1 ratio of housing was forced on us at the last minute in 1969 and had been a product of backroom politics, with Lindsay caving in to pressure from his new Democratic allies. I emphasized that the ratio was never the subject of discussion but presented to us only as an ultimatum. It had been extremely irresponsible "because every change in the housing mix meant a change in the revenue available for the authority's debt service and in the fiscal return to the city and a change in the ancillary facilities that the authority would have to provide." I also noted that our developers had alerted us to marketing problems caused by the housing mix.

I recounted our success in state-sponsored projects with mixed-income families under the Capital Grant Low Rent Assistance Program, in which we subsidized families with lower incomes living in the otherwise middle-income Mitchell-Lama projects. The federal government had a similar experience with its Section 236 mortgage interest reduction subsidies in which there was a limit of 20 percent of low-income families in a building.

What it came down to was this: "The question is not whether we create an elite group downtown but whether we can create housing at all." I emphasized that with the new ratio, the low-income units would now be built "in an economically and racially integrated, socially desirable, experience-tested setting."

The commission vote was favorable, but we took a bit of a publicity hit the next day when the newspapers harped on the changed housing mix, using words such as "cut" and "slashed." In fact, the City Planning Commission had not actually accepted our argument that we had to change the housing mix in order to make the luxury apartments more marketable. Instead, they based their decision on the prospect that sufficient subsidies for the original number of low-income apartments simply would not have been available.

The Board of Estimate was next on the schedule. I addressed them on July 20. I reiterated the point I had made at the City Planning Commission, and our revision passed there, too.

In October 1972, with the housing ratio readjusted, I told my colleagues at Battery Park City that we were asking the potential developers to plan for luxury units in the first buildings to go up to give the project a bit of a cachet and to test the market for those apartments.

I could not have known in the fall of 1972 just how much ahead of the horse our new-look cart was now running. Manhattan Landing, Westway, and a grossly unrealistic housing mix would pale as impediments to the building of Battery Park City before the disastrous effects of a downward-spiraling economy.

Harry Helmsley, flanked by Governor Rockefeller on the left and yours truly on the right, was a giant in Manhattan real estate in more ways than one.

One might only briefly overshadow Nelson Rockefeller, as I am doing via an accident of nature on the left; or tower over him by an accident of height, as New York City Mayor Lindsay is doing at the governor's left. The governor reigned supreme in New York politics. (International Photos)

We began by creating 8 1/2 acres of new Manhattan real estate at the south end, pumping an acre of sand a day. The bulkhead has been completed in this photo.

"Docking or Berthing" at this spot was academic once we had extended Manhattan's boundary out into the Hudson River, leaving the former shoreline high and dry.

An ad for apartments to test the waters resulted in the post office delivering trays and trays of applications to our office—thirty thousand applications in all.

"If you lived here, you would be home already," was the message to drivers on Manhattan's Lower West Side. That's me in the cherry picker.

Future Battery Park City residents would see from their windows sights such as the *Q.E. 2* heading upriver. Here the great ship passes the lower sixteen acres, contained by a sea wall but not yet filled.

"Archie," a homeless man, created his own apartment on our landfill, becoming Battery Park City's first "tenant."

Chapter 8

THE BEST OF TIMES, THE WORST OF TIMES

When Battery Park City existed mostly on paper alone, it was possible to run the project from the Midtown building that also housed the New York State Division of Housing and Community Renewal. But I always knew that we would need to be on site once the landfill got under way.

Our original thought was that the World Trade Center, then still under construction, would be the logical place for us, and in 1970, 9,500 square feet on the fifty-sixth floor of one of the Twin Towers were set aside for our eventual use. Occupancy was slated for March 1972. But as that time approached, we changed our thinking. The space turned out to be too expensive and inflexible for our purposes, so we began to shop around.

We chose the seventeenth floor of 40 Rector Street, a building on the corner of West Street then undergoing renovation. We leased twenty-one thousand square feet at $160,000 a year, enough space to spare for the new staff members who would be joining us as Battery Park City began to become a physical reality, and we moved in at the beginning of April 1973. Our new quarters overlooked our project area. I would be able to watch from my desk as Manhattan literally grew before my eyes.

Battery Park City Becomes a Full-time Job

My plate was full in those early years of our project, with Battery Park City only one of my responsibilities. Being New York State commissioner of housing and community renewal commanded most of my waking hours, and even that wasn't the end of it. I also served on numerous other committees and commissions related to housing and real estate. For example, I was a member of President Nixon's Rent Advisory Board, which for a while in the early 1970s required me to be in Washington once a week.

But the state commissioner's job and the Battery Park City project were certainly the main calls on my time. My six-year term on the Battery Park City Authority was due to expire at the end of 1974. To ensure that my hand would be on the wheel right through the voyage, Governor Rockefeller, on February 2, 1973, appointed me to the remainder of the six-year term left vacant by Sam Pierce's departure, thus extending my tenure right through the end of 1978. He also named Mario Procaccino to fill out my original term.

By 1973, it was clear that Battery Park City would soon be requiring more of my attention. It was just as clear that, now in my early forties and the father of two young children, I needed to keep an eye on my financial future for my family's sake. My business and profession was real estate, but I had been away from it—at least the private practice of it—for some time. With my position at Battery Park City secure, it was time to make a move.

Early in 1973 I became part of a group negotiating to buy control of Douglas Elliman & Company, a venerable real estate firm that managed market rate cooperative apartment houses in New York City. They did *no* business with New York State, nor were their properties involved in *any* way with any matters I dealt with as housing commissioner.

I discussed the impending purchase with the governor in March and decided that, while there were no legal or moral conflicts involved, there shouldn't even be room for people to imagine that they might exist. With the job at Battery Park City growing in importance, this seemed to be the right time to cut my ties to the state housing division and resign the job of commissioner. Rockefeller asked me to stay on while he selected someone to succeed me.

The Elliman purchase went through on April 16, 1973. In a formal statement of resignation the next day, I reported that I had accomplished the essential tasks Nelson Rockefeller had given me:

helping to devise an innovative urban program in the form of the Urban Development Corporation, broaden the mission of the Division of Housing and Community Renewal, especially in the area of middle-income housing, and bring Battery Park City from the realm of ideas into reality

During my tenure, we had begun construction on 59 subsidized low- and middle-income projects containing 17,500 apartments, including the 5,888-apartment Starrett City in Brooklyn, at the time the largest housing project under way in the whole country. I had also seen the gigantic Co-op City through to completion. New York State had secured $900 million in federal Section 236 mortgage interest subsidy and rent supplement funds on my watch. The default rate on New York City—supervised Mitchell-Lama projects, many conceived in response to politically-driven factors regardless of economic reality, was over 60 percent. But not one of the 238 state projects in the program had defaulted on its mortgage while I was commissioner.

We had also begun a large-scale rehabilitation program. As chairman of the State Building Codes Council, I had also helped to write a new housing code to cover factory-manufactured homes.

I was also personally involved in initiating the end of rent control by the use of vacancy decontrol throughout the state and especially in New York City. Rent control had been instituted in 1943. In the three decades since, the law had kept rents from keeping pace with rising operational costs. Consequently, many buildings had fallen into disrepair or had been totally abandoned. The legislation I developed to remedy this situation did not impose onerous rent increases on existing rent-controlled tenants. It only removed the old controls when an apartment became vacant.

It was a sensible step, but it drew heavy fire Even state legislators who supported the end of controls had been afraid of voter reprisals if they openly opposed rent control, and no member of the assembly or senate wanted the "honor" of having his or her name on a bill that ended the popular program. I volunteered to take the heat by putting my name on the 1971 Urstadt Law that fostered vacancy decontrol and prevented any municipality in the state from enacting controls more restrictive than those existing when the legislation was adopted. There's no telling how many rental units were *not* abandoned since then because of that simple act.

It was not easy shepherding that bit of legislation through the legislature in Albany. In fact, I still have hanging on my office wall a news photograph of me on the floor of the legislative chambers, jacket pulled open to "assure" the members of the assembly that I was not packing any weapons.

The governor graciously wrote to me that "under your knowledgeable guidance and devoted leadership we have dealt with our problems at all levels and the progress we have made in the area of housing and community renewal is the result, in large degree, of your vision."

Now I needed to look forward and get on with the big job downtown. Avrum Hyman would continue to assist me, leaving his state post as deputy commissioner to become Battery Park City's full-time director of public information in May.

I did not want a conflict of interest problem with Battery Park City any more than I did with my position as housing commissioner, so I took measures to cover all bases. On April 18, I informed Governor Rockefeller that I had asked several lawyers to examine my participation in the Elliman Company and my work at Battery Park City to be sure that they did not conflict under Sections 73 and 74 of the New York State Public Officers Law. They found no conflict. I would confine my work on Elliman to weekends and it would in no way interfere with running the Battery Park City development.

Filling in the Picture Downtown

On June 29, 1973, we awarded a contract to bulkhead and fill the north forty-five acres of what was to be Battery Park City, the final large slice of the pie. The low bidder was a joint venture of Edward B. Fitzpatrick Associates and the Schiavone Construction Company. They were scheduled to complete their work in two years.

In August, champing at the bit to actually see at long last some physical signs that a city was taking shape, I wrote to Governor Rockefeller, complaining in my progress report of all the "red tape" we were having to put up with. Now however, we could cut up some of that red tape and toss it up as confetti because we were about to have something to celebrate.

No child building sand castles at the beach could ever have felt the pleasure—no, make that the *thrill*—I had on September 21, 1973, when the hydrobarge *Ezra Sensibar* approached our site. I watched from my office window at 40 Rector Street as the barge was maneuvered into place at what was to be our south sixteen acres next to the seawall, dike, and embankment forming a crib, erected by the George W. Rogers Company. A few hours earlier the barge had been moored in the lower bay, sucking up sand from the river bottom. Now it began to pump that sand into our crib. Land, ho!

The *Ezra Sensibar* could handle as much as seventeen thousand cubic yards of sand on each trip. By October 15, working day and night, after three weeks and forty-six trips back and forth from Staten Island and just off Coney Island, an area we had also been authorized to tap, the barge had pumped 660,000 cubic yards of sand and we completed landfill of Battery Park City's south section. We had added sixteen acres to the island of Manhattan. Whoever said land is valuable because "they ain't making it anymore?"

On the day we began the landfill operation there had been a sign on the bulkhead off our south end warning mariners, "Docking or Berthing at This Pier Prohibited." With the sixteen acres filled, the sign was left stranded, five hundred feet inland. Although I knew better, I hoped that the red tape that had impeded us so far would be beached with that sign.

I was elated, and on October 24 sent Governor Rockefeller a photo of "the miracle at Battery Place." At the time this addition was worth about $160 million. And we did it by pumping sand into what had been a water-filled bathtub that we had also created.

Completing the bulkhead would not be without its adventures. In the course of its construction, we had to install a fifty-six-inch main through it, leading to the World Trade Center. The air-conditioning system in the Twin Towers required it. To protect the main's opening to the river, we installed a wire mesh gate weighing several tons. That was on a Friday. By Monday morning it was gone. Either someone in the construction crew had made a nice killing in scrap metal, or we had been victimized by a thief or thieves who had given new meaning to the term "strong-arm."

But overall, bulkheading and filling would be the smoothest, most successful part of our entire operation. Once we got past the bureaucratic impediments, the technical aspects of the task proceeded more or less according to schedule, and we would bring the operation in under budget.

As 1973 ended, all of the space between our south end and the landfill we inherited from the Trade Center excavation, excepting less than an acre adjoining pier A, where the city docked its fireboats, was filled in. That gave us forty contiguous acres of land. By the spring of 1974, the Fitzpatrick-Schiavone joint venture was at work filling in our northern end. Fortuitously, at the same time, they were simultaneously building a water tunnel that would bring water south from upstate, and they took the rock they dug for that tunnel and barged it down the Hudson to build the stone berm for our north seawall. In fact, the first "structures" to go up at Battery Park City were three-story-high piles of this rock, stored temporarily on our new, south sixteen acres, until they were ready to be processed and crushed for the seawall.

All that remained to be accounted for were the six acres over the area containing the Hudson Tubes, directly in front of the World Trade Center. In July 1974, that contract also went to the Fitzpatrick-Schiavone joint venture, the low bidder for the job. They would dredge around the tubes, build platforms that would span them and connect with the landfill to the north and south, and pour fill into the area between the tubes. As I've mentioned, we had planned low-rise buildings housing cultural activities for this area. In the end, ironically, the World Financial Center, containing Battery Park City's biggest structures, would end up right there.

A Shift of Emphasis

The action on stage center was encouraging, but it was being played out against a backdrop that increasingly featured dark storm clouds. We watched helplessly as the real estate recession slowly tightened its grip on the city. The bottom was dropping out of the commercial market in particular. "Glut" was the buzzword heard everywhere. Harry Helmsley was as good as they come when it comes to developing and filling commercial space, but he couldn't walk on water, and he couldn't produce a prime tenant out of the increasingly thin air. A full development contract, not just a letter of intent between Battery Park City and Helmsley, began to look less and less certain. And Lew Rudin was not to be heard from despite his previous aggressiveness.

By mid-1973, just as ominously, Moody's, one of the two major bond rating services, was moved to comment on the implications of the recession for moral obligation bonds. "What amount could or should a state add to its tax rate in time of economic stress for an unplanned debt service outlay?" they wondered. "Could there possibly be a selection among the various programs for subsidization, if more than one were to suffer reverses at any one time?"

That's about the last thing I wanted our bondholders to be reading. But on September 28, 1973, I was informed that they were going to be seeing something worse. We heard from Moody's that day: "We wish to inform you that our Rating Committee has reviewed and is revising the rating on the Battery Park City, New York, bonds from *A to Baa*."

They cited an "increasing amount of uncertainty" with regard to the downtown office space market—the completion of the Trade Center with the vast footage of space it would have to rent would not help—and were disturbed by the changes in our housing mix. Moody's also mentioned continuing delays and changes in our master development plan as factors in the downgrade, as well as their perception that state support for our bond issue was soft. All this in the context of their increasing discomfort with the whole concept of moral obligation bonds.

It was small comfort that the other rating service, Standard and Poor's, maintained our "A" rating. The delays, red tape, and incessant politicking also bothered us. We needed to build buildings, not butt heads with yet another bureaucrat. But we were even more concerned now about the real estate market. The financial linchpin of our project was to have been the office space, the ground rent from which would help pay our debt service, allowing us to use the bond money, in turn, to build the infrastructure that would support the residential units and also to pay our administrative expenses. Once the houses and stores had been built and the landfill dotted with structures throughout, the project would become financially self-sustaining and eventually produce the surplus we had promised to the city. In normal times that would have happened, and ultimately it did.

But these times were far from normal. With no office development on the horizon, we were forced to take a long hard look at our priorities. We couldn't just sit around, waiting for the office market to revive. Increasingly, the residential units would loom large as the source of at least some revenue to keep our administrative expenses and interest payments on our bonds from eating too far into our $200 million bond sale proceeds. Not only would building housing help our cash flow, it would also give developers and the public a sense of the project's sustained momentum. Commercial developers would be more likely to come aboard eventually if they saw visible signs of our viability and not just empty landfill.

By 1973, as well, we had been in business for several years and if something vertical besides a sign didn't start appearing soon on our landfill, political pressure might begin to grow to drastically change the project. I knew that there were people in the city's government then who would be pleased with our demise. What of the future? Some bureaucrat or politician might seek to make headlines at our expense.

In a February 8, 1973, memo to the governor, before the debt market turned sour, I sought to get things moving on the housing front. We had been successful floating a bond issue that would largely be devoted to project infrastructure and now, I felt, economic conditions warranted our going the same route to secure funds directly supportive of housing construction. Another bond issue would enable us to lend directly to developers to entice them to start building middle-income, assisted housing on the site. I suggested $500 million as a target figure. I preferred the authorization be allocated directly to our Battery Park City Authority but would settle for a transfer to us of the $500 million in borrowing power the State Housing Finance Agency had been authorized to use but, I knew, was not going to tap. I wanted it allocated to us because we could put that money to work a lot faster if we could control it directly and not have to go through the established State Housing Finance Agency and the Division of Housing and Community Renewal bureaucracies

The governor was willing, but we were almost tripped up in the state legislature, which had to authorize the transfer of borrowing power. Conservatives feared that small homeowners would have to pay higher real estate taxes to support the limited profit housing units, liberals wanted state funds devoted to housing at other locations and for other constituencies, and the Lindsay administration didn't want anything at all overshadowing its phantom Manhattan Landing project. On May 22, this curious confluence of contrariness was enough to defeat the transfer authorization in the state assembly.

That was our wake-up call. The next day I was in Albany with several of my staff, intent on reversing the decision. According to the *Village Voice*, I "lobbied like a son-of-a-bitch." I don't know about that. But when you come to the state capital without a change of underwear and unexpectedly find yourself in a five-day battle for votes, it does wonders for your motivation. Avrum Hyman, our director of public information, was with us and his credit card bought shirts, socks, and underwear for our stranded staff.

After almost a week of cajoling, educating, and arm-twisting, with a great deal of help from Perry B. Duryea, speaker of the assembly, we got what we came for, reversing the vote and securing $400 million of the $500 million in borrowing power we had requested. It figured to be enough to get limited profit housing under way on our landfill.

Besides possibly supplying a loan to developers, we could also offer them some good news. While the city's economy gradually worsened, there were positive signs over the summer and early fall of 1973 that the hotel and retail space that our residential developers were going to build along with the housing could prove lucrative.

In May, Larry Smith & Company, real estate consultants, reported on the feasibility of a hotel on our site. Despite the down market in the city, "the aggregate demand for hotel space to be located in the Lower Manhattan area is considered to be extremely strong," they advised. "Lower Manhattan presently has 37 percent of the Manhattan office market, but no major hotel facility." Admittedly, weekends would present a problem, since the city's main cultural and entertainment facilities were in Midtown. But, all in all, they suggested that a 350-room hotel should be successful.

The outlook for shopping in our area also was looking up. Not only would the Trade Center provide a massive infusion of stores, we figured to add to the aggregate. In September, Macy's was expressing strong interest in locating one of their stores on our premises.

Lefrak/Fisher

The Lefrak/Fisher joint venture was, of course, our immediate hope when it came to residential development. In hindsight, "immediate" was quite a stretch. From the time we had chosen them to develop Battery Park City's first housing, hotel, and retail store units, through their signing of a letter of intent on July 12, 1973, and long afterward, our dealings with them involved a continuous string of delays on their part as they maneuvered to bring the buildings in at the lowest possible cost.

Minimizing costs is naturally the aim of any developer. But there is also such a thing as reasonableness, good faith, and a commitment to getting things done. It's my firm conviction that Sam LeFrak often strayed from some of these professional guidelines in his negotiations with us. At one point, the *New York Times* would characterize our relationship as a battle between the practical, penny-pinching LeFrak and the architect's visions of grandeur, with me as a kind of Solomon between them. If so, this Solomon must admit that there were times he was tempted to use the sword not to "split the baby" but rather to slice and dice the developer from Queens.

In truth, it couldn't have been too comfortable for Lefrak/Fisher to have to work within the stringent parameters of our master development plan. The limitations began with very specific directives about preservation of sight lines to the waterfront from points along Broadway outside the project area, which limited building locations. The developers also had to maintain the north-south spine concept and plan for the two access levels, vehicles on one and pedestrians on the other. The fixed location of ramps leading to the World Trade Center garage also affected how buildings could be placed on our site. Even building on landfill itself could be problematic. Piles might need to be redriven or realigned, especially on the unconsolidated landfill area created by excavation for the Trade Center. Getting on the same page with all of these and many more requirements meant they would submit plans only to have them returned for redrawing to fit our specifications.

But most of the matters we constantly sparred about with them were much more conventional. It began with the administrative and legal structure they set up to oversee their work on the project. There were two new corporations, one for each partner in the joint venture, and we learned about them only when we suddenly began to see references to them in their communications with us. Would these shadowy entities alone have liability for possible nonperformance regarding construction?

What if they lacked the capital to cover it? Would liability then extend to the original participants, Lefrak and Fisher?

What exactly should the ground rent for the buildings be? What were the land and apartments worth when stacked up with comparable locations and accommodations in other parts of Manhattan? How long should the developer's subleases run—for the full ninety-nine years of our lease with the city or some shorter period?

For a full year and more after the Lefrak/Fisher joint venture signed the letter of intent, we skirmished over these and other issues, as well as on the details of the plans they submitted. The height of the buildings they were to erect exemplified the kind of contention that permeated our dealings. The master development plan required only varying heights, without specifying numbers. When such a vacuum exists, opinions pour in. I had always aimed for high-rises, with plenty of open space between them. I thought this was the most efficient way to build and to preserve the vistas that made our location special in the first place. But John Zucotti, who had become head of the City Planning Commission in the new Abraham Beame administration, leaned toward the ideas of urban planner Jane Jacobs, who stressed organization on a small scale, with the "stoop" the paradigmatic urban form. Zucotti, in Jacobs' spirit, was pushing us to put up uneconomical, low-rise, wall-to-wall buildings.

Sam LeFrak also wanted to hold down the heights, but only because he wanted to limit his costs. By the spring of 1974, he knew our exact specifications for Pod III, our designation for the neighborhood of residences and commercial space the Lefrak/ Fisher joint venture was to construct: 1,624 subsidized units, 696 market-rate (luxury) apartments, and 35,000 square feet of neighborhood shopping. In May 1974, I pushed him to give us plans finalized enough to get a building permit and to file with the City Planning Commission.

Lefrak looked at the 696 luxury apartments and came back with a counter suggestion of 600 units. Why the difference? Because to give us 696 meant they would have to add a few stories, pushing their buildings over three hundred feet, the line at which the cost increased substantially per floor. Consequently we spent a good deal of time revising and re-revising the plans, trying to squeeze as many apartments as possible into a height that would stay within the three-hundred-foot limit. And every revision ate up more precious time.

The developer also needed to do test borings for foundation design in May 1974. Managing the Lefrak/Fisher Battery Park City affairs was a young urban planner named Richard Kahan. When our technical liaison, William T. Maley, questioned Kahan about these borings, he couldn't get a straight answer. Kahan, according to Maley, "did not know what action was going to be taken or whether it would proceed." Two months later, my chief assistant, Tom Galvin, asked Sam LeFrak directly about those test borings at a meeting, but LeFrak referred him back to Kahan. Time was closing in on us, and they wanted to play project ping-pong.

In mid-June, we held a meeting at our offices with representatives from the developers to discuss details of the financing of construction. Kahan was delegated to write up a memo summarizing what transpired. He did a sloppy job and got the facts all wrong. We set out to get the details straight.

By July 1974, we thought we finally had the details of a development agreement in place, but Lefrak/Fisher kept sending it back, quibbling over details and constantly asking us to extend their letter of intent. The Lefrak motto on their logo was "Labor Omnia Vincit (Labor Conquers All)." That's a nice sentiment, but if their logo had reflected reality, it would have depicted a foot dragging across a barren landscape.

In August, it was the test borings again. This time we suddenly noticed that legal documents from the developer related to this issue were referring to a new corporate entity, the "Battery Park Construction Company," of which we had never heard. How was it related to the "Battery Park Housing Company," with which we had supposedly been dealing? Who were its principals? It didn't make sense to make us play "Twenty Questions" with so much at stake. But that's how it was.

Refining Our Plans

While the 1972 revision of our original 1969 master development plan improved the guidelines for Battery Park City, we and our developers were still finding them unnecessarily rigid. The cumbersome plan would have had to have been reviewed and amended each time we sought a building permit for each parcel of land, so tight were its strictures. On this, at least, the city agreed, and by the middle of 1972, we were working with it to replace the master plan with a more fluid special zoning district.

By late 1973, we had arrived at more flexible parameters for just about everything except the public areas of Battery Park City. These were now spelled out in detail. For example, the new district would require amenities such as art galleries, boutiques, and restaurants on the building frontages along the esplanade. The new plan enhanced the esplanade, already an important feature in 1969, and today one of the glories of Battery Park City. Better pedestrian access to the waterfront and more open space was also built into the revision. Although design elements such as the hexagonal theme on the office towers were dropped, site lines throughout the project were laid out in minute detail. Ironically, the new plan emphasized smaller buildings and maximum sunlight in the area just west of the Trade Center. Today, Battery Park City's most massive buildings stand there and, after the collapse of the twin towers, have more sunlight than anyone ever bargained for.

The City Planning Commission, after its usual delay to quibble over minutia, accepted these changes on November 14, 1973, and passed them on to the Board of Estimate. In that august body, at issue would be not only changes in our plans for Battery Park City but also a new element in the financial relationship between the project and New York City.

As 1973 drew to a close, it was clear to everyone that our original idea of having revenues from the office buildings play a major role in financing the infrastructure for the rest of the project would have to be shelved. In this recession, commercial buildings were a nonstarter. This new set of circumstances put the expenses for the roads, sewers, schools, and other necessities of urban life in a different light. What was the best way to fund them, given all that had happened? The answer was the new civic facilities agreement we worked out with the city's Office of Lower Manhattan Development.

The driving force behind the agreement was the city's recognition that it needed the housing we were prepared to build, and we needed a new source of financing to help build the infrastructure that would support it. The solution—a temporary one—was that the city agreed to pay up to $10 million a year for this infrastructure until conditions would enable us to develop the office space that we had originally intended would pay for these improvements. The *Daily News* termed the agreement a "bailout," but it was really just a recognition that changing circumstances required a temporary midcourse correction. Ironically, four years later, this civic facilities agreement would become a brief impediment to the beginning of housing construction on our site.

The collapse of the market for office space also necessitated one more change. Our lease required us to begin certain payments to the city upon completion of the project, then projected for June 1983. Clearly economic conditions had rendered that date inoperative, and so we were granted an extension to June 1986.

The Board of Estimate gave its approval to all of these revisions on December 28, 1973, the same day it also approved some changes to the plans for Manhattan Landing. The difference was that at Battery Park City, you could already walk on the land where once there was only water. Manhattan Landing, on the other hand, remained a mirage unless you could walk on water.

The Economic Outlook Worsens

It appeared at the end of 1973 that the start of housing construction at Battery Park City was imminent. With that in mind, we made an essential addition to our staff in early November. I had come to know Henry Nussbaum at the New York State Division of Housing and Community Renewal, where he had been director of our finance and audit bureau. He was a specialist in subsidized housing, a dedicated professional with impeccable credentials, and he now joined us as a consultant in his area of expertise.

We also hired Jack Rosen, most recently at Alcoa, to work with Avrum Hyman and take charge of community relations. As Battery Park City rose from the water and became part of New York City, we needed to pay more attention to the public's perception of us and encourage interaction between New Yorkers and this exciting new piece of New York. Jack, gifted with superb "people skills," was the man for that job.

So, with our landfill under way, new flexibility in our plans, a new financial arrangement for the project's infrastructure, and new authorization to borrow money for housing through another bond issue, we were making important progress despite the recession. With things looking up, and even more talent to draw from at Battery Park City, I had no reason to feel that Nelson Rockefeller's resignation as governor on December 11, 1973, should be an omen of anything bad for us. His replacement, Lieutenant Governor Malcolm Wilson, also supported the project. Maybe I should have been more superstitious, because Wilson's tenure would be brief and the man who would replace him as governor a year later, Hugh Carey, was to be a whole other kettle of fish.

Meanwhile, the economy and the real estate market continued to worsen. In October 1973, against a backdrop of mounting political crisis in Washington, as the Watergate scandal deepened, Vice President Agnew was forced to resign because of his involvement in a separate scandal in Maryland before he came to Washington. Pessimism grew when a crisis abroad seriously undermined the American economy and, incidentally, any hopes we had of seeing a recovery any time soon in our bailiwick. The Arab states declared an embargo on oil shipments to the United States because of our support for Israel in the Yom Kippur War.

Gasoline prices were already rising as 1973 drew to a close and, thanks to OPEC, gas rationing was in the works. By February 1974, more than half the gas stations in the New York City metropolitan area were closed, and lines at the ones that managed to get their supply of gasoline stretched for as much as six miles. The total embargo ended on March 19, but fuel prices remained high, bringing inflation in their wake. In July, a Gallup Poll would show that a majority of Americans thought that inflation—almost 14 percent for the year—had supplanted the energy crisis as the nation's number one problem. Two months later, in separate speeches, President Ford, who had succeeded to the office upon Nixon's resignation in August 1974, and Secretary of State Henry Kissinger, warned of the real danger of a worldwide depression.

"Live today. Tomorrow will cost more," went the 1974 slogan advertising Pan Am, then still a major airline. Just as certainly, if developers didn't build today in a time of rampant inflation, tomorrow would cost more. The longer Battery Park City existed as a site without height, bare land without buildings, the more it was likely to cost everyone concerned.

Dig We Must

The year 1974 had barely begun when in a speech to the Rotary Club, I promised that tenants would be moving into Battery Park City apartments by 1976. I was off by seven years. But a timeline projection was the least of my worries. Keeping the development alive was a bigger concern. Forces were brewing that would aim to scuttle the whole thing. They were as nearby as the looming gubernatorial election.

If it was at all humanly possible, I was going to get some construction going on that landfill, and soon. I had to, or I would give the lie to the 1974 Interfaith Movement's Award for Humanitarian Service, presented to me by Mayor Beame in March. For I was receiving the award, which in the past had gone to Governor Rockefeller and Boston's Cardinal Cushing, among others, in part, because Battery Park City "will do much to bring credit to our city and create an oasis of happiness that makes for democracy in action . . . ." By oasis, I don't think they meant just that largely empty stretch of sand extending into the Hudson River.

To help put something on the landfill, I had hired Thomas Galvin to serve as my right-hand man, with the title of general manager and assistant to the chairman. He would coordinate all the facets of building such a complex project. Tom, an architect, had most recently served as executive vice president of the New York City Conventions and Exhibitions Center Corporation, the mission of which had been to produce an exhibition space that would enable the city to capture some of the lucrative shows, conventions and business that were bypassing Gotham because the city's convention facility, the aging coliseum at Columbus Circle, was woefully inadequate. The proposed center had run into community opposition to its originally intended site on the Hudson at West Forty-fourth Street, and delays in securing congressional approval to build on the water at that location. Tom was a former president of the city's chapter of the American Institute of Architects, and had experience building Mitchell-Lama housing. He had also been an unsuccessful candidate for city council president in 1973. I knew by now that political experience, even in a losing cause, was a plus, given the people with whom we had to deal.

Increasingly, flexibility was becoming the key to Battery Park City's survival. After all, when a good quarterback can't bring off the exact play he called in the huddle, he has to go for option two or three. That may mean calmly changing signals at the line of scrimmage, or even scrambling after the ball has been snapped, picking out a different receiver or changing a pass play to a run on the fly.

In fact, I wasn't just changing a play. I needed to shift our entire game plan. When external economic conditions had squelched the possibility of putting up office buildings first, as we had originally aimed, we switched the focus to housing. Now I made a fundamental decision not to wait passively while our developers got their act together. The price of building materials was only going to climb higher as Lefrak delayed and the long and involved process of securing Mitchell-Lama mortgage and tax benefits inevitably dragged out. We had millions of dollars in bond money that we could put to work to get those buildings started by pouring their foundations. It would give us a head start on construction and provide a jump-start to a project in danger of finding itself dead in the water. The wording of our bond prospectus was sufficient to justify this expenditure, especially since the developers would reimburse us once we arrived at a contract.

In truth, there was yet another reason why I wanted to get this work under way in 1974. The reconstruction of the West Side Highway still loomed out there somewhere, sometime as an apparition that could suddenly take a disturbingly real form and direction, causing us serious harm. I had heard that Ed Logue had not given up on the option of running this road through the middle of our landfill. As they say, there's nothing like "facts on the ground" to help you establish a position and hold it. Now we had the ground, and we could create the facts in the form of cold, hard steel. A few I-beams sticking up out of the ground directly in the middle of a prospective right-of-way would do wonders to deter even the most avid road builder.

We made the public announcement about ordering the steel for the foundation on July 12. The Bethlehem Steel Corporation was going to ship us three thousand tons of steel piling for the foundations for six buildings, three of which we figured, at this point, would rise thirty-four stories. There would also be three smaller structures. We applied to the city's Buildings Department for a permit—only worms can dig a hole in Manhattan without one. And on August 1, we filed with the City Planning Commission an "intention to develop" the first residential neighborhoods at Battery Park City, as required by the Special Battery Park City District Zoning Regulation

A few days later, City Planning Commission Chairman John Zucotti responded with a demand for more design details and information about what our plans were for energy use in these buildings. The reality was that he had no right to insist on such specifics at this point and, calling his bluff, I told him so. We soon got the certification we sought. But the Buildings Department dragged out the permit process for a while.

The piles began to arrive on our site in August. Virtually nothing comes easily when you build in New York City, and that goes double when what you're doing involves the International Brotherhood of Teamsters. Knowing what can happen when a developer gets caught between union locals involved in a jurisdictional dispute, I had already met with John Cody, head of the brotherhood's Local 282, to make sure we were on the same page. I told him that Teamsters from Pennsylvania would be driving the trucks carrying the steel into New York City. Cody countered with a demand that we off-load the steel in New Jersey so that his men could bring it across the river into our site. That, I protested, would drive up our costs to the point of making the operation prohibitive. And if there was no foundation and possibly no project, there would be no jobs for anyone.

I thought we worked out a reasonable compromise. The Pennsylvania Teamsters would bring the steel right to a single location at our site, but Cody's men, now or in the future, would do any moving of the piles on the site. That's why I was flabbergasted the morning of the delivery to look out of my office window and see a parade of forty flatbed trucks loaded with steel piling, halted along West Street just outside our project area. Their engines were idling and so were the trucks and their drivers. They were just sitting there, mere yards short of their destination. What the heck was this about?

It turned out that this was about the crane operators, whose job it would be to hoist the steel off the trucks. They objected because the drivers delivering the material onto the site came from another jurisdiction. We had a standoff, but not for long. Determined not to be thwarted by this last-minute nonsense, I immediately called Cody, who was at a Teamster's conference in Rancho La Costa, California. Since it was six o'clock in the morning out there, you could say that it was truly a wake-up call. I reminded him in a tone of voice that was less than friendly that we had an agreement. I threatened to go public with this incident and to take it up with Harry Van Arsdale, Peter Brennan, and the city's other labor titans. He said he would see what he could do.

No more than ten minutes later he called back and as he started to speak, I saw, seventeen stories below, the long truck caravan begin to move onto the landfill. Maybe Cody made the crane operators an offer they couldn't refuse.

On September 20, 1974, we held a groundbreaking to celebrate the beginning of the foundation work. We had set up a tent at the foot of Liberty Street and nearby, Governor Malcolm Wilson pressed a button to start driving the first pile. The governor, Mayor Beame, and Robert Moses were among those speaking at the event.

Moses was never one to mince words and the "Master Builder" set the beginning of construction on our landfill against the backdrop of a city in crisis. "This is a period of high prices and shortages. There are, it is true, businesses quietly leaving town, families moving out, and staggering increases in welfare and public aid," he said, pulling no punches as he depicted a people in pain. Yet, he noted, in the face of the need for action, all he heard was, mostly, carping. "We have too many abject apologists and critics who build nothing," Moses complained. But at least, "Here at the Battery the dirt is flying."

"Flying" may have been an exaggeration—Moses was sometimes prone to flights of rhetorical fancy. But the dirt was certainly beginning to move, and the start of foundation work, combined with our continuously expanding landfill, gave us cause for optimism as well as pride. By November we were well into the foundation building process and anticipating the start of work sometime soon on the infrastructure. It was time to hire an agent to perform the hands-on management of this work. We were still in the process of hashing out a contract with Lefrak/Fisher. Presumably, they would be the developers at some point—hopefully soon. Lefrak certainly had all the experience one could hope for to manage such projects. And we wanted continuity once they signed a contract to actually erect the buildings. So, despite some misgivings on my part, they were the obvious people for the job.

On November 29, 1974, we signed an agency agreement with Lefrak/Fisher authorizing the joint venture to oversee the initial construction work. They would get 2 percent of the construction cost, payable at the rate of $40,000 per month.

Keeping in the Public Eye

In politics, perception can go a long way toward influencing how things turn out. We needed to build a public constituency for Battery Park City so that it would be difficult for those who wished us ill to determine the future of the development. That's not easy to do when external events, over which we had no control, had made it as yet impossible to construct the buildings we had promised would by now be rising from the landfill.

In this work, Avrum Hyman and Jack Rosen excelled. Avrum diligently worked the public relations angle to squeeze the maximum public exposure out of what we had been able to do so far. My files still carry long letters he wrote personally to average citizens who wrote to us with suggestions, complaints, observations—whatever. On the other end of the media spectrum, he placed me on a steady stream of radio and TV programs, and captured for the project plenty of print space to make our case and bring to the public the good word that something wonderful was stirring on the waterfront downtown.

In the spring of 1974, Avrum also began to turn out a project newsletter, the *Battery Park City Beacon*. In our inaugural issue, anticipating the 200th anniversary of our nation's independence, we optimistically dubbed our first residential neighborhood the "bicentennial phase" of the project. I guess it's a good thing that in 1976 they didn't tell the captains of the tall ships participating in "Operation Sail" to orient themselves in the harbor by the tops of our buildings.

Speaking of the harbor, what better place could there be for Battery Park City to make a splash than in the midst of the very physical feature that most distinguished our site? We had a truly splendid view of the harbor once the old piers were out of the way and our landfill was in. And what's the prettiest thing one sees out there amidst the whitecaps, under a pale blue sky? Sails!

Everyone loves to see a trim yacht slicing through the water. Bunches of them are even better. We would stage a yacht race in the harbor near our building site. Not only would it be fun and build morale, it would also be picturesque enough to all but guarantee us coverage by the media. I laid it out in a memo to Jack Rosen and he got working on it. Jack did such a good job that it would become an annual affair around Labor Day, known as the Battery Park City Governor's Cup Race.

In truth, as a former All-American swimmer, my first thought had been to set up a race *in* the water, not *on* it. But the pollution that was then still so characteristic of the Hudson River precluded that approach. As a former naval person, I was certainly not unhappy with option number two. Several yacht clubs in Sheepshead Bay, Brooklyn, agreed to administer the event, co-sponsored by Battery Park City along with, appropriately, Virgil Conway, chairman of the nearby Seamen's Bank for Savings, who contributed the trophy cup.

Governor Malcolm Wilson was then beginning his election campaign for a full term in Albany against Democratic Congressman Hugh Carey, so it was not hard to convince him to snare a little positive publicity for himself by kicking off the race on September 14, 1974. Spinnakers never looked so good in the lower bay as they did on that gorgeous afternoon. And with their help, we got the publicity for which we had aimed. In fact, we were a photo on the front page of the Sunday *New York Times* and shared the Sunday *Daily News* centerfold the next day with the America's Cup Races.

Had we known what was coming, we would have probably appreciated even more such good times, good weather, and good news. Things had been tough for us as 1974 went into its second half, but not as tough as they were to become. We had weathered some squalls, but now we were going to hit a real northeaster. And most of the news would be bad.

Battery Park City's director of public information, Avrum Hyman, in the suit on the right, worked tirelessly to get the word out about the project. Here he shows students the Lucite model that did not quite reflect the correct dimensions of the buildings.

A groundbreaking was always one good way to keep us in the public eye. From left to right: New York City Mayor Abraham Beame, New York State Governor Malcolm Wilson, myself, and builder Samuel J. LeFrak. (Jules Geller)

The Labor Day Governor's Cup Race off the Battery Park City landfill in the mid-'70s.

I'm flanked by fellow members of the Battery Park City Authority: Alfred S. Mills on my right, and Mario Procaccino on my left. Landfill can be seen from the window.

Part of my job was to be the public spokesperson for Battery Park City. (Jules Geller)

Chapter 9

CIRCUMSTANCES BEYOND OUR CONTROL

Early in 1975, we discovered that we had put Battery Park City on the map—literally. On February 1, the annual edition of the U.S. Department of Commerce's National Ocean Survey Charts came out, and there we were. We had officially changed the contours of Manhattan Island. The Hammond Map Company, acknowledging this prodigious feat, presented me its "Earth Shaper" Award.

On our now immortalized site, the Cobra Pile Driving Corporation was beginning to change the configuration of our landfill, sinking the foundation piles that would support our first housing units. All in all it should have been a time of considerable satisfaction for us, but it wasn't.

A series of events and trends were making it seem as if the very gods were conspiring against us. The Urban Development Corporation, after recklessly underwriting infeasible projects, for all intents and purposes, defaulted on notes it had issued in anticipation of its moral obligation bonds. In the process, UDC's failure tarred us as an arm of government that had also marketed debt backed by the moral obligation of the state. There was no valid comparison between Battery Park City, where we had $125 million in cash invested and earning 12 percent, and Ed Logue's bankrupt UDC, but the bond market lumped us together, and consequently we took our lumps.

We would also be hamstrung for several years because of our connection, however indirect, to New York City. Although we were not in any way a part of the city's governmental apparatus, Gotham's well-publicized economic collapse brought us under the thumb of the catch-all State Emergency Financial Control Board, as well as the city's Office of Management and Budget. This would, in turn, help to put us at the mercy of an unsympathetic governor.

Elected in November 1974, Hugh Carey would become a problem for us beginning with inauguration day. It is axiomatic that no politician wants to carry out a project that his predecessor has started. That's even more the case when it is as large, as visible and as publicized as Battery Park City. Carey was nothing if not a good politician. He was a great guy with whom to sit down and have a drink, which I have done on several occasions, but in the political arena he had been not entirely inaccurately characterized by journalist Doug Ireland as "a man of unbelievable dullness punctuated by frequent improvidence." Carey was damned if he were going to just sit there and sign off on something so completely identified with Nelson Rockefeller.

It was bad enough to lack support from above, but we also had to watch out for sniping from below. Developer Sam LeFrak, the driving force behind the Lefrak/Fisher joint venture, should have been behaving as a friend and ally in our struggle to get the project off the ground. Sometimes that was the case. But too often, his minor-league scheming and meddling were a distraction. He was quick to claim credit for accomplishments that were not his, went behind our backs in discussing the project with the new governor, and even threatened the relationship with the construction unions that I had worked hard to strengthen.

The Fallout from UDC

The Urban Development Corporation, under Ed Logue, had sold $1.1 billion worth of moral obligation bonds. But many of his projects were not financially workable and their mortgages were shaky. Cash flow became an iffy thing for the UDC as the Nixon administration began to rein in housing grants early in 1973, and a number of the corporation's economically unstable projects were unable to pay their way.

I never had any doubt that the UDC's concept and basic structure was sound, but Logue was profligate in running it. At Battery Park City, our bonds were keyed to a specific project and we had spelled out the revenue stream that would—we had every reason to believe—pay for the debt service on them. But the UDC's bonds were backed not by individual projects and specific anticipated revenue, but by the agency as a whole. They were, in effect, general obligation bonds of the corporation. This allowed Logue to overextend himself and build some projects that were ill-advised and poorly thought out. Most egregiously, his staff did not sufficiently analyze the market in which each project would be built. They did not carefully match the income of their prospective tenants to the rents required to pay off the UDC's debt.

Why should a UDC crisis become a problem for Battery Park City? Because the UDC, like our project, had sold moral obligation bonds. If the UDC should default, confidence in our bonds would skid. Bond buyers would wonder whether legislators, faced with a theoretical collapse of several agencies financed by such bonds, would vote money that might be needed elsewhere to pay off bondholders. The state's obligation, after all, was "moral" and not legally binding. In fact, the general concern over New York State's indebtedness had played a role in Carey's defeat of Malcolm Wilson for the governorship. Eventually that concern would drop the price of our bonds to little more than $37, even though we had $75 in cash behind each bond.

As 1975 began, I was already worried about Carey and how he would perceive the situation, even assuming he approached it with some objectivity. I wrote to him on February 5. Unlike the UDC, I assured him, we would be building our Mitchell-Lama units with a careful calculation of costs versus the rental income we could expect, and that we would sell housing bonds not as unsecured general obligations of our authority, but rather as debt backed by the revenue stream from our developers. In effect, our bonds were like familiar real estate mortgages, tied to a specific property. The moral make-up provision was merely a second line of defense. It was extremely unlikely that the state would ever have to make good on a shortfall.

I also asked that the new governor meet with us so we could bring him up to speed on our project. Carey's icy reply was that he was setting up an investigation of the past use of moral obligation bonds and we could speak to the man chairing it to convey our views. Antagonistic right out of the starting gate, Carey would consistently make trouble for our project over the next three years through his pointed lack of support.

. On February 25, the UDC missed a $135 million interest payment on its bond anticipation notes. That let loose the deluge, and a hue and cry was raised throughout the financial world against "back-door financing," putting us and other agencies that had prudently used the moral obligation concept, in the same bed with the tarnished UDC. Bond salesmen on Wall Street who had made handsome commissions marketing such instruments of finance, and politicians in Albany who had voted to support them, now ran helter-skelter for the sidelines.

In a dramatic show for their constituents, state lawmakers voted to cap our original authorization to sell $300 million in bonds to pay for project infrastructure at the $200 million we had already sold. They also capped the more recent authorization of $400 million in housing bonds at $85 million, leaving enough only to fund the Pod III housing, the foundations of which we had begun.

In truth, however, selling even this amount of moral obligation housing bonds aimed at bringing in the developer for Pod III was now impossible, given the atmosphere created by the UDC default. But without that construction, and stymied in our efforts to attract commercial tenants to our office space, Battery Park City might be stopped cold.

Holders of our 1972 Series A bonds were letting me know personally that they were unhappy and nervous. One wrote in April that he was "shocked" at the declining value of his investment. His broker had recommended that he sell, but he wanted to go to the top to find out. "How much trouble are we in?" he wanted to know. Another, in a hand-written note, said he had put $20,000 into our 1972 issue. "Their present price is deplorable, as you know," he reminded me. I knew.

Bond salesmen were no more pleased. One of them, in Municipal Research at Shearson, Hayden, Stone, wrote to me in March 1975. He asked, "How long could the authority sustain itself under present circumstances?" He had been down to our site and was disturbed that "a visual inspection indicates little progress."

I reassured each, pointing out the difference between the Urban Development Corporation and us. I told them, in effect, what I told the Municipal Forum of New York in a speech on April 11. There was nothing inherently wrong with moral obligation bonds "as long as the authority which has a moral make-up available to it does not use that make-up without regard to the normal prudent practices of financial security and the marketability and feasibility of the product which the bonding authorization is being used to finance."

I reiterated that message in our 1974 annual report, issued early in 1975. Urging people not to equate us with the UDC, I noted that we had "consistently taken prudent, conservative steps in advancing the Battery Park City development to avoid similar problems. Our management is cautionary and our construction program to date is well within our budget estimates," an approach that ought to reassure investors.

But it was like trying to douse a firestorm with a bucket brigade. The UDC—provoked panic was even threatening the New York State Housing Finance Agency bonds. The HFA had issued $4.2 billion of these instruments since authorized to do so by the Public Authorities Law of 1960. The most spectacular use of this money was to make possible the building of Co-op City in the Bronx and a host of state mental health facilities.

This financially unwholesome atmosphere created by the UDC was straightjacketing more than just New York State agencies. Thirty states had sold $9 billion worth of bonds with moral obligation make-up provisions. The panicky debt market was closing down to them as well.

By April, contractors working on the foundations of our apartment units were asking the Lefrak/Fisher agency team supervising them if we were solvent and had enough money to cover their work. Indeed we were, with $126 million from our bond issue still in the bank. But if you read all the downbeat stories in the financial section of the newspapers, you might wonder if anything would ever be built anywhere.

Gloom and doom were in the air. If we had maintained any hope that an upswing in the office rent market would pull us out of this morass any time soon, it had been dashed for good in October 1974. James D. Landauer, our real estate consultant for office space, had chimed in with a stark reassessment of the survey of market conditions it had done for us in 1972. "Whereas in 1972 we foresaw the Downtown office market reaching a state or relative equilibrium by 1976, the many unforeseen occurrences of the last two years have now rendered that prediction unattainable," it gravely acknowledged. "It is now our best estimate that it will take a minimum period of three or four years for the Downtown Manhattan office market to reach a point whereby new office construction can be economically justified." This time the consultants would be on the money.

In 1972, they had estimated the office towers in the south sixteen acres would be completed by 1979 and would produce an annual ground rent of $5,230,000. Now they saw us completing the buildings in 1984, with a ground rent of $4,174,000 per year.

Their conclusion was especially sobering: "We cannot fully discount the possibility that the Downtown office market may not rebound even to the degree to which we are now assuming since the foregoing represents our most optimistic effort."

So much for Harry Helmsley and what he might do for us in the short term. We would have to get that housing going. It alone could not entirely pay our way. But it was reasonable to assume that once some development was under way on our landfill, we would prove more attractive to commercial developers when that market did revive. And others might perceive us as an appropriate place for development for endeavors we hadn't even considered. While I had a game plan—much of which was written into our master development plan—it was by no means anchored in cement. I had always liked the creativity and flexibility that the field of real estate demands, and I was going to get an opportunity to exercise it.

We Apply for FHA Insurance

The question of Battery Park City's future had more riding on it than just our bondholder's investments and the jobs of our staff. In 1974, we had secured building permits for 5,600 residential units, one-third of all such permits granted by the city for the entire year. With unemployment in the construction industry pushing 50 percent, we were almost the only show in town, the only substantial hope for these men and their families. We needed to find a way to keep going.

What to do? Who was it who said, "When you have lemons, make lemonade?" I would never have taken the route I was now to traverse had I not been forced to, but there really was no choice. The only possibility of raising the money we needed to jump-start residential construction would be to sell bonds that had a backing that investors perceived to be more solid than "moral make-up." On March 11, 1975, I met with former New York State assemblyman William Green, now regional administrator of the U.S. Department of Housing and Urban Development. The subject was Federal Housing Administration insurance to back the mortgage that would finance the construction of housing in Pod III.

In truth, the FHA, created by the National Housing Act of 1943 and administered by the Department of Housing and Urban Development, had never backed a mortgage on any single project to the tune of $80 million, which is what our first residential units would cost. Another obstacle would turn out to be the financial structure of the Battery Park City development. Ordinarily, the FHA insured a mortgage with the proviso that in the case of a default, the federal agency could seize the property, which was collateral for the mortgage loan. That didn't exactly square with the setup at Battery Park City. The city owned the land, we leased it from the city, and the developer subleased it from us. FHA rules required that the mortgagee own the land directly, or in "fee simple." They did not insure leaseholds because the FHA might be too far removed from the title to the land in the event of a default.

Other issues would also be sticking points. There would be some technical questions about the environmental impact of our housing, but since the Army Corps of Engineers had already examined us, we didn't initially think that would be much of a problem. There was also the question of just how much of the mortgage the FHA would agree to insure.

The FHA would also have to be reassured about the marketability of our apartments. I had heard specific mention of the problem of competition from Independence Plaza, the New York City—financed Mitchell-Lama project inland to our north. In support of our application for FHA insurance, I wrote to HUD, pointing out that the city's development, going up in the midst of the old "butter and eggs" warehouse area, did not have anywhere near as attractive a site as we did, especially with regard to proximity to the waterfront. Battery Park City was directly on the water, while West Street stood between Independence Plaza and the Hudson River. We were also considerably closer to Wall Street and thus could truthfully advertise our site as one that allowed residents to walk to work.

Our status as a lessee seemed at the time to be the most serious impediment to securing the insurance, but we were confident that the rule could be bent if we could show that the project was viable and that the federal government's interests would be protected. On March 18, we filed an application with HUD's New York Area Office for certification as an eligible mortgagee under the FHA program.

On April 15, not yet completely sure of which course to take to secure the financing we absolutely needed, we publicly announced that we were reassessing our approach. We mentioned the FHA strategy but also suggested we might use the bond money we already had to begin construction of the buildings and not just the foundations, or we could secure private bank loans, albeit at a greater cost than selling bonds. Another alternative was to terminate the project, a move that would just about put a lid on new middle-class housing in New York City, and call upon the state to pick up the moral obligation to meet the debt service on our outstanding bonds.

In truth, building the housing units ourselves with the money from our first bond issue entailed considerable risks. They included possible bondholder lawsuits, the loss of federal tax benefits and the general risks involved with construction that would otherwise be borne by a private developer.

The *New York Times* covered our statement, placing it in the context of various other agencies that were now strapped for cash in the wake of the UDC's default. That smoked out the governor—not the first time he would respond to nothing less than the suggestion that we might default—who now said publicly that termination was "*not*" under discussion at the moment.

Meanwhile, we worked to mobilize support for our new direction. The *Times* published a letter from State Senator John Marchi on June 30 calling for FHA insurance for Mitchell-Lama mortgages. On the same day I wrote to now vice president Nelson Rockefeller, asking for his help in swaying the FHA. "At the present time," I put it to him bluntly, "this is the only solution I can see to our problems."

While we awaited word from the Federal Housing Administration, the debt market continued to dry up. In early July, the *Wall Street Journal* reported that New York State's Dormitory Authority could not sell all of the short-term notes it had put up for bid, and the part they could market was at an onerous 10 percent interest. "Investors have been increasingly leery of most New York fixed-income securities ever since both the city and the UDC narrowly averted defaulting on their debt obligations," the *Journal* commented.

Tom Galvin went to Washington later that month to lobby on our behalf, meeting with Congressmen John Murphy, in whose district we were, and James Delany, who was on the House Rules Committee. Delany warned Galvin that we were encountering guilt by association with New York City, which was now losing control over its financial affairs to the state. Galvin also met with the city's chief Washington lobbyist, Bruce Kirschenbaum, who was very much behind our efforts. How ironic it was now to have a friend at city hall in the Beame administration and an opponent in the statehouse in Albany, originally our stronghold until Malcolm Wilson lost to Hugh Carey.

We made a concerted, organized effort to overcome resistance at HUD to our FHA application. My staff developed a detailed organization chart of that agency and with the help of many friends in government and business, we pushed and pulled wherever it might do any good in mustering support for our cause. We also worked on members of the House and Senate, whose committee assignments put them in a position to have any effect on the outcome.

I made Carla Hills, the secretary of housing and urban development, my own personal target for persuasion. On August 6, I wrote to her, stating our case. I explained that even with the reduced authorization of $85 million in housing bonds, we had enough to put up our first residential units, but we needed FHA backing to sell the bonds. That insurance would reassure bondholders, who were avoiding moral obligation debt like the plague. Some housing agencies in other states had already been able to re-enter the bond market using FHA insurance as security, I reminded her.

I acknowledged the technical problems we had encountered in our own application for that insurance for Battery Park City. But I wanted her to have a sense of what that project meant, "psychologically and financially," to New York in the present economic climate. What we were seeking "would not constitute a gift or grant, or subsidy with an adverse impact on the Federal budget or deficit but would, rather, be revenue-producing for the benefit of all concerned," I assured her. I concluded with a request for a meeting so that she and I might discuss the project.

We cleared the first hurdle in mid-August 1975. On the fourteenth, we were able to announce our preliminary acceptance as a mortgagee, eligible for FHA insurance. Well, what it meant was that we qualified and were acceptable enough to go ahead with our formal application. But just how qualified was "qualified," how far away we still were, was clear from Carla Hills's reply to my August 6 letter, which I didn't receive until September 3. "There are many underwriting and legal problems that must be resolved before the project may be considered eligible for mortgage insurance," she bluntly wrote.

We weren't the only ones pressuring HUD to devote more efforts and resources to supporting new housing construction. In November, the *New York Times* reported that a number of state housing agencies were criticizing HUD for not taking full advantage of the Housing Act of 1974 to get things moving. They were particularly steamed about HUD's failure to effectively use Section 8 of that act, which they could have employed to spur the availability of lower-income units through direct rent subsidies to private owners and developers.

Carla Hills replied to the paper that she was interpreting the intent of that act to encourage landlords to rehabilitate already existing units, not for the federal government to back new construction. Increasingly, I began to go public to counter that pusillanimous policy. When the *Wall Street Journal* reported on November 7 that the president's Labor-Management Advisory Committee could come up with no new ideas for aiding the housing industry, I fired off a letter to its chairman, John Dunlop, who was also secretary of labor, urging the federal government to shoulder more of the risk of housing construction. One way to do that would be to add federal backing to state moral obligation bonds.

On December 1, the *New York Times* published my letter commenting on an article by Ada Louise Huxtable on the city's housing crisis. I pointed out that New York City "was losing 30,000 units a year, replacing them with only 5,000 units annually." Even more reason why Battery Park City deserved support. "Our construction program is providing the City with a dynamic sign in a highly visible location," and the scope of our planned housing units compared to what developers were doing elsewhere in New York made us "the only game in town."

I knew Carla Hills and other HUD officials read the *Times*. But I was not relying on newsprint alone to sway opinion high up in the councils of government. On November 30, we released a new poll of potential tenants for Battery Park City. Of the 26,000 people who had answered our ad in 1969, asking if they were interested in living in this new-town in-town, 9,500 had moved or couldn't be located and another 8,000 had lost interest. But 8,500 families and individuals still hoped to rent one of our apartments. We received the biggest response from singles and couples without children who already lived in Manhattan. The next day the *New York Times* ran a story about it and I hoped this would speak to any fears HUD had about our units' marketability.

By December 1975, HUD was leaning toward a waiver for us on the leasehold issue. But they were so far proving surprisingly intractable on our environmental impact. They still insisted that we duplicate the work of the Army Corps of Engineers.

We were also having trouble satisfying them on the issue of minimum property standards. These involved physical standards of construction, including measures to withstand earthquakes that were not applicable to New York City. In fact, some of their standards with regard to other factors, such as fire safety, were at variance with New York City building codes, which we of course adhered to in our plans. Further, by now, our foundations were already in place and rebuilding them to fit someone else's "standards" would be expensive and time consuming.

As the year ended, we seemed caught up in HUD's vast bureaucratic web. This application process could—and would—take time. Meanwhile our funds were slowly draining away, public and political pressure was increasing for some visible signs of progress other than landfill, and wrestling with HUD over our qualifications for FHA insurance wasn't the only major governmental problem we faced.

Ford to City: Drop Dead

That New York *Daily News* headline was one of the decade's most melodramatic and memorable. Something less than a subtle analysis of the relationship between the federal government and the municipality of New York City, it nevertheless captured part of the spirit of the times.

New York City was on the ropes and desperately needed help. I've discussed earlier the social forces that were stirring this crisis. By 1975, they came to a head. Over the previous decade, the city's long-term debt had ballooned from $4 billion to $14.6 billion, primarily because John Lindsay had used long-term general obligation funding to meet daily operating expenses. By the early 1970s, New York City was balancing its budget by resorting to short-term, tax-anticipation notes, debt purchased by banks in anticipation of a tax revenue stream that would pay them off. But that tax revenue scenario did not figure on an economic downturn and on OPEC and its effect on the national and local economy. When tax collections dropped below normal, the banks balked and New York City was staring at bankruptcy.

The buck could no longer be passed to future administrations. Now was the time for solutions, no more budgetary sleight-of-hand. Help had to come from somewhere. Washington didn't want to hear about it, hence the *Daily News* headline. It would, instead, be the state that put the city's affairs in order. But the price was high: Gotham went into receivership.

By mid-1975, Governor Carey had convinced the legislature to set up the Municipal Assistance Corporation, which converted the city's short-term debt into bonds guaranteed by the corporation and backed by the city's sales tax, now collected by the state. The Emergency Financial Control Board that instituted draconian economies on all of the city's expenditures complemented this move.

The first inkling I got that we would be drawn into what seemed to be strictly a city matter was a letter to us from Mayor Beame and City Comptroller Harrison J. Goldin in March 1975.

They wanted detailed information about the authority's affairs because the city was being sued for issuing debt that exceeded its limit. Our tenuous connection to this issue was supposedly that we leased city land and issued debt that helped us to pay for the land.

A few months later, the connection was just as tenuous, but the consequences were considerably more significant. We became the *only* state agency placed under the supervision of the new Emergency Financial Control Board. As I told the Fifth Avenue Association in a speech in September, "I can only trust that the inclusion of the Battery Park City Authority was not politically motivated but rather a case of an innocent bystander hit by a stray bullet." Privately, I had my doubts.

I summarized for my audience the city's mishandling of its Mitchell-Lama projects and inability to get a handle on rent control as factors in bringing it to this crisis point. Compared to the government of New York City, the Battery Park City Authority had been a beacon of light in a fiscal and political environment of descending darkness.

The Financial Control Board would have the power to scrutinize, delay, and prevent any substantial expenditure we planned to make in the foreseeable future. It was the ultimate bureaucratic nightmare. It did not keep us from using available funds to cover contracts we had already undertaken, but it would prove a hindrance and possibly an absolute roadblock in negotiating and executing future contracts. Indeed, it would delay us from building part of our infrastructure and it would drive up our costs.

When word got out, the construction industry showed that it realized the significance of this decision. On September 10, the New York Building Congress sent a telegram to the governor protesting our inclusion as a supervised agency. They expressed fear that such a move "would adversely affect the only substantial construction now existing in New York City and would likewise hurt the construction industry." It was to no avail.

Sidney Schwartz, acting special deputy comptroller for New York City, officially informed us on September 25 that we were under the Financial Control Board's control. He wanted financial information about our project. We cooperated, but under protest. We challenged our inclusion as a supervised organization and reminded him that our revenues, after expenses and required payments to the city, were legally pledged to our bondholders and could not be touched by the Emergency Financial Control Board. (It was reported to me that the revenue-starved city fathers as well as the governor had given some thought to somehow gaining access to our approximately $120 million in cash.) This cooperation in supplying information, along with the protest, was to become a monthly routine for the next several years.

But I didn't just leave it at that. I took it up a notch and challenged New York State Senate Majority Leader Stanley Steingut to explain why we were subject to this control. He replied that "the debts incurred by the Authority through its bonding power adds to the combined total debt of New York City and is an additional factor in the financial difficulties of the City."

That was nonsense. "The bonding power of the Authority is not connected in any way with the City of New York," I informed the Speaker, who simply didn't have the facts, "and does absolutely nothing to add to the City's combined total debt." We weren't spending city money. Even should we default on our bonds, the city would have no legal or moral obligation to pick up our debt service, as a reading of the master lease between us and the city would make clear to anyone. It would go on that way for the duration of my tenure with the authority. The simple facts of the matter were never going to deter them.

Who's in Charge Here?

Meanwhile, our relationship with our potential developers was at best mixed. The Lefrak organization oscillated between cooperation and delaying tactics.

With the Carey administration in Albany leveling its guns at us, the last thing we needed was a loose cannon on our ship. Perhaps we should have tied Sam LeFrak to the deck once the storm hit.

Then he might not have made the speech he delivered on March 12, 1975, to the Women's Financial Association at Fraunces Tavern.

With the media present because LeFrak had promised an "explosive statement about UDC," Sam was in his element. He did criticize Ed Logue's mismanagement and compared UDC unfavorably to Battery Park City. At that point he should have said "thank you" and sat down to lunch.

But Sam didn't stop and instead began to rip into the construction unions, talking tough about how he was going to handle them on our project. Hardheaded Sam was going to stick it to the hard hats. He promised "two six-hour shifts at regular time." They weren't going to mess with *him*. "The time has passed for the no-shows, the featherbedding and the parasites," he grumped. "If they wanna eat, they gotta reform . . . ."

Fortunately, I was not present or I might have strangled him. As he knew, we were just then engaged in delicate negotiations with the unions, trying to convince them to make concessions on work rules in order to hold down our costs. When Avrum Hyman handed me a transcript of LeFrak's public posturing, I hit the ceiling.

The next day I drafted a letter to LeFrak but decided not to mail it, venting my anger instead by swearing at him over the phone. What the heck did he mean by his "ill-advised, unwarranted, untactful, self-defeating and gratuitous statements to the press concerning our negotiations for a project labor agreement"? These talks were vital to our entire endeavor, not just his corner of it. His performance had suggested the behavior of an out-of-control child trying to grab the steering wheel of a moving car.

When Sam wasn't making a spectacle of himself in public, he was not above going behind my back to make mischief. Two incidents were particularly annoying. The first had occurred in the fall of 1974. One October day, in the lobby of 40 Rector Street, I ran into Martin Bandier, LeFrak's son-in-law and lawyer, who told me that should Carey be elected, he might replace Mario Procaccino on the authority with someone more to Carey's way of thinking. But how did Bandier know that? There was only one way.

Two days later, I encountered Sam LeFrak at a social function. In the presence of Tom Galvin, I confronted the developer with my suspicions that he had been conniving with Carey concerning Battery Park City. I got my confirmation when LeFrak reassured me that he was only trying to help and that whomever Carey might appoint in Procaccino's place, "it would be someone we could get along with."

Sam was compulsive when it came to plotting. In the spring of 1975, I discovered that LeFrak had paid a personal call on Governor Carey on April 18, toting with him a model of Battery Park City. Naturally, he never mentioned this to anyone at our project. Knowing about LeFrak's propensity for grandiosity and fearing that could play into the governor's antipathy to our undertaking, I needed to counter any mischief the Queens developer had created.

It took me the whole month of May to contact Carey's counsel, Judah Gribetz, to exercise some damage control. I made it clear to Gribetz that LeFrak had a letter of intent with us, not a contract, and was at that point serving only as our agent to supervise construction of the foundations for our first apartment buildings. "In my opinion," I told Gribetz about our negotiations with LeFrak thus far, "his present prices contain an exorbitant amount of profit to which we cannot agree. Secondly, he has a strong tendency to cheapen the buildings by eliminating many of the architectural amenities which the location calls for and the people of the city deserve."

LeFrak set a tone for his organization that reflected his own style of operations. Even when they were working out in the open where we could keep an eye on them, they could be, like their leader, troublesome. For example, in a telling incident, there was a question of who should be a party to a contract for a radio paging service at our site, Lefrak or us. The developer's lawyer, Martin Bandier, unilaterally decided that we should have our name on the contract. Our attorney, Jerry Sindler, immediately disabused him of the notion that such decisions were his company's to make.

And for the future, Jerry reminded him, remember "that the final determination as to the form and content of contracts imposing obligation on the Authority will be made by this Authority," not by Lefrak/Fisher.

A more serious argument arose over our payment to Lefrak/Fisher for its service as our agent supervising construction work. We had agreed to pay them $40,000 a month on account. But when we hit a snag in the summer of 1975 and the work was temporarily delayed, we notified them that we were suspending payment because of an "imbalance" in the amount they had received compared to the work they had performed.

Through August 31, they had already received $342,000 from what had been our automatic payments of $40,000 per month. But with little or no work to supervise at this point, they were now collecting but not rendering services. We held up the payments until the work resumed at a normal pace of construction. Otherwise, as I wrote to them, we would end up paying them "for all the services contemplated long before such services would ever be performed." They took the matter to arbitration, as provided in our agreement with them, and the upshot was a compromise. We agreed to pay them $10,000 a month until construction resumed at its normal pace, at which time the amount would revert to $40,000.

A Struggle for Power

The year 1975 even brought turmoil and conflict where one might not have expected it. Ordinarily, the choice of a method for heating and cooling apartments in a development would not become as big an issue as it did at Battery Park City. But at this time, in this city, with these politicians and bureaucrats, it truly became a struggle for power.

The highly respected engineering firm of Syska and Hennessey had studied the issue for our project and in the fall of 1974 reported that a combination of electric heating and gas for cooking would be the wisest way to go for our initial housing units. Although electric heating rates might be higher than the cost of oil or gas heat when our first tenants moved in, the lower construction costs entailed by the use of electricity would make for a lower overall cost for the project, thus holding down rents.

We submitted this choice to New York City Municipal Services Administrator John Carroll, who was also chairman of the city's Interdepartmental Committee on Public Utilities. He had to approve our decision, and he did.

With OPEC dominating the news, energy use had become a hot, contentious topic. Sure enough, by April our energy choice was drawing fire from several sources. At the end of the month, the *New York Post* ran a story that called our choice into question. I replied, citing the eight-month, $75,000, 215-page study on which we based our decision. The numbers did add up.

I also pointed out that "most high cost, electrically heated buildings cited by critics are not designed to the high standards of insulation, double-glazing, limitation on window sizes and ventilation, as are incorporated into Battery Park City." Our heating would be computer-controlled and we would be able to buy electric power in bulk for further savings.

In Battery Park City, electric heat would best meet the criteria New York City had set for us: it minimized the waste of natural resources, was best for the environment, and also came in the overall least costly of all alternatives. I would have heated the buildings with sterno if it had proven to be the cheapest and least environmentally problematic.

Objections also arose from some mechanical engineers, presenting themselves as energy professionals who had independently examined our energy policy and found it wanting. But they turned out to be people who worked for companies that installed oil-fueled heating and cooling systems in the metropolitan area.

Our lease required that we get the approval of the City Planning Commission for our energy policy for the first set of residential units. Chairman John Zucotti had already let it be known that he was unhappy about electric heating at Battery Park City. When delay followed delay and we still didn't have that approval by fall,

I sued the commission in New York State Supreme Court. That got their attention and the commission gave in, approving our choice of electric heating on November 13. They did it, as Tom Galvin put it at the time, after indulging in "outright distortions and misrepresentation in attacking the Authority's compliance with the Commission's own criteria set forth in the Master Development Plan."

Our December request for a minor modification in the number of apartments in our first unit from 1,625 to 1,642 shows just how hard it had become to deal with the City Planning Commission on anything. Architect William Halsey from our staff attended the session at which it came up and reported that one of the commissioners, Gordon Davis, tried to hold up any action by resorting to a pedantic disquisition on the word "shall" in our lease in reference to the commission's approval. That was almost a quarter of a century before Bill Clinton was to mesmerize America with his public contemplation of the word "is."

Amazingly, as 1975, this most difficult of years, ended, we were still making progress, uphill though the path might be. We were pouring concrete for the foundation walls of the first residential units and had driven in the steel foundation piles. We had extended the landfill inherited from the Trade Center excavation out by one hundred feet and had added a sewer outflow extension. Pod III would make use of some of this new land. Work was proceeding on the piles and platforming that would span the PATH tubes in front of the Trade Center, and to the north, the forty-one acres that would bring us to our upper boundary were shaping up. About 80 percent of the rock embankment that would contain it had been put in place, and 75 percent of the ultimately 2,690,000 cubic yards of sand that would fill it had been poured into the site.

Considering how much of the rest of New York City was virtually moribund, we weren't doing so badly.

Chapter 10

FLEXIBILITY BECOMES OUR BYWORD

B ig issues monopolized most of our time in the mid-1970s, but running a huge and complex development such as Battery Park City meant dealing every day with many smaller details, too. Even they could be potentially explosive if they got out of hand. That was literally true when a lawyer filed a complaint with the U.S. Coast Guard in 1975 that the Fitzpatrick-Schiavone team was improperly handling fuel for its pile drivers while bulkheading and filling our northern section. We saw to it that they shaped up before someone got blown up.

And there were surprises. There could be mystery in a memo or a potential whodunit when we opened the morning mail. For example, in October 1975, I received an anonymous letter from "Inspectors at BPCA Project," written in broken English. It accused a project employee of corrupt dealings with a major contractor. Was this a crank letter? A baseless charge by a former employee of the contractor? Or was there substance to the allegation? Most likely, it was one of the first two, but I couldn't overlook the possibility that this wisp of smoke might be signaling fire. I delegated Tom Galvin and Jerry Sindler, our counsel, to look into it. The charges proved groundless.

There were also distractions that did not prove as serious as they first seemed, but which claimed financial and human resources that we could ill-afford to expend. Here's a good example: In September 1975, the House Ways and Means Committee approved a measure that would have phased out the residential real estate tax shelter, a provision of the revenue code that attracted developers to state-subsidized middle-income housing. The developer's return on equity was not enough to make these projects lucrative on their own.

We followed this development closely, taking time away from other matters. In fact, all state housing agencies were up in arms over this issue and descended on Washington. Carla Hills, something of a nemesis for us on the FHA loan, was at least on the right side of this battle and the measure was eventually fought down.

And then there was Operation Sail. The celebration of our nation's bicentennial on July 4, 1976, was going to take place right on our doorstep. With a view of the parade of tall ships on the Hudson River from, literally, out *in* the Hudson, the Battery Park City landfill was the perfect spot to observe the festivities. The people organizing the gala obviously thought so and contacted us with a request to install upward of sixteen thousand bleacher seats on our site for both the afternoon's event and the grand fireworks display that evening.

It seemed to offer us a great way to promote the project and further community relations. But Jerry Sindler, our counsel, who was paid to see the dark possibilities in all seemingly bright things, raised strong objections, peppering us with words like "accidents," "negligence suits," and the like. Heeding his dire warnings, we restricted our participation to the daytime part of the show. And participate we did, hosting sixteen thousand ticket-holding spectators almost at water's edge, with the proceeds going to Operation Sail to help defray its cost.

But the evening brought more than fireworks. On the one hand, there was the chain link fence on our eastern boundary along West Street, sufficient under most circumstances to provide security for our site. On the other hand, about one hundred thousand people surmised, correctly, that the landfill would be the perfect place to see the rockets' red glare and assorted, multicolored explosives bursting in air over the Statue of Liberty. The other hand won. The fence was ten feet high, but the crowd went over and under it, so strong was their desire to get a good view of the show.

Miracle of miracles, there were no injuries or lawsuits. Nobody fell into the river and nobody drowned. Had we been so lucky with the course of our project's development, the story of Battery Park City's first years would have had been a lot different.

Build It Here!

While the biggest story of the 1970s, the real estate recession, compounded by New York City's virtual financial collapse, seemed to cast us constantly in a reactive mode, we also launched some unplanned initiatives that came close to pulling our irons out of the fire. Hard times called not only for hard decisions but also for a certain amount of "give" in our approach to what we might build on our landfill. Just as we had shown flexibility as we changed our financial strategy in midstream with the FHA option, we also had to be prepared to pounce on any development opportunity that surfaced. As we made clear in our 1975 annual report, released at the beginning of 1976, "We do not believe that we are entitled to just sit back and wait for times and conditions to improve."

In late 1975, the search for a new site for a New York City convention center would show that serendipity had its role at Battery Park City. The city's coliseum, at Columbus Circle, which this new structure was destined to replace, was obsolete almost as soon as it opened in 1956. Before long it became clear that big, lucrative trade shows and other events were bypassing the Big Apple because its premiere exhibition space was just too small. By the 1970s, the idea of replacing it with something bigger and better had become a planning staple These plans began to materialize with the formation of the New York City Convention and Exhibition Center Corporation, the executive vice president of which, as I have noted, had been Tom Galvin. That group came up with a site involving the piers around West Forty-fourth Street and the Hudson River.

The City Planning Commission approved this location for a new convention center in 1973. But New York City's financial crisis threw a log across the road, and in October 1975, Mayor

Beame announced that he was putting the $231 million project on hold. That's where matters stood a month later when Tom Galvin and I were at the office of John Zucotti, chairman of the City Planning Commission, to conduct some other business. Zucotti interrupted our discussion to speak briefly to someone about the convention center and it's as if a light bulb had suddenly been switched on in my head. Without missing a beat, I turned to Zucotti and on the spur of the moment, suggested that I had the perfect location for the new center.

As soon as I could, I gathered my staff to put this idea into the workaday language of a detailed proposal. The convention center would fit nicely into the northern sector of Battery Park City, north of Vesey Street, where the landfill was almost complete. We could accommodate a structure similar to the one they had intended for the Westside at Midtown: 750,000-1 million square feet with 2,000-2,500 parking spaces. There could also be a hotel with 3,000-4,000 rooms on top. Our bond proceeds would finance the infrastructure. Either the Port Authority or bank financing would pay for construction and the Port Authority would run it. It would all work out for us as long as we could be assured of ground rent from the facility that would at least equal what we would have received from the 5,100 Mitchell-Lama apartments originally slated for the location.

At the time—late 1975—such a project might have been our salvation. In fact, Tom Galvin, in a memo to me, wrote that the center "may well hold the key to our future success as well as our ability to survive." Resurrecting the convention center project would be extremely important to the city, as well. It had been projected to draw $770 million in new business annually to the financially strapped metropolis, not to mention creating twenty-five thousand new jobs.

John Zucotti, now one of Mayor Beame's deputy mayors as well as head of the City Planning Commission, strongly backed our proposal. Our ability to supply roads and utilities at a low cost made it especially attractive to him and he quickly convinced his boss that this was the way to go.

On December 12, in the lobby of Twin Tower One, I stood with the mayor and Port Authority Chairman William Ronan to announce that the Port Authority would conduct a $100,000 study to determine the feasibility of building the convention center at Battery Park City. We felt we were in.

But we had not figured on competition from Donald Trump. In March 1975, "The Donald," as the New York press was later to tag the celebrity-developer, had agreed to pay $62 million for fifty acres of land on West Thirty-fourth Street near the river, part of the railroad yards of the bankrupt Penn Central Railroad. Trump, too, thought he had the perfect site for a new convention center. Six days after our news conference he held one of his own, at which he said it would be "a tragic mistake" to put the new facility in Battery Park City.

The media were quick to side with him. NBC TV broadcast an editorial calling for a new convention center at the Thirty-fourth Street site. They rejected Battery Park City and the financial district in general as "a cultural desert at night and overcrowded by day, a ten-dollar cab ride from midtown." ABC joined in, finding the subway downtown "overloaded," and said that we couldn't handle large crowds.

Their language was remarkably temperate, contrasted with the demagoguery from then assemblyman Andrew Stein, a very young man in a very big hurry to go places in politics. Stein called our proposal "an irresponsible attempt to bail out two other fiscally unsound government projects—the World Trade Center and the Battery Park City Housing Project." (The Trade Center was still very far from fully rented.) Stein described our environs as a "desolate part of Manhattan," and further labeled our proposal "a fraud on the taxpayers of this city" and "a fraud on the Battery Park bondholders, as well."

The image of us camped on the outer edge of nowhere is amusing in the light of what it's like today to trek to the present convention center on the far—very far—Westside, located near . . . nothing. In a letter to the *New York Times*, Trump brazenly claimed that Midtown's entertainment offerings were at the "doorstep" of his patch of land. That was true only for a giant with enormously long legs swinging open a door reaching from here to the moon. As for public transportation, we had four subway lines and the PATH tubes at our door, while the nearest Thirty-fourth Street subway stop was on Eighth Avenue, almost a mile from Trump's location.

This battle over where to put the new facility was to drag on for some time. The longer it did, the more time Trump had to mobilize some of Midtown real estate's heavy hitters on his side, such as the hotel interests headed by Robert Tisch. Trump also had the advantage of support from the *Times*, which itself had major real estate holdings in Midtown and was thus no more objective than we were.

The "paper of record" weighed in against us and in favor of the Trump site on January 19, 1976, but at least they also published my letter challenging their judgment. What really hurt, though, was an aside in the editorial that described us as "foundering." To counter that notion in this most influential molder of opinion, I wrote a personal letter to editorial page editor John B. Oakes, a cousin of the publisher.

I pointed out to Oakes that any assessment of our project had to be placed within the context of the economic downturn that would surely run its course. I reminded him of the city's delaying tactics through just about the entire life of the project. They had left us considerably more vulnerable to inflated construction costs than we should have been. Besides, with still more than $100 million in the bank and having just changed the map of Manhattan, "foundering" seemed hardly the way to describe Battery Park City.

But the damage had been done by Oakes's paper and now, I told him, "bankers, bond-holders, underwriting syndicates and investment counselors will assume that we are foundering and our ability to raise financing will be jeopardized." Contractors might avoid us and potential renters would look elsewhere. Given the *Times*'s influence, we were powerless to fully correct this deeply damaging distortion of the facts. But Oakes stuck by his editorial's assessment of our condition.

The next month we saw an example of just how such "common knowledge" could be propagated. The *Architectural Record*, in an article on where to put the new convention center, noted Battery Park City's "reported financial difficulties."

Donald Trump's campaign bore fruit, and in March 1976, the Port Authority delayed its feasibility study so as to include his Thirty-fourth Street site in the mix. At the beginning of June, they released their conclusions: they couldn't choose between us. Trump immediately went on the attack. In a letter to the *Times*, he claimed that building the convention center as part of our Battery Park City project would force the insolvent city to spend an enormous amount of money to renovate the West Side Highway. I replied that the road was going to be renovated anyway, no matter what we did.

At that point, the Downtown Lower Manhattan Association took up the challenge and commissioned its own study by Vollmer Associates, an architectural engineering firm. A year later, in March 1977, they endorsed Battery Park City as a more appropriate place to build.

It seemed that everyone was determined to hand down an opinion on the subject. In January 1977, New York State constituted a commission made up of City Planning Commission Chairman Victor Marrero, Deputy Mayor Osborne Elliott, State Housing Commissioner John Heimann, and Felix Rohatyn, head of the Municipal Assistance Corporation, to look into the competing proposals. In addition to our site and Thirty-fourth Street, they included the original location at Forty-fourth Street and also considered the possibility of simply enlarging the existing coliseum at Columbus Circle.

In May, they issued their report, naming the original location in the West 40s as the best place to put the new structure because it would strengthen the midtown area. The 1970s had not been good to the city's fabled Times Square and its environs. The sex industry dominated Forty-second Street, drug sales were rampant, and "seediness" had become a byword in anything written about it. The commission feared also that somehow a Battery Park City convention center would hurt the Westway highway project, and also worried that putting the convention center in Battery Park City would draw restaurants and hotels away from Midtown. But they also dismissed Trump's proposal as having no beneficial effect on *any* area.

The *Times* and the *Daily News* endorsed the commission's choice. The Downtown Lower Manhattan Association wrote to both papers, pointing out that the Vollmer study showed that the sponsors of many of the trade shows that did not then come to New York City favored the Battery Park City site.

And that wasn't the end of it. Choosing a site for the new convention center had become a growth industry. In October 1977, Mayor Beame appointed his own panel, headed by Richard Ravitch, former chief of the UDC, to investigate potential sites, limited to Battery Park City, Thirty-fourth Street, and the original location in the 40s. But Beame's tenure in office was almost up, and his successor would be the one to choose the final site.

Ed Koch, elected mayor in the fall of 1977, was initially wary of Battery Park City. He had no ties to our project, knew us only from what he had read in the papers, and viewed the civic facility clause of our lease as a possible drain on the city's revenues. In hindsight, we never had a chance. He had promised during the campaign to get the convention center built and he went right at it as soon as he took over. Narrowing the choice down to the Forty-fourth Street site or the old Penn Central yards, he announced in April 1978 that Trump, who benefited to the tune of a $500,000 fee, had triumphed. By then, we were completely out of the picture.

The FHA Story Goes On . . . and On

The beginning of 1976 brought prospects of a housing partnership with another major developer at Battery Park City. On February 4, flanked by Robert Olnick and Henry Benach of the Starrett Housing Corporation and Andrew J. Frankel of National Kinney Corp., I announced that these companies were forming a joint venture to build 1,854 residential units in the northern sector of our landfill. They proposed to put up six buildings on nineteen acres at a cost of $75 million.

Their plan was predicated on the use of Section 236 subsidies of the National Housing Act of 1968 to reduce mortgage interest. This measure aimed to continue the federal government's subsidy of low- and moderate-income housing without having Washington actually choose the tenants. The Starrett plan also proposed to tap Operation Breakthrough, HUD's 1969 program, to encourage factory-assembled housing.

While we continued to explore any development possibilities that seemed at all reasonable, the epic struggle to secure FHA mortgage insurance for our initial Pod III residential units dragged on. On February 18, 1976, the *Wall Street Journal* reported that HUD would co-insure mortgage loans made by the Massachusetts Housing Finance Agency, the first such instance of FHA backing for a state agency's projects. Surely, this boded well for us.

Not necessarily. A month later, HUD assessed our prospects as mixed, estimating that we would need three years to rent out the apartments in Pod III, casting a shadow over our insurance application. But on March 17, Kuhn Loeb gave us some good news. In their opinion, with FHA backing, we could sell our housing bonds at an acceptable 7 percent interest rate.

May brought some support for our cause from the outside. The *Daily News*, worried about the dearth of new housing and the similar scarcity of construction jobs, urged both Albany and Washington to do whatever it took to expedite the building process at Battery Park City. On our site on May 26, New York Congressmen Peter Peyser of Westchester County and Mario Biaggi of the Bronx addressed a rally urging a jump-start for our development, the convention center, and the West Side Highway renewal project.

But it seemed that for every step forward we were able to take, something popped up to drag us back. Now it was Co-op City, the huge Mitchell-Lama project in the Bronx, where tenants were withholding maintenance payments, protesting increases in their monthly charge. This seemed to have rattled Carla Hills, who spoke increasingly of being more conservative with FHA funds, pushing the states to shoulder more of the burden of new housing construction.

All too slowly, we continued to work our way through the HUD bureaucracy. In the summer of 1976, we were still stymied by the issues of minimum housing standards and our impact on the environment. Another sticking point had become the fact that we had already built the foundations for our units, while FHA insurance usually went to projects on which construction had not yet begun. Nor had we completely resolved the sublease issue. But the biggest stumbling block, it increasingly appeared, was the issue of marketability.

Downtown Lower Manhattan Association Chairman Howard Clark wrote to Carla Hills in July, restating the difference between Battery Park City and Independence Plaza, the development to our north that really *was* floundering. That project's failure so far was being used as a weapon against us. Its inability to attract a sufficient number of tenants was considered a bad omen for our prospects. To counter this impression we weighed in with another study by real estate consultant James Felt, estimating that we would come close to fully renting our apartments about eighteen months after we completed construction, not the three years that HUD had envisioned.

But so far, even Vice President Rockefeller couldn't budge the HUD bureaucracy. By mid-1976, we had already spent a year and a half wading through that morass. I had concluded that the agency was rife with incompetents and hoped that it would be given a thorough cleaning out should Gerald Ford, who had succeeded Richard Nixon as president in 1974, win a term of his own in the November presidential elections. So many of the bureaucrats we had to deal with opted for the safe road of inaction. Having run a state housing division that had had produced 120,000 residential units without a default, I could muster very little sympathy for their molasses-like modus operandi.

Just how bad was it? We had sent HUD a check for $65,000 in January, covering the application fee for a conditional commitment on mortgage insurance. More than six months later, HUD's local office in New York claimed they had never deposited it because of all the outstanding issues I have discussed. Fortunately, I was able to produce the cancelled check to show how wrong they were.

This agency had paper records in its main Washington headquarters and field units combined that filled 253,000 cubic feet. For that figure, we can thank the Paperwork Management Branch in the Management Systems and Organization Division of the Office of Organization and Management Information in the Office of Administration at the Department of Housing and Urban Development. I wonder how much of that paperwork was devoted to *their* letterhead!

With construction workers desperate for work and construction on new middle-income housing virtually at a standstill, our application was still going nowhere. Carla Hills's letter to me, dated July 19, 1976, was a low point in this saga. She was ready to return our $65,000 processing fee because of all the problems I have noted. She said that HUD's market analysis, including comparisons to other projects, "indicate that the project could be rented up in the near future only at rent levels which would support a radically reduced mortgage amount." She estimated that we would have to go up to $180 a room to support a $65 million mortgage.

I replied a few days later, suggesting that her people were using faulty figures in reaching this conclusion. For example, they appeared to be confusing gross total rent with shelter rent—rent less the cost of utilities. Nor did they seem to take into account our plan for individual tenant metering of electricity. They were also assuming we would need to pay 8 percent interest on our housing bonds, far above the Kuhn Loeb estimate. As for marketability, I quoted from the mercurial Ada Louise Huxtable, who only the day before in the *New York Times* had declared, "Even at $130 (currently) a room, there should be a stampede for these apartments."

I wasn't going to lose this battle on the marketability issue. Throughout the first half of 1976, we had continued to follow up on our 1975 recanvassing of the people who had responded to our original ad for apartments. We were concentrating on small samples of several hundred to be able to make more accurate, detailed projections of potential tenant interest. By the end of the summer, we were able to forecast, with a comfortable degree of reliability, that we could rent 2,900 apartments, substantially more than the 1,642 that would be available.

We also managed to keep just enough pressure on Carla Hills, with Vice President Rockefeller, New York's Senator James Buckley, and Congressman John Murphy among the prominent people who labored on our behalf. Finally, on October 18, I was invited to Washington to press our case directly with Hills and her staff. I urged her to speed up the application process. Although sticking to her guns on each of the now all-too-familiar issues, Hills now told us to file a formal application for a firm commitment of FHA insurance for Battery Park City. This meant we could avoid a long-drawn-out Sight Approval and Market Analysis, known as SAMA. Here was progress of a sort, and this time HUD set up a special full-time task force just to process our application, under the direction of Deputy Director Alexander Naclerio.

Senator Buckley and the *Daily News* prematurely announced that our FHA insurance would be along shortly. Had that been true it would have been a beautiful bit of timing because less than two weeks later, on October 27, 1976, we held a ceremony on our site to mark the completion of the landfill. Where once 12 rotting piers dominated the shoreline, 3,646,457 cubic yards of sand, 50,806 cubic yards of concrete, 33 miles of concrete piles, and 801,052 cubic yards of stone and rip rap, at a cost of $49,052,847.75, had produced Manhattan's biggest real estate bargain since the original 1626 purchase of the island from the Indians.

"Proud" is too mild a word to describe my feelings that day. But "sobering" is how I viewed the letter I received from Carla Hills just after our Washington meeting. She reiterated the need for an environmental review, called for us to renegotiate our lease with the city to protect the federal government's interests should we be granted FHA insurance for the mortgage, and reminded me of the federal fire safety standards that clashed with the city's varying set of safety measures that we had already met in our plans.

How did I keep going in the face of such dark tidings? Perhaps there's a clue in an award I received at the end of 1976. The Optimists Club of New York City named me "Optimist of the Year." I won't be falsely humble: that year, I truly deserved it!

I would continue to need that optimism. Just when we were becoming accustomed to dealing with Carla Hills, Jimmy Carter defeated President Ford in November, leaving us to deal with a new head of HUD, Patricia R. Harris. What's more, the agency would be going through reorganization, meaning that we would also have to be working with new contacts.

Thanks to Henry Nussbaum, our housing financial consultant, we would negotiate with Harris from a stronger position on the question of apartment marketability. In September, Henry had suggested that we could make a better case if we began to take actual applications for apartments accompanied by a $50 good faith deposit. As they say, "money talks." On October 27, during the ceremony marking completion of our landfill, we announced that we were doing just that.

Labor Peace

We had to assume that through determined effort we would overcome the economic, political, and bureaucratic roadblocks that were holding up construction at Battery Park City. Once we did, we hoped to get off to a quick start and keep going. Toward that end, we were moving to ensure that labor strife would not delay us once that happy day arrived.

It was the right environment in which to negotiate a labor peace accord, similar to the agreement that Robert Moses was able to work with while preparing the 1964 World's Fair. We held out to the unions the prospect of a potential 6,200 jobs involving 760,000 man-hours of work. With construction industry unemployment at a sky-high 50 percent, this was El Dorado for them. In return for this employment bonanza, we wanted to be able to work free of petty stoppages.

Our negotiations with Peter Brennan, president of the 250,000-member Building and Construction Trades Council and former secretary of labor in the Nixon/Ford administrations, bore fruit on February 24, 1976, when the council's delegates ratified a productivity and continuity understanding. On March 8, the membership ratified this first-ever labor peace agreement to cover housing and related construction. The agreement was designed to prevent strikes, lockouts, waste, and delays.

The *Daily News* hailed the agreement as a model for how to conduct labor-management relations in tough times. The paper wrote, "It is the only way to revive an industry that is desperately ill, and in which unemployment is brutally high." But this opinion wasn't unanimous. There was, after all, the long letter in the Communist Party's the *Daily World*, denouncing the pact as "a sell-out class collaborationist agreement." We decided we would go ahead with it, nevertheless.

Albany: Everything but a Ball and Chain

The previous year, 1975, had presented us with the prospects of working with a hostile governor while trying not to be dragged under by a municipal government drowning in red ink. Now, 1976 would confirm just how damaging these circumstances were going to be.

We had hoped the labor peace agreement would smooth the way in advance for actual building construction. While we were finalizing that pact, we also ordered the steel we would need to begin the infrastructure of roads and utilities to support the apartment houses and to block Westway. On January 5, 1976, we placed an order for 3,700 tons, with delivery anticipated from Bethlehem Steel in April.

The state's Emergency Financial Control Board had to approve our order. In submitting the contract to them on January 26, I noted that Bethlehem guaranteed the quoted price for the steel for only four months, after which inflation, which was then a big concern, would almost certainly increase it. We therefore requested the board to act with dispatch. Our contract with Bethlehem did not come before the board until February 25. On March 27, they told me they would need at least another month to consider it. New York City informed us on April 27 that the board was further delaying its decision until the city showed how *our* contract fitted in with *its* financial plan. On April 30, the city finally submitted the contract for the board's approval.

Did this get the ball rolling? It did not, because now the state was in the process of reassessing the viability of our development, and no contract approval would be forthcoming until the Carey administration could be convinced to accept our project's continued existence.

The state began to hack away at us on February 25, 1976, when State Comptroller Arthur Levitt's office issued a report on the audit it had been conducting of Battery Park City. Although acknowledging that economic conditions beyond our control had prevented us from keeping to our original construction timeline, Levitt's report nevertheless portentously put us at a turning point. It described our problems as "deep-seated," with a possible default by 1984 if we didn't get development going soon. He prescribed a long, hard look at our viability by the state, which should consider whether the social benefits of our continuing the project were worth the risks involved. The comptroller's office also portrayed us as stubbornly sticking to our original plans and simply waiting for the direction of the wind to change.

Perhaps the comptroller's people had cancelled their newspaper subscriptions, leaving them uninformed about our FHA application, the well-publicized search for a new convention center site, and the Starrett proposal to put up more than 1,800 additional units of housing. But even without the reading matter, all they would have had to do is to come down to our site and open their eyes. They might then have noticed that we had added over $100,000,000 worth of new land to Manhattan Island. Imagine what we could have done by then in better times!

The *New York Times* front-paged the comptroller's report on March 1. Not only did this endanger our steel contract, it also jeopardized some intense negotiations I was carrying out in secret with a potential major tenant for our long-dormant commercial space. EBASCO Services, a three-thousand-employee engineering firm, was assessing the possibility of relocating its headquarters to Battery Park City. But the public bad-mouthing we now underwent cooled their interest.

The next day the *Times* gave my side of the story. In addition to listing our accomplishments and favorable cash position, I let on that we had a potential commercial tenant without revealing their identity for fear that other states might go after them as well. I also noted that I had been keeping Governor Carey fully apprised of these negotiations.

While I was doing that, Governor Carey was sharpening the blade. The comptroller's report had emboldened him, and on March 10, the *New York Post*, in a story attributed to Carey staff members, said that the governor "may eliminate the troublesome project altogether in the near future." I quickly fired off a letter to Carey, reminding him of the potential consequences of publicly denigrating Battery Park City. It was not just his housing policy, construction jobs, and Battery Park City bondholders that would be hurt by these tactics. There was also the moral obligation of the state to make good on our bonds if the rug was pulled out from under us. I urged the governor to discuss these matters with me face to face. I got that meeting on April 28, but the usually inscrutable Carey gave us no satisfaction

Having heard from the heavy artillery from upstate, we next dealt with a popgun. Later in March, first-term member of the state assembly Elizabeth A. Connelly wrote to us, stating that she was co-sponsoring a bill to abolish Battery Park City. She envisioned the possibility that the one hundred acres of sand could be put to "recreational use." For what, a second Coney Island, hard by Wall Street?

Increasingly it was looking as if we would have to carry that steel from Bethlehem on our backs over a bureaucratic and political mountain if we ever wanted to see it put to good use on our site. In April, Governor Carey formed the Council on the Economy to consolidate the work of various governmental bodies working to pull New York City out from under its debt. Carey himself headed the council, which would be directed by State Commerce Commissioner John Dyson. Almost immediately, on April 30, a subcommittee of the new group, headed by Municipal Assistance Corporation Chief Felix Rohatyn, was formed specifically to deal with us.

Also, on April 30, the *New York Post* raised an issue that would prove a major stumbling block in getting top city and state officials to fully back us on our application for FHA insurance. The paper quoted Michael Bailkin, counsel to the mayor's development office, on the issue of the civic facilities agreement we had worked out with the city in which the city would temporarily subsidize part of the infrastructure we were going to build to support development on our site. Bailkin wanted to scrap the 1973 agreement because it was unfair and unaffordable under the present circumstances.

Tom Galvin answered for us, pointing out that we had factored the city's payments, limited to $10 million in any one year, into our financial plan. Even so, we were more than willing and able to delay those payments until the municipal crisis had passed. We would repeat these reassurances over the next two years but met with recurrent fears and resistance on this issue.

On May 3, I sent Rohatyn a Mailgram, asking for quick action from the economic council so we could finally buy our steel and get back to the business of building. I pointed out that should his subcommittee's study drag on, we might be faced with winter construction work, which was more expensive than building in fair weather. He replied that the details of our steel purchase order were for the Emergency Financial Control Board to deal with, while he and his colleagues were going to take a more "general" look at our enterprise. That was ominous.

In a meeting at Felix Rohatyn's office on May 10, I got a good picture of how the Council on the Economy viewed us. The memo they handed me rehashed all of the points that the comptroller's office had made in its audit, adding some new factual errors about Battery Park City. But it did acknowledge our "strong and stable short-term financing position."

Then our prospects with the council worsened. On May 27, Frank S. Kristoff, director of housing at the UDC and a respected and influential figure in the housing field, wrote about us to Herbert Ellish, director of the Municipal Assistance Corporation. Kristoff contended that our Pod III housing was not "a financially viable project in terms of obtaining the necessary occupancy to pay for rentals required to meet debt service payments, payments in lieu of taxes, and all operating costs including necessary reserves." He, too, cited the failure of Independence Plaza to rent its apartments the previous year, and concluded that Battery Park City "would not obtain sufficient rents to support itself." Here was more ammunition for the Council on the Economy's subcommittee on Battery Park City.

Kristoff's confidential letter had fallen into our hands from an outside source. I wrote to Felix Rohatyn, informing him that we had seen the letter and complaining that we had not been given an opportunity to rebut it. I reminded him that if the letter got out, it could endanger our application with HUD for mortgage insurance.

Fortunately, Kristoff listened to reason. After examining the June report from the James Felt Company that established the viability of our housing in the market, he changed his mind and agreed that our units were at least "arguably marketable." That at least removed one of numerous obstacles to progress.

But although we had undone this damage, it didn't move us forward. We couldn't order our steel from Bethlehem because the

Emergency Financial Control Board was awaiting a clean bill of health for us from the governor's Committee on the Economy. And what would cause the committee to smile in our direction? HUD's commitment of FHA insurance for Pod III. But HUD was being influenced by the constant bad-mouthing from various elements in the state government. Round and round it went.

Meanwhile, in May, Carey had obtained a direct foothold in our operations. Mario Procaccino's term as a member of the Battery Park City Authority had expired and the governor appointed John F. Hennessy, of the engineering firm of Syska and Hennessey, to fill the position. He was an able and likeable individual, but there was no doubt whose interest he would be representing.

The Headache That Wouldn't Go Away

Consistency is often a virtue, but not when it means you've been force-fed a steady diet of nonsense and trouble. Sam LeFrak and his associates had been so consistently a nuisance that we almost severed relations with them entirely. In fact, on April 9, 1976, we returned their $250,000 deposit as a dramatic statement that we wouldn't put up with the continuing lack of cooperation.

That storm passed, but Sam continued to be a thorn in our side. On May 31, he appeared on the cover of *Business Week* under the headline, "Real Estate Bargain Hunter." He was photographed on a boat with the Battery Park City bulkhead in the background. The picture had been cropped to show only his upper body, with no sign of the boat, giving the impression that Sam, never one for modesty, might be walking on water.

The magazine's story began, "The survivors of the historic 1973-75 real estate slaughter are glumly seeking to save what they can from the carnage." Sam, a "vicious negotiator," according to one unidentified developer quoted in the piece, was negotiating to buy the Uris Building Corp and also wanted to develop resort villages for Club Med, which was just then seeking to enter the U.S. market. With the article was another photo of Sam LeFrak, with a caption stating that he "bets he can help pull Battery Park

City out of its financial troubles," and that he would like it to become the "jewel in the Lefrak crown." Further, the article stated, *he* had already "poured foundations," and *he and the joint venture* had about $5 million of their own money tied up in the work completed so far.

Some people have no shame whatsoever. I had Avrum Hyman write to *Business Week* to temper some of Sam's self-aggrandizement. Referring to that figure of $5 million, Avrum informed the editor "that this is probably a typographical or transmission error, as a more accurate guess would be in the vicinity of $5 thousand. The change may have crept in because it is so hard to associate Mr. LeFrak with such a small figure."

As Ada Louise Huxtable had written in her piece on us in the *Times* on July 25, 1976, "New York is supposed to thrive on adversity, and adversity is one thing Battery Park City has had plenty of." So far, we had risen above just about everything else, and there was no reason to believe that my friend Sam would be the exception.

Peter Brennan, president of the 250,000-member Building and Construction Trades Council, signs our historic labor peace agreement in 1976.m

A labor rally on our site in May 1976 supported our application for an FHA mortgage guarantee.

The urban myth persists that the entire Battery Park City landfill came from debris resulting from construction of the World Trade Center. That debris provided only the middle twenty acres—and we had to rework that section to turn it into viable landfill. (Thomas Airviews)

It was necessary to shore up the landfill provided by the construction of the World Trade Center. (Christian Science Publishing Society)

Chapter 11

THE CLOCK IS RUNNING

E arly in 1977, the New York City newsletter, *Economic Conditions Quarterly*, reported that "the City's construction industry was severely depressed during 1976 as both government and private sector building slowed to a trickle . . . The construction of new residential buildings showed little improvement over 1975, itself a year of below-normal activity." In fact, our building permits accounted for half the city's total.

As the decade wore on and economic conditions remained adverse, we were severely challenged to keep on course and continue to move ahead. In a covering letter to Governor Carey accompanying our 1976 annual report, I noted that we had been forced "to fit our development program to a procrustean bed not of our making." The prolonged real estate recession had made us improvise, with a financing strategy that now hinged on the FHA-insured mortgage and an approach to development that left us hunting opportunities, such as the convention center, we had never dreamed of when we drew up our master development plan.

Any opportunity to advance our project in any way was welcome, even a temporary one, if it did us some good and did not hinder our work of actually building Battery Park City. For example, since our project's inception in the late 1960s, the politics involved had sometimes resembled a circus. There often seemed to be no lack of clowns ready to impede our progress for reasons that were truly laughable. All the more appropriate, then, that our still largely empty landfill should host a little gem of a real circus in 1977.

That summer, passersby saw a large green tent on our site. It was the first home of the Big Apple Circus, which later became an entrenched New York City institution, to the delight of so many people of all ages. The Big Top was erected on the southern portion of our site and the show had a seven-week run. We provided the space at the request of Mayor Beame, without charge. What we got back was goodwill and a chance to introduce our project to the crowds that flocked to the performances.

When Governor Carey, in February 1977, advanced New York State as a possible site of the 1984 Summer Olympics, I volunteered Battery Park City as the perfect place to erect housing for participants. I wrote to Carey on February 23, making the case for our development as an ideal Olympic Village, pointing out that the buildings could eventually be incorporated into Battery Park City's permanent housing stock. I'm still waiting for a reply.

We even contributed to the city's efforts to draw film companies to New York. Well, in truth, few people remember *Bye Bye Monkey*, a French/Italian hodgepodge of a movie, filmed partly on our site in 1977 and starring Marcello Mastroianni, Geraldine Fitzgerald, James Coco, and Gerard Depardieu. Leonard Maltin's popular *Movie and Video Guide* charitably rated it a "bomb." I won't even attempt to summarize its bizarre plot. But it did get us more newspaper space and it briefly left its mark on our landfill in the form of a fifty-foot ape. I will resist the temptation to even suggest which prominent political figures the Styrofoam simian might have resembled.

We not only hosted culture in the late '70s, we rescued it as well. The Brooklyn Academy of Music found itself in a fix in 1977 when an old water main burst, partially flooding the hall and undermining the street outside. Suddenly, there was a demand for landfill in downtown Brooklyn. We had sand to spare and donated seven thousand cubic yards of it. In a relatively short time, BAM was able to reopen its doors to the public.

We responded to any reasonable request for assistance. But sometimes we had to say "no," especially when the appeal was ill conceived and impractical. On January 19, 1977, for example, we got a call at 3:50 p.m. from CBS TV. They wanted to know if they could shoot a sequence for one of their dramatic programs on our site at 6:30 the next morning. The caller had not taken into account the need to arrange insurance against injury or damage, a city permit to film on our landfill, and the task we would have of blocking out space that would not put them in the path of workmen on the site. The bottom line: they shot elsewhere.

Our landfill was also in demand by still photographers. The previous spring, in May 1976, *Newsday* ran a photograph of a group of nude men, women, and children sunbathing alfresco on our sand beach a la Riviera West. The photo, picked up by the Associated Press, carried a caption explaining that the group was "demonstrating for the establishment of a clothes-optional bathing area in Manhattan. The demonstration was also held," the caption continued, "to reportedly promote National Nude Beach Day, scheduled for August 8, 1976." As far as I could tell, the naked political ambition that clearly motivated some of our opponents was nowhere in evidence in the image.

That FHA Insurance: Same Plot, Different Players

But these were diversions. In what was becoming an off-Broadway show that threatened to run as long as *The Fantasticks*, we kept getting the same old rigmarole in 1977 from HUD on our application for FHA mortgage insurance, although now the cast changed. A new president occupied the Oval Office after January 20, and he would be staffing government agencies with his own people.

The February issue of *House and Home* quoted Jimmy Carter on our nation's housing situation. "We've got a very dormant construction industry because of an absence of homebuilding incentives," the incoming president said. "The FHA and HUD both, in my opinion are an administrative shambles . . . With a very minimum amount of investment of taxpayer's money, you could have a quick stimulation of the housing industry which could be almost entirely in the private sector."

Amen! *We* had a project that linked the public sector to the private, but that would depend mostly on the efforts of private developers to actually put up the buildings. FHA mortgage insurance, for which we had already paid more than $195,000 in application fees, would get us going. The starter's pistol was cocked and we could "go" if someone would only pull the trigger.

Carter named Patricia R. Harris to replace Carla Hills as secretary of housing and urban development. We were determined that Harris would have a harder time holding us off with the marketability issue. At the beginning of January 1977, we put ads in the *New York Times* soliciting the apartment applications, along with the $50 nonbinding fee, that we had announced at the ceremony marking completion of our landfill. We were going to present her with facts on the ground. Besides applications from individuals, we also invited interest from companies needing corporate apartments for temporary housing.

As soon as Carter named the new HUD chief, we sent her our congratulations. In a letter on January 19, I also filled her in on the nature and importance of our project, our progress to date, and the already long and tortuous history of our FHA insurance application. I also reminded her of the still massive unemployment in the New York City construction trades—50 percent!—and the need for more middle-income housing. We were potentially a big part of the solution for these problems. We already had 2,100 applications for apartments in hand, with application fees in escrow deposits in the Seamen's Bank for Savings. Battery Park City, I suggested, presented her "with an opportunity for action" without having to actually spend federal funds.

By now I knew that private persuasion would not be enough so I also released the letter, along with relevant data, to the press, resulting in a *Daily News* article on January 24. It reported that applications for apartments were pouring in at a rate of one hundred a day and that if we got quick approval of the mortgage insurance, some of those applicants might be moving in as early as the end of 1978.

If Harris had been unfavorably swayed in advance by some of the disparagement of our project that had gotten around, the February 11 *New York Times* article on how construction was being stymied almost everywhere should have put the bad-mouthing in perspective. The story described projects of all kinds being delayed or terminated by the economic blight that had beset construction through much of the decade. It also made particular mention of our situation, relating how the UDC fiasco had undercut our ability to go back into the bond market, making it necessary that we secure FHA mortgage insurance first.

On February 1, the acting director of HUD's Office of Loan Origination in Washington replied to my January 19 letter to Harris, informing us that "the processing of the Battery Park City project is going forward." That was fine, but forward at what rate? What new approach could we expect to expedite matters?

On April 15, Rolf Jensen & Associates', HUD consultants, submitted a report to the agency on the fireproofing of the first residential buildings we planned for our site. They stipulated a myriad of details that they thought we should change. On June 16, we were officially informed about these upgrades. I handed the matter to the Lefrak/Fisher team that was temporarily supervising our construction for a cost analysis of these new requirements. They pointed out that our plans as they then stood met the rigid standards of the New York City Building Code, the city's special zoning regulations, the city's Housing Maintenance Code, the New York State Multiple Dwelling Law, and the state's Mitchell-Lama Design Criteria. They also reported that the Jensen suggestions "are exceptionally excessive, require maintenance, are unsightly in appearance and will produce marketability resistance in renting." The new and elaborate sprinkler system Jensen called for would alone increase costs from several hundred thousand to a million dollars per building.

Yet, even with the bar possibly set higher for us, depending on how rigidly HUD wanted to hold us to these new standards, there was a small sign of progress in July when our mortgage loan application was granted "preliminary" approval. The catch was that no dollar amount was specified. We needed at least the $65 million backing we had originally requested and now the figure was to be determined later. That part of the process, we were told, would take another two or three months.

On July 27 Mayor Beame joined union leaders and several hundred construction workers—and just as important, members of the media who reported it—on the landfill at Battery Park City in a demonstration to keep the federal administration's feet to the fire. At the rally, I announced that we already had in hand apartment application number 3,000, raising applicants to almost twice as many as the number of units that would initially be available.

Something, probably the new Carter administration's close ties to organized labor, made the people at HUD sit up and take notice because now the New York office was told to take control of the processing of our application and to expedite it. We met with the local HUD officials, headed by Alexander Naclerio, on August 25. They said that now we were all right on the environmental issue. As for the sublease, HUD's position was that it could live with it. That wasn't firm enough for us, but when we pushed them, all we got was "It's not too much of a problem." But after everything we had done to demonstrate the marketability of our units, marketability somehow remained a sticky issue. And property standards were still in the problem category.

Time was working against us. Our capital was slowly draining away and the political winds were becoming increasingly unfavorable. The longer this struggle with the federal bureaucrats dragged on, the less viable Battery Park City would appear to be. At this point, I attempted to cut through the red tape. At least give us "conditional" approval of the specific amount we had requested, I asked. "Final" approval could be left pending as we, hopefully, worked out the bedeviling details.

Their response was to ask us to file an entirely new application for the mortgage insurance, with the promise that now things would move. We were, of course, anxious to get off the starting block and whisk this thing over the finish line. Our contact person at HUD was to be a Mr. Walter Bond. He was supposed to get in touch with us, but a week went by following the August 25 meeting and we heard nothing from Mr. Bond, despite repeated calls from Henry Nussbaum. Finally, Henry was reduced to writing to him to get things going.

By mid-September, we had a clear idea of where we stood, or so it seemed. Within sixty days of receiving all the requisite documents, HUD promised us, they would complete the processing of our conditional loan commitment. The two-month processing period would begin on October 4. Meanwhile, there was a stack of new forms to fill out and conditions to meet. And we upped the amount of insurance we were requesting to $69 million to allow for inflation.

It was in a spirit of dark humor that we read the HUD October newsletter. It described some of the measures the department was taking to reorganize mortgage insurance application procedures on the local level to spur processing. The newsletter said that the changes had been required because of a breakdown in communications between central headquarters and field offices that they ascribed to "management problems." No comment!

By now, I knew that complying with HUD regulations in our reapplication would be no small formality. Making our floor plans acceptable, for example, would mean indulging in micro-minutia. Their objections included, "Change Prof. Apt. label to Prof. Suite." If HUD had been in charge of this nation's settlement of the West as we expanded in the nineteenth century, we would never have made it to California.

Nevertheless, optimist that I was, I hoped to get that conditional approval within the promised sixty days. In a November 3 letter to Justin Murphy, president of the Downtown Lower Manhattan Association, I wrote, "We are progressing nicely with the FHA." I continued, with too much optimism, that I was "confident that we will have our conditional commitment in

December and if we continue to work with persistence and determination, construction of the superstructure can start shortly thereafter." Fat chance.

Mounting Political Opposition

Not only could we expect no help from the governor's mansion, I was increasingly concerned that Carey might be emboldened to undercut us entirely. I spoke to him in late February 1977 and, sure enough, discovered that he was reevaluating our master development plan! His advice to me was to put off the residential units and return to the office building construction that we had originally planned for our starting point. He suggested that we needed a high visibility tenant, such as the New York Stock Exchange. What he didn't mention was that the office market was still virtually nonexistent.

I wrote to him on March 2, explaining that changing the master plan now would be extraordinarily expensive. It had taken several years to produce and the process had cost several million dollars. Numerous governmental bodies and consultants had reviewed it along the way. Even Ada Louise Huxtable approved of it! And the plan was tied to our master lease, another complicated document. Initiating basic changes at this point would be a death sentence for the project, "leaving the State with the moral obligation to pick up the entire debt service on our $200 million of outstanding bonds," I pointedly reminded the governor.

Of course, we would love to bring an institution such as the New York Stock Exchange to Battery Park City. In fact, we were now actively pursuing the American Stock Exchange. But we were ready to go with the Pod III housing, lacking only the mortgage insurance. We had already put in the foundations for 1,642 units. It had been over a year since we had submitted for state and city approval our order for steel to build infrastructure. If he really *wanted* to help, Carey could expedite that approval and give us his strong backing for that FHA insurance. Meanwhile, we were spending $23,000 a day on debt service and operating expenses, and inflation was constantly raising the price of everything for which we would eventually have to pay.

If our bond proceeds were slowly eroding, the drain on our political capital was mounting at a disturbing rate. Although some former opponents, such as Percy Sutton, now strongly supported Battery Park City, politicians of all stripes looking for an easy target found one in us. And the more we were publicly denigrated, the easier it became for even minor politicians to lash out at Battery Park City, getting their names into print and scoring cheap points with their constituents.

One of them was Queens Councilman Arthur Katzman, who during hearings on charter and government operations on March 15, declared us "dead as a dodo." Constant repetition of that false picture of our status threatened to create its own reality, and I wrote to him with a long list of facts that belied his glib remark.

Much worse was a March 27 story—hatchet job, really—in the *Daily News*. The story behind this story began in 1976, when a "sunshine" law that came out of Albany opened public agency meetings to the public and press. We, of course, complied, and in February 1977 discovered that we had an almost permanent visitor to our offices. *Daily News* reporter Claire Spiegel, obviously smelling blood in the press reports and politician's comments that had us barely clinging to life, virtually attached herself to us.

Spiegel didn't just cover our meetings; she also pestered Avrum Hyman, our information director, with phone calls, constantly asking about everything we were doing. Then she planted herself on our premises, often late on Friday afternoons, perhaps in the hope, vainly, of catching some of us stealing away early for an extended weekend. It soon became clear that we had a genuine snoop in our midst. Our patience with her wore thin, and then wore out. Finally, Avrum told her, "Our people are not experimental animals to be put on display and exhibited like monkeys in a zoo." She was no longer welcome.

By late March, Spiegel apparently felt that she had managed to dig up whatever dirt she was burrowing for. Her "exposé" appeared in a Sunday edition of the paper under the headline, "Weak Battery City Gets $1.6 M—a—Year Juice." She briefly outlined our situation, editorialized that we were tossing good money after bad, and falsely reported that neither city nor state had any control over our wild spending. (I wonder what the people on the Emergency Financial Control Board thought about that!) Along the way, she smeared us with a series of quotes from the always convenient and "anonymous," highly placed sources. One higher-up in the state housing division said it was common knowledge that we were floundering.

On March 30, I fired off a five-page, single-spaced rebuttal to *News* editor Mike O'Neill, in which I suggested that someone higher up at the paper seemed to have it in for us. The article itself, I charged, had been "pieced together with innuendo and partial truths and could cause us serious damage." Our offices were not even remotely "posh," as Spiegel had described them. In the article, she had also confused a depreciation figure of $63,000 with office "improvements," which we had not made.

Spiegel had zoomed in on a few social functions for which we had bought tickets, implying that we were living it up at our bondholder's expense. But anyone without an axe to grind could see that the groups hosting them and the audience attending were people we needed to mix with to advance Battery Park City. A prime example was one at which I was able to meet James Sawhill, president of NYU, whose business school was near our project and whose institution was a likely candidate to rent space on our site. I had also attended a dinner for the head of Merrill Lynch, who would be influential in deciding where the New York and American Stock Exchanges would relocate, if they moved. (Merrill Lynch would eventually become a prime tenant in Battery Park City's World Financial Center.)

She had also complained that we had spent money on a van. But I put that in perspective. For a project that had raised $200 million through a bond sale, had added one hundred acres to Manhattan's configuration, had already put in the foundations for 1,642 residential units, and was preparing a development that would ultimately house some of America's major financial institutions and would be home to thousands of New Yorkers, that vehicle was hardly a luxury item.

O'Neill insisted that Spiegel reply (privately) to my letter. In her rejoinder, she stuck to her story, remarking that many of the unnamed people in government she had interviewed thought, "Battery Park City should be junked." She questioned whether anyone was going to put up money to help finance the project and doubted that enough people would ever want to live there. Then she said that our expenditures would only be justified if the project we were planning ever came to fruition. Well of course, that was and is the raison de'etre for *any* expenditure on *any* project. Did she think merely wishing would create Battery Park City? Even by her own standards, those expenditures were an enormous bargain. Today's Battery Park City is the proof of the pudding.

In a cover letter with Spiegel's reply to my letter, *News* editor Mike O' Neill put his finger on the size of the perception gap we were facing. He mentioned that the political figures he had talked to about Battery Park City said, "It still does not have the ingredients for an economically successful project." Here was the heart of the problem. We knew that enthusiastic backing from Mayor Koch and Governor Carey would almost surely speed the FHA insurance through the pipeline. But they were not yet giving us that support. Then they disparaged our prospects on the basis of our not having the economic backing to which they themselves were the key.

Five weeks later, the man who had almost certainly been Spiegel's anonymous source in the state housing division for her original article came out of the shadow and let himself be quoted directly in her May 25 story in the *News* that again questioned why we should continue with our work. He was State Housing Commissioner John Heimann.

The only thing new about Heimann's opposition was his owning up to it in public. I had heard from him on January 7, when he wrote to me about the drop in our bond price. "The following two research reports of the First Albany Corporation should be of some interest to you," he all but sneered about what he had enclosed with his letter. The reports concluded that our prospects were "dim" and suggested "that investors steer a wide path around BPCA's . . . ." The attitude behind his missive seemed not so much "here's something FYI," but rather, "aren't you in a pretty fix, so why don't you pack it in?"

In fact, he had been bad-mouthing us for some time, although with a certain amount of reserve when quoted in print, as in an interview published in *Barron's* in April, in which he said the state was closely watching us. Now, in Spiegel's May 25 piece, he really let loose. Likening us to the UDC—that albatross we couldn't shake—he suggested that the state would do well to cut its losses and close us down. This from a man whose background was in banking, not real estate.

Spiegel also quoted State Assemblyman Edward Lehner, who represented a neighborhood in Upper Manhattan, in her May 25 piece. Lehner, chairman of the assembly's Housing Committee, chimed in that, while "there is no crisis yet, it obviously will come and the taxpayer will be left with the bill." It would not be the last we heard from Assemblyman Lehner, who would shortly do his best to see that we had that crisis.

Meanwhile, with city hall and the state house up for grabs in the fall, I wrote to all the candidates in August, explaining our plight and enlisting their help if they won. In this particular election year, we followed the candidates with close interest, but not just because they held the key to our future. One of our own was among them. Tom Galvin had taken a leave of absence to run as the Republican candidate for borough president of Queens, a race that, unfortunately, he lost to Donald Manes.

Forebodings

As 1977 drew to a close, optimism at Battery Park City was in short supply. December 4 would mark the end of the sixty-day period in which we had been promised action on our FHA application. But in an October 30 story in the *New York Times*,

HUD's Alexander Naclerio was quoted to the effect that a decision should not be expected before the end of the year. The question now had become, would we get the word before it was the end of us?

As if we didn't have enough enemies, the *Times* piece also quoted Herman Badillo, an unsuccessful candidate for mayor in the Democratic primary and former Bronx borough president, who hoped we would be just as unsuccessful at HUD. Badillo felt that we would be using resources that could be better applied to the city's poorer areas. He incorrectly characterized residential construction at Battery Park City as "luxury" accommodations, which, ironically, would be true only after control of the project passed into other hands. Again, Battery Park City was being described as part of a zero sum game in which we were somehow stealing from the poor. It may have made good copy, but again, it was wrong. Our financing came from a bond issue, not government subsidies.

It's a good thing that I'm not superstitious. In November, the city's Department of Ports and Terminals, repairing pier A at our southern end, placed 20 twelve-by-twelve timbers against our bulkhead, damaging it in the process. And the apartment application sign we had affixed to our main sign on the property fell down and was left lying on the ground, facing skyward. In a memo to our property manager, Richard Rowe, I asked that "it be aimed at potential tenants instead of seagulls."

But a request we received in November from Assemblyman Edward Lehner, whom I have mentioned, threatened much greater damage. His committee wanted detailed information about Battery Park City, flaunting Arthur Levitt's 1976 report in our faces for emphasis. He was going to come after us with public hearings. When we didn't move fast enough on the request for information, the counsel for the committee, David Sweet, got a bit antsy.

By December, the Lehner Committee had the information they wanted, along with a warning from me. I advised Mr. Sweet of the potential damage he and his colleagues could do to our chances of getting that FHA mortgage insurance if they made reckless charges and rushed to judgment with unwarranted conclusions that seeped into the media. In fact, the hearings and constant demand for information that flowed from the Lehner Committee would be only one of the negative forces with which we would have to contend in 1978. Crunch time for Battery Park City, and for me, was just over the horizon.

Chapter 12

CRUNCH TIME

On November 30, 1977, we received a letter from Conway Publications, asking for information about Battery Park City. "This inquiry is addressed to the developers of large-scale projects which suffered through the 1974-77 real estate depression—worst in a generation," they began. "Our purpose is to identify those projects which survived and to determine how they stand today."

We checked the option, "Project still in jeopardy, must have funding or additional equity before _____," and filled in the blank with "1984," when our bond money would run out unless supplemented by new revenues. In truth, 1984 was only the technical deadline. We didn't have that long because political pressure on us to show "results" would surely close us down before then. In fact, we really needed to get something going in 1978. Even if my term on the Battery Park City Authority had not been due to expire at the stroke of midnight on December 31 of that year, I would have felt that this was it. The steady tom-tom beat of criticism in the media was having its effect. We had to have something to show for our efforts besides the one hundred new acres of land, and we had to have it soon.

Forecast: Wind

At the beginning of 1978, the city's Environmental Protection Administration warned us that we had a "blowing sand" problem that could adversely affect air quality in nearby neighborhoods.

We had relented on accommodating a helicopter service temporarily at our site, and the rotary blades from craft using the heliport supplemented nature's force in blowing the sand around. Perhaps we should have added camels as ground transportation.

It wasn't hard to deal with the blowing sand—just a matter of adding some fencing in the right places. But we were also faced with another kind of windiness that was not as easy to contain. This kind emanated from a forty-five-year-old New York State assemblyman who had only been in office for four years.

As it prepared for joint hearings on Battery Park City with the Standing Committee on Corporations, Authorities and Commissions, the Lehner Committee, chaired by Assemblyman Edward Lehner, sometimes gave the impression that it was the gang that couldn't shoot straight. Their preparation for the hearings was almost as dismal as their command of English. Mimicking the complaints of other critics, they challenged us on the potential marketability of our apartments, questioning the validity of our ads soliciting applications and deposits. "In view of the fact that we understand that the projected rents were not included in the advertisements," they sputtered, they remained unconvinced. "In view of the fact that we understand . . . ?" Understanding had little to do with it, and "facts," nothing at all. The rents were *in* the ads. Hadn't anyone bothered to *read* them before casting aspersions?

David Sweet, the committee's counsel, kept asking us for documents and wanted a schedule of our Battery Park City Authority members meetings so they could have someone sit in and observe. For the first three months of the year, they also tied up the schedule of *our* counsel, Jerry Sindler. So copious were their demands that Jerry had to stay late at the office through an early March snowstorm and then come back on the next working day, though quite ill, in order to meet their deadlines for submitting documents. Meanwhile, we needed Jerry's services ourselves as we approached the endgame in our battles with city and state politicians and Washington bureaucrats. It was like trying to run a race with a log tied to one leg.

Lehner himself really gave the game away when he signaled where he was coming from on March 7. About to chair an inquiry into a subject about which he was presumably impartial until the evidence was in, the chairman wrote to Port Authority Executive Director Peter Goldmark, suggesting that it would be better for all concerned if the landfill we had so diligently worked on for several years be given over to an industrial park rather than Battery Park City. He invited Goldmark to testify at the hearings—an invitation Goldmark wisely rejected—then scheduled to open on March 23 at the World Trade Center, and to speak to Lehner's suggestion for small industries and warehouses at the doorway to America's financial district. Quite a setup, I would say: Lehner was casting himself not only as judge—a position he later attained— and jury, but also would-be executioner.

After sending copies of his vision for an industrial park for Battery Park City to every major city and state political figure, Lehner informed us on March 10 that "invited" speakers would be heard at the March 23 hearings and that an additional session on April 14 would accommodate anyone else who wanted to speak. But they had yet to publicly announce this and I knew that many of our allies in the construction industry and civic organizations would want to have their say. I immediately sent a telegram to the assemblyman to that effect. Lehner replied that they were working on getting out the word, and that labor leaders Peter Brennan and Harry Van Arsdale were on the list of invited speakers for the first session on the twenty-third. Meanwhile, they put the second session, when they were likely to hear comments favorable to Battery Park City, off till May and moved it up to Albany.

In writing to me on behalf of his chairman, Committee Counsel David Sweet said, "I believe you will agree, after the hearings have been completed, that a full and fair hearing was given to all points of view." But I already had knowledge of Lehner's missive to Goldmark advocating beforehand that we be turned into an industrial park. Under the circumstances, I think I was justified in having a somewhat more jaundiced view of the so-called fairness of these proceedings than did Mr. Sweet.

Meanwhile, the questions and requests for documents kept coming. Now the committee wanted to know about Mario Procaccino's term of service on the authority. What, for instance, was he paid? The answer was that the former Comptroller of the City of New York received all of $100 per diem when meetings were held. He would have to seek his fortune elsewhere. They also wanted to look at every document in our files. Having kept careful and complete records, we had them to show, right down to who ordered which sandwiches on our annual employee boat ride.

Just before Lehner's hearings began, I wrote to Governor Carey, complaining about the stacked deck. I referred to Lehner's letter to Peter Goldmark advocating an industrial park for our site as "ill-considered, ill-advised and ill-timed." Were he to get his wish, an eyesore would have been placed at the very entrance to New York City. Heavy trucks would once again clog the streets of Lower Manhattan, which was one of the main reasons for moving the Washington Street Produce Market to Hunts Point in the Bronx. Lehner's folly would also see garbage burned to generate electricity, right next to the World Trade Center.

Moreover, the whole point of an industrial park is to build on cheap land because such a facility covers a great deal of space and the use of much of the space, such as for parking lots, is not cost-efficient. Here was Lehner wanting to put his industrial park on some of Manhattan's most valuable and visible property.

Clearly, the hearings that were about to commence were no more than window dressing for conclusions that had already been reached. They could also be the final blows to our attempt to get FHA mortgage insurance for our residential units. And they might undermine our negotiations with potential commercial tenants, just when the commercial market was showing signs of coming to life.

On the day I wrote to Carey, Lehner held a press conference laying out his plan of attack. He cited State Housing Commissioner

Heimann's comment on our inability to market apartments at rents sufficient to cover our costs. Heimann's internal report, to which Lehner referred, had been initiated at Carey's request and was almost a year old at this point. It had never been made public. Why was Lehner bringing this hash to the table now? He weakly replied to a reporter who asked that "it's unfortunate the report was never released." But the real reason was that the figures didn't stand up then and had even less validity now.

Lehner also held up for criticism the agreement that would have the city temporarily laying out some of the costs of the infrastructure we were going to build. He ignored our offer to forego such assistance until the city could afford it.

Fortunately for the future of Battery Park City, the Lehner Committee hearings turned out to be a fiasco. I almost felt sorry for Lehner because surely he never knew what hit him. Labor leaders Peter Brennan and Harry Van Arsdale testified, as promised, on March 23. But, unbeknownst to me, they also brought along some "friends": about two hundred burly boisterous determined out-of-work construction workers. Wearing their hard hats and wielding picket signs, they burst into the hearing room at Two World Trade Center, letting Lehner know in no uncertain terms that he was threatening their livelihood and the jobs of thousands of their fellow workers. A confrontation with union members was about the last thing that any elected New York City Democrat wanted.

The hard hats were a consistently demonstrative presence in the audience. So demonstrative were they that speakers who tried to undermine our efforts had enough trouble being heard at all and could not make their points against Battery Park City. It may not have been quite according to Hoyle, but Lehner wasn't dealing off the top of the deck himself.

When it was my turn to speak, I went after Lehner's rationale for these hearings pointing out the obvious. Lehner was the chairperson of the Housing Committee, but he was undercutting the only large-scale middle-class housing development in the works now through his schemes to foist an industrial park on Lower Manhattan. He was throwing outdated figures at us from Heimann's internal report, trying to disprove our contention that Battery Park City apartments were marketable. We had, after all, three thousand actual applications in hand for those units.

Dr. Frank Kristoff, who followed me, supported my testimony. This was the respected state housing expert who, it will be recalled, once challenged us on the marketability issue but had been persuaded by the facts to reverse his position. And to top it off, a representative of the FHA assured the public that the granting of mortgage insurance to us would under no circumstances reduce the potential resources available for low-income housing in other parts of the city, a red herring that Lehner had clearly been counting on to build opposition to Battery Park City.

Lehner may have anticipated his hour in the sun—he had invited his mother to attend and watch him in action—but what he got was a cloudburst directly over his head. The next day the *Daily News* pictured him dejectedly holding his head in his hand. The caption explained, "Mr. Lehner was continuously heckled by construction workers for expressing reservations about the project."

The second hearing was pushed back to May 17. But by then the political climate had changed in our favor, and that hearing was mostly a formality. The starch had been removed from Assemblyman Lehner's sails, and his ship was dead in the water. He would no longer threaten the building of Battery Park City.

Showdown

Despite the bureaucratic morass at HUD, we were confident we could extract a decision on the mortgage insurance in our favor if we could bring the mayor and governor on board. Their support would push us over the top.

The mayor, Ed Koch, had not displayed the overt hostility that had been directed at us by Hugh Carey's stand-ins, nor the personal antipathy the governor clearly had for Battery Park City, but he would still be a problem. Koch had not had the time to immerse himself in the issues related to our project and thus depended on others in his administration to advise him. Chief among them was Robert Wagner Jr., the new chairman of the City Planning Commission, son of a former mayor and a close friend of Andrew Stein, who was about to roll a boulder into our path.

On February 28, Wagner wrote a memo to Mayor Koch that was extremely critical of Battery Park City. The occasion was our application to the Board of Estimate to execute the street mapping that we needed before putting in the roads to provide access to our first residential units. Koch had asked Wagner to bring him up to date on where things stood.

Wagner was not as conversant with our status as he should have been. He, too, relied on Arthur Levitt's 1976 audit and the comments made by several political figures about our marketability "problem." In his memo, the new city planning commissioner cited the now familiar travails of Independence Plaza to our north and the similar inability to rent apartments experienced by the city-administered Mitchell-Lama Manhattan Plaza development in the West 40s in Midtown. Wagner was also worried about the city's commitment to help finance our infrastructure, despite our reassurances that we would not ask for money while the financial crisis persisted. Still another of his concerns was the possibility that a financial crunch might push us into requesting Section 8 funds under the federal housing act that would best be spent on housing in lower-income areas in the city. To top it off, Wagner suggested to Koch that the city should not support our application for FHA insurance until the results of the Lehner hearings were in.

If Ed Koch wanted an excuse to let us founder, there it was. Sure enough, the day he received the memo, he wrote to David Rockefeller, one of our prominent supporters, enclosing a copy of Wagner's warning. "I believe the recommendations which he makes are sound, and it is my intention to accept and implement them," he declared.

This was, as Laurel and Hardy would have put it, "a fine kettle of fish." I wrote to David Rockefeller that Wagner's recommendations to Koch were "indefensible to anyone possessing knowledge of the project." The issues Wagner raised had been "discredited previously."

On the morning of March 8, I met with Bobby Wagner and members of the staff of the Downtown Lower Manhattan Association in my office. I reiterated our willingness to postpone the city's payments toward the project's infrastructure until the fiscal crisis had passed and reassured the city planning commissioner that under no circumstances would we try to tap Section 8 funds. Impressed with what he heard, Wagner agreed to reassess the marketability issue.

The next day, David Rockefeller wrote to Mayor Koch, questioning the factual basis of Wagner's memo, and expressing the "dismay" of the members of the influential DLMA over the lack of support we were getting from city hall. Rockefeller told the mayor that the memo raised questions "as to why it is so easy to stop progress in the City and so hard to get anything done."

In a crucial turn of the tide, we now benefited from what appears to have been a split among Koch's advisors as to how to proceed on Battery Park City. On March 13, Deputy Mayor Robert Milano, a good friend of Assembly Speaker Perry Duryea who supported Battery Park City, and whose job it was to facilitate economic development in New York City, told Koch about our negotiations with Ebasco Services to bring that large engineering firm in as a prime commercial tenant. He also systematically criticized Wagner's memo, point by point. Milano cautioned the fledgling mayor that failing to support Battery Park City would send the wrong message about New York City, demonstrating an "inability to grow" and, not incidentally, would display "indecisiveness and timidity" on the part of the new administration.

Milano pushed all the right buttons with Koch, and it was soon apparent that the newly-elected mayor would not be a lost cause after all. But we still had a harder nut to crack. Hugh Carey would simply not listen to reason, continuing to hem and haw about supporting us on the FHA application while at the same time undermining us. Finally, it became evident that to crack this nut, we would need a nutcracker. Fortunately, I had one at my disposal.

Should everything fail and the project come to a grinding and sickening halt, the Carey administration would not be left unscarred. Our moral obligation bonds, the interest from and principal of which had to be repaid, was a kind of doomsday machine we could stick in the governor's face. Should we default on those bonds—our next interest payment would fall due in May—New York State was morally obligated to make up the shortfall. That would be a disaster for the Carey governorship. Was he ready to walk to the edge of the cliff, and possibly over it? We would see.

In a March 22 letter to the new state housing commissioner, Victor Marrero, I set the stage for the ultimate push with Carey. I knew that the only grounds the governor might be able to give for withholding his support at this point was the marketability question. But Marrero and his boss would have Henry Nussbaum's detailed memo, which I enclosed with my letter, offering the views of all the experts who had undercut this argument, including the most recent survey by our real estate consultant, James Felt & Company.

On April 10 I messengered to the governor's counsel, Judah Gribetz, with whom I had served on the aircraft carrier USS *Bennington*, a letter informing him that the mayor had shifted his position and was now actively supporting us, and that we needed to bring Carey aboard as well.

I laid out our case to Gribetz in stark terms. In the two years he had been in office, the governor had sidestepped our request for support, but now the dance was over. An interest payment of $6,200,000 on our Series A bonds was due on May 1. Our bond resolution stated that I had to certify that the payment was "proper." Housing was the linchpin of the whole development now and I didn't feel I could make that certification without at least a conditional OK from HUD on that FHA insurance, allowing us to go ahead with the building of Pod III. Without that insurance, the interest payment would not be a "proper charge" against the Construction Fund, into which we had deposited the proceeds of the bond sale, and we would therefore have to dip into the Debt Service Reserve Fund. In keeping with the moral obligation to repay our debt, the state would be obligated to replace any money withdrawn from that Reserve Fund. Since the Reserve Fund had to contain an amount equivalent to the interest and bond retirement payments due that year, any drawdown from that fund would automatically trigger the moral obligation make-up clause. So, Carey could either give us his unqualified support, or sign off on the unanticipated appropriation of millions of dollars of the taxpayers' money. He could put up, or pay off.

Gribetz immediately assured us that we would have the governor's support. He pleaded with me to literally take back the letter and he agreed to my demand that the governor publicly endorse the project. Two days later, Carey addressed the New York City Chamber of Commerce of Industry. In the middle of lauding his own administration for getting New York City moving again, he said, "We have held discussions with Mayor Koch on Battery Park City. An application has been filed with HUD and we hope to be able to announce a detailed plan to go forward with this important project. When you can't borrow, you can't build. Battery Park City emphasizes the special urgency of the city's needs." Carey no doubt finally realized that the project he had helped to stymie might now prove useful to him, especially with unemployment in the construction trades still running high.

But that wasn't enough. Alexander Naclerio, the local HUD director with whom we dealt, had told us that he was understaffed and could not give us the priority we had asked for and deserved. What would break the bureaucratic deadlock and get the ball rolling? Only a *letter* of strong support from the governor of New York. Well, Carey had clearly mouthed some positive words, but where was the letter? Maybe the dance wasn't over.

I ratcheted up the pressure. I had Avrum Hyman draft a press release announcing that we would draw our payment for the May interest on our bonds from our Debt Service Reserve Fund instead of the Project Construction Fund. "The significance of this action is that the State would become liable for replacement of the $6,200,000 [in the Debt Service Reserve Fund] and perhaps for the entire obligation of $200 million," I explained in the release. With Carey's lack of support for the FHA insurance endangering the entire project, I had to protect our bondholders. Lacking Carey's letter of support, I was prepared to issue the release, forcing Carey's hand.

On April 17, I applied the final squeeze. I called Judah Gribetz and left a message in which I explained the situation and let him know about the press release. I concluded, "I can't make the interest payment under these circumstances." I also wrote to Victor Marrero, state commissioner of housing and community renewal, reminding him that HUD had yet to receive that letter from Governor Carey.

On the eighteenth, we secured the mayor's formal cooperation. We had amended the municipal facilities agreement to guarantee that the city would have no liability for infrastructure at Battery Park City until after the municipal finance crisis had passed, and had given Mayor Koch an unambiguous pledge not to seek Section 8 funds for our project.

At 11:15 a.m. on April 19, I was preparing to hold a press conference in conjunction with the Associated Builders and Owners of Greater New York at our headquarters to hold Carey's feet to the flames. As in an old movie cliffhanger, Victor Marrero, finally realizing that I wasn't bluffing about a "default" on our Battery Park City bonds, appeared at the last minute with a telegram from the governor expressing his full support for our FHA application, and stating he would communicate that support *directly* to HUD

Secretary Patricia Harris. At 12:50 p.m., the governor himself called to express interest in what I would have to say at the press conference. I told him I was going to thank him and Mayor Koch. Exactly what would I thank him for, he asked (and well he should!). Why, his "support" for Battery Park City, I replied. How I kept from choking on that word I will never know.

Struggling with HUD, Right down to the Final Form in Triplicate

Now the ball was back in HUD's court. They had viewed, reviewed, and re-reviewed our application, and then had done the same after we reapplied. It had been like a horror movie in which the bureaucratic monster would not die, and now we were living through sequel VI. The governor and the mayor had endorsed our project and there was simply nothing more we could do to secure at least conditional approval of the FHA insurance. At that April 19 press conference, I said as much, challenging HUD to sign on the dotted line.

They had been dragging their feet since the beginning of the year. On February 25, the *New York Times* had reported that HUD was saying, "it will be a while longer" before we got an answer. On March 13, HUD Assistant Secretary Lawrence B. Simons had written to me, complaining about how the transition from one administration to another had slowed operations. The bottom line was that this was holding up our application.

The stakes had been raised in March when William Halsey told me that at least two major corporations had let it be known that they would be very favorably predisposed to sign leases at Battery Park City if we could finally get construction going on the Pod III housing. We had to take advantage of the momentum generated by our political success in Albany and city hall.

On April 20, the day after my press conference, I wrote a memo to Tom Galvin, directing him to "push HUD . . . as hard as you can with everything you've got. This includes everyone on the staff, political, labor and civic groups."

But two days later, the *Times*, in an article headlined "U.S. Doubts Intensify About Battery Park City," reported that HUD was now holding up the insurance, fearing that Westway, now planned to be built east of Battery Park City in the existing West Street right-of-way, would reduce access to Battery Park City during the road's construction, making it harder to rent apartments. The paper was citing the views of HUD Regional Administrator Thomas Appleby. Koch had dropped his opposition to the new roadway the previous day. So now Westway was being used against us, even though that project's executive director, Lowell Bridwell, had confirmed that access to our project would be maintained.

I couldn't let myself be sidetracked by the objection du jour. On May 8, I wrote to Margaret Myerson, HUD's acting area director, imploring her to *act*. I stressed the urgency of securing the mortgage insurance to back our planned sale of nonmoral obligation housing bonds before interest rates rose.

That same day, fate struck us a cruel blow. Alfred Mills suffered a fatal heart attack. He had served with me on the authority for a decade and had matched my dedication to getting the job done. As I wrote to his widow, "He was the dearest, most even-tempered gentleman I've ever had the privilege of knowing." We were so close to our goal, but he did not live to see the final fruit of his labor.

Time had taken a friend and colleague, and it would bring down the curtain on our project if things didn't break our way soon. In one of life's sad ironies, we reached that goal just four days after Alfred's death. On May 12, almost a month after Carey finally dropped his passive resistance to Battery Park City, the day arrived that some on our staff had doubted they would ever see. HUD conditionally approved us for FHA mortgage insurance for Pod III. "We're very thrilled," I told a reporter from *Newsday*. Boy, were we, and after a more than three-year struggle, a little weary!

I reordered the steel from the Bethlehem Steel Corporation that we needed for Pod III's infrastructure. I also placed ads for bids for the construction of that infrastructure. Ever the optimist, I suggested that we might be able to start building the roads and utility systems on July 1. Meanwhile, on the fifteenth, in yet another media vote of "no confidence," a *New York Post* editorial "Wrong place, wrong time?" suggested that federal money would be better spent on upgrading deteriorating housing and neighborhoods. They just didn't get it. They would never get it. FHA insurance did not mean yet another federal expenditure.

Wrangling with the City

Our celebration was brief. As I wrote to my staff after a weekend to absorb our success in this long-fought battle, "Before the first tenant can move in we will have to obtain various approvals from the City, we will have to sell eighty million dollars in housing bonds, we will have to strike a deal with the developers, and we will have to get work started on the roads and utilities."

In hindsight, "obtaining various approvals from the City" sounds way too perfunctory, as if it were a matter of filling out a few forms and perhaps making a few phone calls. Various politicians and bureaucrats in America's greatest metropolis would make sure that we would continue to live "in interesting times."

The city's Office of Management and the Budget and the New York State Emergency Financial Control Board, even at this late date, had still not approved any expenditure for our Pod III housing units related to road and utility construction. This was one logjam we absolutely had to break because the steel we had reordered from Bethlehem had begun arriving at our site on June 12. On July 6, I reminded Donald Kummerfeld, the Financial Control Board's executive director, that we had another interest payment due November 1, and once again, I threatened default.

On July 17, I wrote to Mayor Koch, asking him to intercede with the OMB. We had announced Lizza Industries' low bid on the construction of the Pod III roads and utilities on June 13, and had forwarded the contract to OMB on the twenty-third. But they had refused to revise our financial plan, thus preventing us from building on our own land with our own money.

Koch himself might still be a loose cannon. We heard that he was worried about the amount of tax abatement for the commercial parts of Battery Park City and the length of the period during which the FHA mortgage insurance would cover the Pod III housing. The mayor feared that the city could not make accurate fiscal projections without this information, and according to him, the city lacked the data. In fact, we had long since given it to the appropriate people.

For a while, things really got complicated—and bizarre. There was actually a period in which the following was in effect: OMB would not approve our financial plan until we secured from the Board of Estimate their approval of the streets we were going to build on our site as infrastructure for the Pod III housing. Our request for this street mapping had been before the board since December. Why hadn't the board authorized the mapping of these streets? Why, they said their approval was contingent on the city's OMB approving our financial plan. The Emergency Financial Control Board, on the other hand, was holding back *its* approval until *both* the OMB *and* the Board of Estimate had assented. This was not so much urban planning as a previously undiscovered chapter from *Alice in Wonderland*. All we lacked was the Mad Hatter.

By mid-August, this deadlock was almost as tight as a hangman's noose. We didn't have forever to clear up these loose ends. Our FHA insurance approval was *conditional*. We originally had until August 11 to fulfill those conditions, one of which was to get the Board of Estimate's approval for that street mapping, but I had been able to secure a sixty-day extension.

An August 21 article in *Business Week* served to roil the waters a bit more. It recounted our history, quoted me on the numerous political roadblocks we had been forced to go around, and once again referred to the anonymous officials who doubted our viability.

It may have been a blessing in disguise that a labor dispute had shut down New York City's newspapers, sparing us more journalistic doom and gloom about Battery Park City's prospects.

But despite the naysayers, we were edging toward the goal line. We finally got the Board of Estimate to put our street mapping on their calendar, along with our rewritten municipal facilities agreement with the city. A member of our staff, attorney Frederick Hyde Farmer, met with Lloyd Deutsch of the city's Corporate Council Office to hammer out the details of the street-mapping agreement. Farmer met unexpected resistance as the city tried to use its leverage—withholding the street mapping—until we agreed to details they wanted in the next amendment of our master lease. On August 15, just when it looked like we were making progress on this issue, City Planning Commissioner Robert Wagner called to say all deals were off until the city got its way with the wording of the amended lease. Again, I had to threaten default to keep us from being nitpicked to death.

By September, we had 2,400 tons of steel piling on our site. But it would stay there unused until we at least cleared our street-mapping hurdle at the Board of Estimate. Meanwhile, unbeknownst to me, although we had yet to get the streets mapped, the phantom streets were already being named. The Manhattan borough president's office had forwarded these names to us. As a sop to Battery Park City, there would be an Alfred Mills Place. But as I later discovered, there was also to be a street named for a labor friend of Carey's, and another named for the governor's late wife. For some reason I could not determine, this document never crossed my desk and I was presented with a fait accompli.

On September 12, First Boston informed us they were "optimistic" they could market $80 million of our nonmoral obligation housing bonds at 6.75 to 6.875 percent. Next up, on September 14, was the crucial Board of Estimate hearing on street mapping for Battery Park City. I testified at the hearing, answering questions at what I thought would be a perfunctory session leading to quick approval. I had not counted on being put through the meat grinder by City Council President Carol Bellamy.

I didn't—and don't—know what provoked her ire. I was discussing our moral obligation bonds and pointing out that they involved the only commitment on the part of city or state to Battery Park City, when she interrupted me. Bellamy, who had previously represented one of Brooklyn's upscale brownstone neighborhoods in Albany, rebuked me. She said, heatedly, "to talk about moral obligation bonds as though they have no impact at all on the state when we can see what happened in the state—I was a state legislator at the time. Let us not get carried away with a statement of that kind."

Refusing to be baited, I simply reminded her that the state's obligation was quite limited. That really got her goat. "Well," she snidely retorted, "maybe we'll have Comptroller Levitt in to comment on the moral obligation." Then she got to her real agenda, making it clear that she had serious doubts to begin with about whether we should proceed with our project at all.

Becoming increasingly belligerent, Bellamy pushed me to completely waive the city's obligations under the municipal facilities agreement, even after the financial crisis had passed. I said that wouldn't be fair to our bondholders. Anyway, the mapping we were requesting applied only to the roads we were about to build and for them, the city had no liability. We would have to return to the Board of Estimate in the future for approval of any other infrastructure expenditures, thus providing the board with control over our spending and, by extension, the city's liability to reimburse us for any of it. But she wasn't—and couldn't be—convinced.

Then she tried to browbeat me on the issue of tax abatement. We were getting the standard Mitchell-Lama rate of 10 percent of the shelter rent, that is, the rent minus utilities, another condition for securing our FHA insurance, and that annoyed her. She felt the FHA was dictating the tax abatement rate to the city.

Finally, we got down to the nature of Battery Park City and whether it was a good deal for all concerned. I put it to her: Would she rather the city have retained the rotting piers we had replaced? Or should the city be "willing to bring in a billion and a half dollars [from developers], produce housing for 16,000 people, produce jobs for 30,000 construction workers . . .," but she appeared not to be listening.

She wanted to pose *her* question to *me*, and became yet more irritated when I refused to opt for either of the choices *she* offered: which would hurt the city more, a Battery Park City default or New York City failing to balance its budget in the next four years, preventing it from returning to the bond market? (At least I had offered her one positive option with my question!) Her assumptions were skewed. Continuing with Battery Park City was not going to place New York City in any kind of danger, and she ought to have known that.

Robert Wagner Jr. followed my testimony. Finally satisfied on all issues relating to our project, he supported Battery Park City and the points I had made. In casting a "no" vote on our mapping request, Bellamy characterized us as "Fire Island West." But she could denounce us all she wanted to now: the street-mapping measure passed, 9-2 (as council president, Bellamy had two votes). The municipal facilities agreement sailed through, as well.

Despite the Board of Estimate's approval, we still couldn't start to build those roads. The board's vote should have been a "go" signal to the Emergency Financial Control Board, but they wanted more information about our finances and the Lizza construction contract. Yet, they had all the information they needed about Lizza since we had determined on June 13 that theirs was the low bid. And the OMB, which was represented on the Emergency Financial Control Board, had been sitting on our 1979 financial plan since April 28.

Without the Emergency Financial Control Board's approval, we couldn't go to market with that $80 million bond issue. And our contract for work on the roads and utilities we were putting in would expire on October 11, after which the cost would almost certainly increase. We were scheduled to go before the Emergency Control Board on September 18 to make our case, but because of the request for more information, that was delayed.

On September 21, I sent Deputy Mayor for Finance Philip L. Toia, a member of the board, a ten-page, single-spaced review of our finances containing everything they could possibly want to know about our project from a fiscal angle. On September 28, at long last, they approved our financial plan and our contract to build the roads and utilities for Pod III. By early October, Lizza Industries would be busy building roads on our site. Compared to the bluster of the politicians, the sound of Lizza's construction equipment would be music to our ears. I'd rather hear building than braying, any day.

From Pad to Pod

The Pod III housing was our first priority, now that we had earned a respite from the political wars. But there were other distractions.

Our strategic location and the landfill we had painstakingly constructed made us attractive to those with other priorities. For example, as far back as 1974, the Port Authority had operated a temporary helicopter service from Battery Park City. In March, the Port Authority let us know that they wanted to build a more permanent heliport for New York Airways on our site near pier A, and the city urged us to accommodate them. By May, they were operating expanded service from New York City's airports, which are owned and operated by the Port Authority, to our landfill. Always on the lookout to promote our project, Avrum Hyman, our director of public information, told one of New York Airway's officials that I had recently used the service myself, flying from JFK right to the doorstep of the World Trade Center and Manhattan's financial district. But I had noticed upon alighting from the craft that no sign informed travelers that they were setting foot on the future home of Battery Park City. This sandy space was a place of some significance, and visitors to the area ought to know it.

But the whirlybirds would very soon have to find another roost. By mid-May we informed the Port Authority that New York Airways had to terminate operations at the site on June 5. We needed to prepare for the construction that we hoped and anticipated would soon occupy our site.

For a while, our attention shifted from the sky above to the earth below. In July, Governor Carey signed a community gardening act that might have required us to permit a garden on any vacant piece of our property. We had just evicted the helicopters, and now, we thought, we might have to be concerned about tripping over carrots and celery as we prepared the way for the largest urban development in America. But that "danger" soon passed.

It was almost beyond belief that the helicopters we thought we had banished in June flew back into the picture in December. The City Planning Commission, backed by the Board of Estimate, granted New York Airways another two years to use Battery Park City as a heliport. And we were about to build apartment houses, with cranes reaching skyward, just downwind from where thirty-passenger aircraft would land and take off! Didn't anybody in government know which end was up?

A Done Deal

Meanwhile, we were still working furiously to line up our subleasees. The terrible real estate market, both commercial and residential, was finally loosening just as we were discarding the bureaucratic shackles that had held us back from exploiting what developmental opportunities there might have been.

By June, we had become less optimistic about luring Ebasco to Battery Park City. That engineering firm, despite the attractive ground rent and tax equivalency payments we had offered, appeared to be leaning toward renting space at the World Trade Center or moving to New Jersey. But we were still in hot pursuit of the American Stock Exchange, and hoped to put together an enticing package for them.

Again, I was summoning all my real estate creativity to fill our buildings with quality tenants. Reinsurance was a big issue then in the state legislature, so I suggested to Albany that Battery Park City would be the right place for a New York State Reinsurance Exchange. But nothing came of it.

We were already negotiating with the Knickerbocker Cove Company, among others, to develop our marina. But when it came to securing sublessees, the developers of Pod III were at the top of our "to do" list. And strange as it seems, in view of all that had transpired over the past half-decade, there was Sam LeFrak, still in position to build the 1,642 middle-income Mitchell-Lama residential units that we had fought so hard to make possible.

Sam had not exactly been in suspended animation in 1978 while we fought for the right to build. A May 29 *Forbes* article reported that the mogul of middle-class housing, still lacking the Battery Park City apartment construction he had hoped would provide a tax shelter for his cash flow from other real estate investments, had branched out into the oil and gas, and even the music recording, business.

By summer, when LeFrak turned his attention again to developing in Downtown Manhattan, it was with a new partner. The Lefrak/Fisher joint venture had to be realigned, as the Fisher brothers as an entity, dropped out, leaving Lester Fisher to continue with Lefrak and opening the way for participation by Robert Olnick, who had been chairman of Starrett Brothers and Eken, a major construction company which in another era had built the Empire State Building and, more recently, Starrett City in Brooklyn.

Negotiations proceeded apace with Lefrak/Fisher/Olnick. On the last day of July, we signed a letter of intent, anticipating a full sublease agreement. The Board of Estimate business over street mapping and tax abatement delayed that document, but by

September, we were back on track. On the twenty-fifth, Bob Olnick informed us that their joint venture had the necessary equity lined up to proceed with building.

Sam LeFrak, of course, could not resist indulging in some of his typical shenanigans, and I wouldn't want to give the impression that everything was completely smooth on this front. The joint venture was also interested in possibly developing some of our commercial space, which was fine with us. But LeFrak jumped the gun, approaching the American Stock Exchange with the misleading impression that I had already authorized him to negotiate with them as our agent on a lease for space at Battery Park City. Typical Sam! He used the same ploy with the Irving Trust Company and Chemical Bank. In fact, another developer had already been in touch with us about Irving Trust. I finally had to rein in the overanxious Mr. LeFrak, as I had in the past, instructing him to wait until we had signed a letter of understanding. And under no circumstances would we actually make him and his partners our agents or brokers on this matter. We were not going to tie our hands when interest in Battery Park City was finally picking up.

Fortunately, this was a mild diversion from our main task, which was to sign up the developers of Pod III and have them begin to build. We were able to get down to serious and fruitful final negotiations with Lefrak/Fisher/Olnick, now operating under the name, Marina Towers. By the end of December, they were set to apply for that FHA insurance that we had almost had to bleed to line up for them. On December 28, all concerned met at our offices at Battery Park City and reviewed the final lease documents for three hours. At 6:00 p.m. we signed the lease. At long last, the deal was done.

Finally, there would be I-beams, concrete, and the beginnings of a skyline in our immediate future. Hard by the Hudson, the sun would shine on structures, not just sand and some tantalizing foundations. But unfortunately, before those buildings could rise to cast their shadows in Battery Park City, something else would darken the scene.

The barge *Ezra Sensibar* pumps sand into the northern end of our property. "Land" appears at the lower right.

Trucks line up to deliver steel for the foundations of Pod III housing.

Caissons (the corrugated iron casings on the right) and the concrete piles on the left form the base of Battery Park City's soon-to-be-famous esplanade.

December 28, 1978: a beginning and an end. Samuel J. LeFrak to my right and Lester Fisher on my left join me in signing the lease for the first residential building at Battery Park City.

Chapter 13

ENDGAME

In its August 21, 1978, article raising questions about Battery Park City's future, *Business Week* had concluded, "Whatever happens, Urstadt may not be around to take part. His term as chairman expires at the end of December, and he claims to have no idea whether he will be reappointed."

And I didn't. For years, the project had struggled to stay alive, but my tenure had been secure. Now, it seemed, the situation had reversed. After a decade of struggle, culminating with the attainment of that FHA mortgage guarantee and the contract with Marina Towers, my future at Battery Park City figured to be limited because I was a Republican appointee living on a short lease from a Democratic governor.

But I hoped to be able to see the project through to at least its early stages of construction. They say, "You should never fall in love with an investment." But I had invested more than twelve years of my life in Battery Park City. We were so close to seeing buildings rise from our decade of bulldoglike tenacity and dodging one bullet after another. Leaving now would be like turning your own child over to foster parents.

In the fall of 1978, Hugh Carey was reelected to a second term, defeating Perry Duryea and thus ensuring that a Republican governor would not be in a position to keep me at the head of Battery Park City. But while there was no chance that Carey would reappoint me for a full term, I was hoping to be kept on for a brief time to provide continuity for the complex undertaking and to get my team relocated in other jobs. In fact, the governor had told

Howard Clark, head of the Downtown Lower Manhattan Association, that he wanted me to stay on for a transition period. The project was enormous and complicated, I had in place an experienced staff that I had assembled over the course of a decade, and we knew what we were doing. Carey had every reason to aim for a smooth transition.

But if I had learned anything thus far, it was not to assume that reason would prevail when politics was in the saddle.

On December 30, the day before my second six-year term was to expire, having still heard nothing, I sent a Mailgram to the governor's secretary, Robert Morgado, in which I officially offered to serve, unpaid, through April 15. That would allow me to protect my staff till they could at least line up other positions.

With no reply from Morgado by 6 p.m. on New Year's Eve, six hours before my term was to expire, I released the text of that Mailgram to the press. I also took the opportunity to "set the record straight," refuting our critics and summing up what we had accomplished to date. Not only was I not "presiding over an undeveloped pile of sand," I think that the snapshot I presented of where we were then still looks impressive, especially in view of what we had to overcome to get there.

Despite all the media reports to the contrary, we were still in good financial shape, with upward of $95 million in cash on hand and ninety-three acres of land, roads, and utilities in place. We had just received a $500,000 first payment from Marina Towers, which was about to begin building Gateway Plaza, Battery Park City's first residential units. We had 4,000 applications, with deposits, for those 1,642 apartments, the foundations for which we had already constructed ourselves, making the construction sites ready to go. Twelve other developers had declared their interest in building Battery Park City's other apartment buildings. And now that we had finally secured the FHA insurance, we were preparing the $80 million bond sale it was meant to support.

Even luck had finally turned in our direction. The office market, a financial wasteland for so many years, the collapse of which was the prime reason for delaying the project, had recently come alive.

Where once even the name Harry Helmsley could not fill commercial space at Battery Park City, we were now in active negotiations with four office building developers and three firms that wanted to put up our shopping center. Major institutions were seriously considering a move to our site.

In my press release, I announced that the next meeting of the members of the authority would take place on Thursday, January 4. We had important business to conduct, which included ratifying the agreement with Marina Towers.

How could I do that with my term set to expire four days before that meeting? The law was on my side, or so it seemed at the time. While the state legislature was on its holiday break, the governor could appoint an interim member of the authority to fill a vacancy—and there was an opening as the result of Alfred Mills's death in May—but could not replace a holdover member. The rules of the authority, adopted in 1973, stated that its members "shall continue in office until their successors have been appointed *and* qualified." [Emphasis added.] I was a holdover and the New York State Senate would have to examine and "qualify" anyone appointed to take my place.

This rule had its basis in state legislation, not in our own ideas about how succession should be handled. Section 39 of New York's State Public Officers Law stated that the governor could make an interim appointment only "in cases of actual vacancies arising from events occurring before the expiration of the term of office."

Carey Makes His Move

On January 2, while the state legislature was on its holiday break, Governor Carey made his move. He informed Comptroller Ned Regan through Robert Morgado that he was appointing Buffalo developer William D. Hassett, who had contributed to Carey's reelection campaign and was acting chairman of the Urban Development Corporation, to succeed me, and Pazel G. Jackson Jr. to fill Alfred Mills's place on the Battery Park City Authority.

The word went to Regan because he had to authorize the payment of salary checks.

Carey was making sixty-eight such appointments to various state positions, gambling that he could get them through as recess appointments. An aide to State Senate Majority Leader Warren Anderson commented on the maneuver to a reporter that "no governor in memory has attempted to make an appointment between January 1 and noon of the first Wednesday of the session." The *New York Times* would report a few days later that senate Republicans regarded my replacement in this fashion as a particularly sticky issue. Meanwhile, the comptroller, in effect siding with his fellow Republicans, was holding off on cutting any checks for these new people until the dust cleared.

Word of Carey's activities reached me through the morning newspaper on January 2. I arrived at the office at 10 a.m., immediately cancelled a previous engagement, and met with Tom Galvin, Harry Frazee, and our attorney, Sam Brooks. Frazee had tears in his eyes at the prospect of possibly being forced to bend to the will of a new administration. Our conversation continued through lunch with an augmented group of Battery Park City personnel, and I was busy with meetings and phone calls till 7 p.m. that evening.

The senate took up the gauntlet on January 3, rejecting Carey's move and threatened in retaliation to delay appropriations for projects important to the governor. Thus began one of the most tumultuous weeks in my life.

In truth, even as the senate stood up to the governor, I knew that my days at the head of this bold and innovative project were numbered. The senate's move would be at best a holding action. Like it or not, I had to immediately enter into discussions with my successor, if only indirectly, as to the conditions of my departure. I did so through Richard Lefrak, who would be handling Gateway Plaza for his father's company. Lefrak, in turn, was clearing these terms through Robert Morgado, the governor's secretary.

Meanwhile, Carey's appointees tried to assert their power. At noon on January 3, our treasurer, Harry Frazee, received a hand-delivered memo from Hassett formally declaring that he was in charge—he had been "sworn in"—and announcing a Battery Park City meeting at 6:30 p.m. that evening uptown at the headquarters of the Urban Development Corporation. Hassett informed the project's officers that the bylaws had been changed and henceforth, a chairman and a president would run Battery Park City. All Battery Park City records were to be turned over to Hassett.

I told Harry Frazee that such a meeting was "illegal" and against the authority's bylaws, and I directed our staff in writing not to turn over the material or to obey any other directive issuing from Hassett, Hennessy and Jackson, "purportedly as the three Members of the Battery Park City Authority." I also got in touch with the banks with which we dealt, informing them that I was still in charge. On the surface, at least, we were entering a crisis of legitimacy.

Simultaneously, I was beginning to negotiate to, among other things, get some job protection for my staff. Two hours after the arrival of Hassett's memo, Richard Lefrak called to tell me that Hassett and his associates had accepted an agenda for discussion that encompassed my concerns. Our employees would be protected and there would be no "bad-mouthing" of my administration. They acknowledged that I was free to take all legal steps available to me to remain a member of the authority. What's more, *entirely at their initiative*, they suggested that I might remain as a paid consultant to the project. Later, Bobby Douglass called to say that he had also been told of this agenda, and encouraged me to pursue negotiations with Hassett.

Almost immediately afterward, Hassett called and he and I had a long—and I thought, productive—discussion as I sat at our conference table, flanked by Galvin and Frazee. Hassett and I agreed to meet for breakfast at the Dorset Hotel at 8:30 the next morning.

Richard Kahan, formerly Sam LeFrak's representative at Battery Park City and now Hassett's choice for president and chief executive officer of the development, joined us at breakfast on January 4. We quickly agreed that all current employees would remain until at least January 30 and be given no less than a month's notice after that. Hassett agreed to my proposal that Avrum Hyman and the UDC jointly prepare a press release attesting to the fiscal health of the project, but Kahan objected, claiming that the state Securities Law mandated that he could not report to bondholders in advance of a closer scrutiny of our operations. They had no problem with my pursuit of the possibility of remaining temporarily on the authority as an unpaid member. That aside, Hassett and Kahan formally offered to keep me on as a consultant to the project.

After an hour of discussion, we shook hands. Hassett said that he had to present our agreement to his "board"—to this day, I have no idea to whom he was referring—but given his title of "chairman" and Kahan's position, that seemed a formality. He would get back to me by noon.

At 1:00 p.m., having heard nothing, I called Hassett. To my shock, the agreement we had carefully negotiated over breakfast had disappeared by lunchtime. His "board" (probably Robert Morgado, the governor's secretary) had rejected it. The authority members meeting I had previously scheduled was now off. With Hennessy clearly part of the new group, I could not muster a quorum. Instead, I met with my staff and reiterated my position, bringing them up to date on whatever I knew. The gist of it was that now, Battery Park City had two chairmen.

Later I called Hassett again but could get nothing more out of him than that I should call Warren Anderson and other figures in Albany if I wanted the lowdown. Mysteriously, though, I could not reach any of them. Meanwhile, I informed my staff again that they were to refrain from cooperating with Hassett and his colleagues, and continue with their work, "business as usual."

I told the *New York Times* that I would remain at 40 Rector Street and on the authority. "I'm a member till my successor is appointed and qualified," I declared defiantly, "and that means approved by the Senate." But the other side was slowly turning the screws, making deals in the legislature to undercut my political support and letting my staff know that the men who would surely be my successors would require their cooperation.

Fighting to stay on now seemed senseless. I spoke to Bobby Douglass on the phone and he strongly concurred. "Resign, you don't need this," he advised. The only question was how to leave gracefully. I called Hassett and agreed to a statement that would have me declining to contest Carey's naming of him to replace me, and I resigned.

Hassett informed the Battery Park City staff that everyone would be retained at least through the end of January, but that anyone who was less than fully cooperative would be immediately dismissed. Three days later, Tom Galvin called to tell me that he would be staying on as Kahan's assistant. He addressed a staff meeting that day "to help eliminate confusion and to boost sagging morale at Battery Park City," as he later told me officiously in a memo. Tom had already been told that if he didn't fully support the new administration he would be gone.

The governor and the senate finally resolved their dispute with a face-saving maneuver. Carey resubmitted his appointments to the senate for its approval. In mid-January, the senate confirmed Hassett's appointment and I sent him a congratulatory Mailgram, promising my full cooperation. As a sad coda to everything that had transpired since the beginning of the year, Henry Nussbaum, our housing finance expert, died that same week.

Avrum Hyman submitted his resignation as director of public information on January 30. We had been closely associated at Battery Park City for a decade, colleagues and comrades in arms in the fight to build this new "city in town," and he could not imagine serving as spokesperson for an administration whose approach and values appeared to be out of sync with ours.

Not long afterward, a reporter asked me, "What was the most important thing you learned in your twelve years at Battery Park City?" I replied sarcastically, "I learned I should have quit after eight." I could have devoted my full time and energy to Douglas Elliman and made a lot more money than I would in the next four years with only a fraction of the stress and strain. But it's not in my nature to walk away from a challenge. I like to finish what I start.

The Ugly Aftermath

In its January 15 issue, *Real Estate Week* reported that the failure of Governor Carey to reappoint me "was a shock to the industry." An editorial declared, "It is a sad commentary on New York that politics has prevented Charles J. Urstadt from concluding the project which he began twelve years ago." The paper quoted me on my regret "not to be associated with the Authority any longer because I've put my time, my life and my heart into it. I've fallen in love with 100 acres of sand and I wish it all the success."

A month later, the Lehner Committee issued its final report, *Battery Park City: A Time for Decision.* Anyone who actually read this thing might be more likely to conclude it was a time to laugh derisively at the report. Having pored over our files, they still managed to get the basic facts wrong, repeating what was rapidly becoming an "urban legend": "The fill that was used was obtained from the excavation of the World Trade Center complex." Their doubts about the viability of the housing component of the project, out of date when they first began their work, were ludicrous now that a boom was in the making.

We had signed the Marina Towers contract in December, but Lehner was still reporting that we had no residential developer. Finally, the most optimistic prospect Lehner could hold out for the landfill was that it should be placed in a land bank until some more appropriate use turned up. Had that kind of boldness typified the city's history, Manhattan would today boast no building taller than a tepee.

On April 8, *The Financial Prospects for Battery Park City Authority,* a report on a three-month investigation by then State Assemblyman Charles Schumer's Committee on Legislative Oversight and Investigations, was also issued. It was no laughing matter.

When Schumer was elected to the United States Senate in 1998, the newspaper stories about his background all touched on his reputation for single-mindedness in advancing his career. I can personally attest to that characteristic. In the course of trying to hitch his star to the perception that Battery Park City was somehow a financial albatross for the city and the state, Schumer had dredged up every misconception and misunderstanding about the project that had been passing for fact. One thing nobody on his staff thought to do was to interview me. But that didn't stop him from pontificating.

Not only were Battery Park City's prospects "bleak," his report contended, "The Authority was managed in an inefficient and wasteful fashion to the detriment of the public interest." Anyone looking for facts supporting these serious charges should have been immediately suspicious when encountering the factual sloppiness on the report's first page. Their story of Battery Park City began with Governor Rockefeller appointing an authority consisting of me, Alfred Mills, and *Mario Procaccino!* The latter, of course, didn't join us until several years into our work. Sam Pierce was the third member when we began.

Schumer contrasted the money we "wasted" on salaries with the fact that the authority's new head, William D. Hassett, was serving unsalaried. This conveniently overlooked Hassett's new salaried position with the Urban Development Corporation, which would have Battery Park City under its supervision in the new setup.

The report went on to lament that there was no construction under way, which was not true. We had put in the foundations of Gateway Plaza and were building infrastructure when the year ended. We had yet to negotiate a contract for the residential units, they reported, which was also not true. Totally pessimistic about our future prospects, Schumer seemed to be unaware of the real estate boom that was gathering speed. According to Schumer, we were headed for default in 1980, an assertion that demonstrated the inability of the assemblyman and his staff to do simple arithmetic.

Any project's prospects are always a matter of opinion, but Schumer didn't put it that way. He construed my end-of-the-year summing up of where we were and what appeared to lie ahead as "a serious misrepresentation" of our financial condition, worthy of an SEC investigation. He went on to attack us for retaining the $50 deposits from four thousand prospective tenants. He neglected to say that they were kept in interest bearing accounts and that depositors could easily cancel them, with a full refund, at any time.

Any project as big and intricate as Battery Park City must have a staff whose size is in proportion to the work to be done. Naturally, Schumer claimed that we were overstaffed and contended that we made way too much use of lawyers and consultants. But isn't it odd that John Hennessey, Governor Carey's Democratic appointee to the authority and an engineer whose concern was efficiency, never made that complaint while serving with us?

What else could Schumer use to conjure up thoughts of waste, possibly even corruption? Entertainment expenses! He found we were spending in that category an average of $2,500 a year. That's on a $1.5 billion project that would ultimately house at least ten thousand people and provide office space for tens of thousands, not to mention the fact that it first had to create out of nothing one hundred acres of some of the most expensive real estate in the world. I have already discussed where that money went and I believe that anyone with an open mind would say that, if anything, given the political opposition we had to parry to get the project under way, perhaps we should have spent more!

Schumer thought he really had us when his staff found a 1974 expenditure for tickets to *An Evening with Lady Luck*. A Broadway junket for a bloated bureaucracy? They suggested as much—again, without checking their facts. Had they inquired, they would have discovered that these were tickets to a National Council of Jewish Women dinner honoring Ed Sulzberger, then chairman of the Metropolitan Fair Rent Committee and thus a man whose influence and possible support could be critical to Battery Park City. Incidentally, the tickets were never used.

In an egregious gaffe, Schumer's staff painted us as wasteful to the point of criminality for a 1974 luncheon for ten we hosted at the Four Seasons Restaurant for $268. It never happened. And that price to feed ten people at that place, even allowing for inflation in the years since, should have raised a cautionary flag. Had they taken the care to unearth the details before making their wild charges, they would have discovered that the records represented a working meeting we had, at our headquarters, with the top officers of the most prominent banks in New York City. We were trying to line up mortgage financing for our housing units and we ate box lunches, delivered from the Brasserie, the "cheap" cafeteria of the restaurant, while we worked. Given the importance of these discussions and the people with whom we were dealing, McDonald's take-out would have been highly inappropriate.

State Comptroller Arthur Levitt had audited us and raised no complaint along these lines. Shouldn't that have been an indication to the Schumer Committee that there was nothing here to unearth? As I said, the assemblyman had a reputation for being single-minded in pursuing his career.

Schumer was right about one thing. The report stated, "The continuing role of New York City as landlord of Battery Park City should be examined to determine the extent to which City interference has been adversely affecting the project."

Hours after the release of the Schumer Report, the assemblyman appeared on the CBS local news. He was shown touring our site, remarking that "the previous owners of Battery Park City considered that they had a two-hundred-million-dollar expense account to do whatever they wanted." He was a great one for punchy sound bites.

Schumer's classical bit of demagoguery spawned an ugly headline in the *New York Post* on April 9, and now it was getting personal: "Urstadt Accused of Living It Up While Project Went Down Drain." Well, I suppose it could have been worse. They could have gone for alliteration and called it "Battery Park City Bacchanal." It would have had the same level of truth as what they did print.

In what way was I reveling in the luxurious perks of office? Well, the *Post*'s reporter breathlessly revealed, I had averaged $700 a year on mobile telephone calls. This was in the era before the cell phone, on a $1.5 billion innovative construction project the size of—and as complicated as—a small city, of which I was, in effect, the CEO. And what was the nature of the "luxury cars" from which I called? Our van and a used Mercury sedan that had already logged eighty thousand miles. But I will confess that the view of the landfill and the Hudson from my office was priceless.

Not satisfied to drag my name in the mud in their "news" story, the paper accompanied it with an editorial headlined, "Ripping Off New York," which denounced our "bloated expenses and ostentatious spending." The editorial posed the question, "Someone must have known this was going on. Who?" Who, indeed. Our books were open, and other investigative reporters had dug in them for dirt and come up with nothing. The state comptroller's audit disagreed only with our assessment of how to proceed with the project, not with our probity.

Overnight, someone at the *Post* put the breaks on this scandal mongering. On April 10, a more balanced follow-up story attributed the lack of construction until the end of 1978 to the real estate recession. It noted how much the market had changed, and with it, Battery Park City's prospects. They even finally got in touch with me for my side of the controversy—they had claimed, falsely, that they had tried to reach me before running their initial piece—and printed a story the next day headlined, "Urstadt Denies Battery Park City Ripoff." But they also restated Schumer's charges.

I was not alone in standing up to the *Post*'s baseless accusations. On April 23, the editors of *Real Estate Weekly* said they were appalled at the "terrible injustice and deep hurt that has been suffered by a public servant of ability, integrity, and devotion." What's more, they declared, Battery Park City was still viable only because of my "courage and refusal to give up." The whole attack on me was, they concluded, "shameful business."

They also printed my letter of rebuttal to the *New York Post* that the *Post* had not seen fit to run. In it, I suggested that Schumer was politically motivated. Not only had he not spoken to me, he had not even submitted the report to the other members of his committee for their approval. Other papers usually called me before going into print with a critical story on Battery Park City, but not so the *Post*. I also noted their false claim that they had tried to reach me, and pointed out that there was no byline on their story. And in the face of accusations that I was living high off the hog, wasn't it curious that I had not received a raise in five years? I was still making the same $68,575, substantially less than what I would have made had I stayed in private business full time. They hadn't mentioned that.

I countered their specific sensational accusations with the facts. One that I especially took pleasure in was replying to the *Post*'s charge that we had indulged in paying for some "fancy dinner," the true nature of which they did not report. Of course not. For one thing, they couldn't tell one end of the day from the other. It was a breakfast, given by the Association for a Better New York. And the speaker was none other than the publisher of the *New York Post*!

And those luxury vehicles in which we were tooling around Manhattan Island on our joyrides? We bought a Ford station wagon in 1973 and after about seventy thousand miles traded it in 1976 for a Dodge van. I rode in the 4-door Mercury I've already mentioned.

I pointed out that not only had State Comptroller Arthur Levitt examined our books, but so had the Assembly Committee on Corporations, the city budget director, the Emergency Financial Control Board, and the city comptroller. None had found anything irregular. "I can't imagine what benefit the destruction of my reputation can render to the City, or to anyone else," I concluded.

Schumer's response was that my rebuttal of his report was "uniformly lacking in validity," and then he simply reiterated his charges. A few years later, in the early 1980s, developer Larry Siverstein, a friend of mine and today the redeveloper of the World Trade Center, arranged for Schumer and me to have lunch with him. It was a civil, if not especially warm, occasion. The up-and-coming politician soon made it clear that he was concerned that I might bad-mouth him while he climbed the political heights. I had no such interest, but couldn't help thinking to myself that anyone who opposed him should realize that one of the most dangerous places to be in America was between this rising politician and a TV camera.

There remained one last hiccup of hindsight criticism, and this came from a Republican, State Comptroller Ned Regan. Traditionally, the comptroller takes a stance of independence from the rest of the state government, even when his own party heads it. In October 1981, Regan issued a report on Battery Park City covering both my tenure and that of my successors. Disappointingly, it reflected both the spirit and substance of the other critiques I have recounted.

Regan faulted our "planning and timing," suggesting that I had not properly "controlled and coordinated" the project. According to him, we showed "a desire to create the appearance rather than the reality of activity in developing the project and getting construction under way." He specifically criticized our lack of action after securing letters of intent (which, of course, are *not* contracts). If he meant that I had instigated the real estate recession of the 1970s that brought construction of all kinds to a virtual halt for several years, I deny the charge!

He, too, questioned some of our expenses, specifically faulting the $1,800 we spent on catering for office receptions. In fact, that expenditure would not have been excessive for one year, given the nature of our work, but it happens to have been spread over an entire decade! I leave it to the reader to decide whether this was reasonable.

Regan also criticized what he deemed to be our excessive reliance on lawyers and consultants. But given the technical complexity of the project, the legal and financial issues involved, and the massive problem of steering our way through one political minefield after another, the only alternative would have been to increase our permanent staff to unacceptable levels.

As for Regan's contention that the $121 million spent on Battery Park City for the landfill, interest on debt, infrastructure planning, and administrative expenses as of the date of his report was excessive, one can only make this response: it turns out to have probably been the biggest bargain seen in town since the Dutch paid $24 for Manhattan Island. Today, the Battery Park City land is worth at least $2 billion.

A Project Left in Process

Clearly, Battery Park City had not progressed according to plan. The new town-in-town that should have already made its mark on the skyline remained largely on the drawing boards.

How did it come to this? We began in the late 1960s with a rare combination of a bold vision and a hardheaded approach to implementing it. Yet here we were, a decade later, with one hundred acres of landfill, foundations for apartment buildings, and a partially built system of roads and utilities.

Two things had brought us to this state. One was the disastrous real estate market of the 1970s, over which nobody had control. The other stemmed from the obstruction of a few well-placed individuals whose ambition was out of control. As Alfred G. Gerosa, president of the New York Concrete Construction Institute, put it succinctly about Battery Park City in January 1978: "What caused a workable concept to be stalled right in its tracks? *Politics.*"

It began with John Lindsay's efforts to overshadow Nelson Rockefeller, and it continued through the duration of my tenure, with the governor's mansion now in Democratic hands and its occupant looking for ways to diminish Governor Rockefeller's legacy. Carey worked largely behind the scenes, allowing surrogates to do his sniping for him and "anonymous sources" in newspaper stories to bring his views to public attention. The consequence was that we might as well have been trying to push a big boulder up a hill while a strong force pushed downward on the rock from above. Under these circumstances, our major and lasting accomplishment was to get as much done as we did, and just as important, keep the project alive so that eventually it could, and indeed, was built.

Chapter 14

THE IMPORTANT THING IS, IT GOT BUILT

As Hassett and Kahan quickly discovered, criticizing and building are not the same thing. They inherited a going concern with over $100 million in cash in the till, and had the good fortune to take over just as flush times for real estate returned after the absence of a decade. But an ambitious project with the size and scope of Battery Park City required as much entrepreneurial skill and spirit as political, administrative, and planning acumen. My staff and I were tested by hard times unimaginable when we started. We kept the project alive through improvisation, imagination, and at times, sheer will power, when conventional financing and planning ran smack up against a disastrous and prolonged real estate recession and adverse politics.

Different times required a different approach. My successors, in my opinion, did their job: they got it built. But the irretrievable opportunities some of them missed along the way through errors of commission and omission and occasional lack of imagination left Battery Park City substantially less than what it might have been.

Early in 1979, there were still many in state and city government who favored folding Battery Park City. The project's continuation was by no means a foregone conclusion. On April 20, Vollmer Associates, commissioned by the Downtown Lower Manhattan Association to reexamine the project, made their report. They urged greater financial support from the state for the development and contended that the more innovative features of the project's plans, such as separate levels for cars and pedestrians, might have to be abandoned to attract a level of developer interest necessary for success. They urged that Pod III—Gateway Plaza—be undertaken as planned, but that the commercial center of Battery Park City be moved from the south end of the landfill to a position opposite the World Trade Center. The latter was a reasonable enough suggestion because of the desire of developers to be near the Twin Towers.

I did not agree that the very nature of the plans had to be altered to deal with developers' perceptions. Developer interest was rapidly growing with the improving economy. But I think they were right in also pointing to uncertainties about the building of Westway and "layers of governmental review" as factors in holding up the actual building of Battery Park City.

Richard Kahan certainly believed that Battery Park City's future lay in a different direction, and he hired the planning firm of Cooper and Ekstut to chart a new course. In October, a new vision of the project was put forth in their report, which was to be the basis for Battery Park City's new master development plan.

Their report criticized the project's "excessively rigid large-scale development format," which was the product of Wally Harrison, Philip Johnson, and the other architects, and pointed to a problem with public perception of the development's "financial stability." At least they acknowledged that the real estate recession played a role. With the beginning of the repayment of bond principal scheduled for 1980, Vollmer contended that a radical departure would be necessary to get enough of the project under way in time for income flow to match expenses.

Cooper and Ekstut proposed to throw out our whole "new-town-in-town" idea, replacing it with typical New York City street grid pattern development. They would replace the separation of pedestrians and traffic with conventional thoroughfares extending into the project from Lower Manhattan. This would also jettison the idea of limited access to a more secure Battery Park City. In other words, Cooper and Ekstut wanted the development to be just another part of Lower Manhattan.

They stressed the development of "small-scale spaces." That may have a nice sound to it, but the result was that more but smaller buildings cut down the sightlines to the river. This partially squandered the project's greatest asset: its position on the shoreline. In fact, only about a third of the windows today have harbor views. Cooper and Ekstut agreed with Vollmer about shifting the commercial center northward. They also proposed the Winter Garden and North Civic Plaza that eventually would be built.

The State Division of the Budget quickly accepted the premises of the new plan and recommended that the project proceed. They suggested that the Urban Development Corporation should acquire the city's title to the land, developers be given financial incentives, and that the state appropriate money to cover debt service for several years until a revenue stream would kick in.

On November 8, 1979, the city and state agreed to the plan. The UDC acquired the city's fee title interest to the land by condemnation, with the city given an option to reacquire it later for $1, a provision I thought unnecessary. The tight zoning district controls that had often hobbled us were dropped. Tax incentives for the first commercial developers were put in place and state funds to tide Battery Park City over for a few years were appropriated. Pier A was returned to New York City, when in fact, it should have been demolished and Battery Park City's esplanade connected to the esplanade at Battery Park, extending the scenic walkway around the tip of lower Manhattan.

On January 29, 1980, the administration of Battery Park City instituted another new policy that would guide it for years afterward. In the project's annual report for 1979, buried on page 10 under the heading of "Summary of Significant Accounting Policies," was this sentence, cleverly employing the passive voice: "The project has been developed to the point where a substantial portion is available for construction of revenue producing facilities by owner-developers." Readers might have wondered if it had been "developed to the point" by an act of God or perhaps through a lesser effort by the tooth fairy. *A decade of work and the people who had done it had become all but invisible.* It would be an attitude that to some extent prevails even to this day, as a visitor to Battery Park City's Web site would have discovered.

The Years Go By and the Buildings Go Up

The new administration found the first residential developer no easier to deal with than I did. In March 1979, they even canceled the contract with Marina Towers to build Gateway Plaza over a disagreement on a payment schedule for $8 million due the authority. Marina Towers insisted on a long repayment schedule, while the administration of Battery Park City wanted it upfront.

It would be May 1980 before everything about Gateway Plaza was straightened out. Three weeks after reaching this final agreement, the project marketed just under $100 million in housing bonds at 6 ¼ percent, backed by the FHA mortgage insurance for which we had fought so long and hard. Work on Gateway Plaza commenced in earnest, rising from the foundations that we had already put in. By 1983, the buildings, many of the construction details of which had been cheapened, would be up and occupied.

On November 13, 1980, Olympia and York was named to develop the office space at Battery Park City. Their pledge to work quickly to put up the structures helped them beat out Lefrak, Helmsley, Tishman, Milstein and several others. The opportunity to develop this space was very much coveted at the time because the office market had heated up and the World Trade Center was fully rented, removing a source of competition with which we had been forced to contend. In this entirely new environment, the developers would eventually be able to secure blue-chip tenants for their World Financial Center, including American Express, Merrill Lynch, and Dow Jones.

We had planned the office development for the project's south end mainly because construction down there would have been cheaper. The bedrock on which the buildings rest is closer to the surface of the water and the builders would not have had to cope with the presence of underground railroad tunnels, the Hudson

Tubes. The view would also have been more spectacular from there, enhancing the value of the office space. And it would have been situated at the most prominent part of Manhattan Island, at the gateway to New York City, making the buildings a landmark akin to the Sydney Opera House. Equally important, the buildings would have been closer to the subway. Nevertheless, I can understand the developer's desire to be near the World Trade Center.

Some things, though, hadn't changed. Ada Louise Huxtable, the *Times*'s arbiter of architectural taste, continued to render her opinions on Battery Park City. On May 24, 1981, she waxed ecstatic over Olympia and York's plans and the Cooper-Ekstut— inspired master plan. "This scheme replaced earlier master plans, which had ranged from daunting complexity to humdrum banality, but all of which had proved equally unbuildable." Could this have been the same writer who had opined about our original master development plan, "Is this any way to build a city? You bet it is!?" You bet she was.

In 1983, Richard Kahan met his own Waterloo at the hands of the new governor, Mario Cuomo. This governor was upfront about his intentions, letting Kahan know in October that he wanted the Battery Park City president's resignation no later than December 31. When Kahan balked, Cuomo wrote to him, "You believe that the public interest requires you to stay beyond that point. This is to tell you as clearly as I can that I do not share your judgment."

Of the people who followed me, Kahan seemed to suffer most from an inability to acknowledge the accomplishments of his predecessors. He even managed to give a talk at New York University in April 1985 in which he evaluated the work done on the project throughout the '70s without mentioning the economic climate of those years. Neither did he acknowledge what would have been the consequences if we had not stopped Westway from slicing us in half lengthwise: Battery Park City would have been just another one of those plans for renewing Downtown that never came to fruition.

More than a decade later, City Planning Commissioner

Amanda Burden, a onetime vice president for planning and design at Battery Park City, managed to will away not only the real estate recession of the 1970s, but even the actual early construction on the project. Burden had a master's degree in urban planning, but she had trouble observing what was in front of her nose. Discussing her introduction to the project in January 2002, she told the *New York Times* that "when we got there in 1983, there was nothing except sand." That's odd. Everyone else at that time was able to spot Gateway Plaza. After all, it isn't easy to overlook three thirty-four-story towers not only already built but also populated by more than 1,500 tenants. Also clearly visible in 1983 was project infrastructure, part of the esplanade and Olympia and York already building what would become the World Financial Center. That's quite a mirage on the 5 million cubic yards of sand and a mile of bulkhead, the product of twelve hard years of work.

As Avrum Hyman, away from Battery Park City for twenty-three years, but still loyal to those who had worked there, wrote, in a letter which the *New York Times* printed: "When we got there a decade earlier, there was nothing there but the waters of the Hudson River and 13 abandoned, dilapidated piers falling into those waters. You have to walk before you can run."

Meyer "Sandy" Frucher, who succeeded Kahan, was up to the requirements of his job. He even had the fairness to acknowledge that he stood on the shoulders of others while blowing his own horn. The project's annual report, published at the end of October 1984, observed that "the inventiveness and imagination of the Rockefeller years gave way to difficult, hard-headed rescue operations under Governor Carey." While such a remark does not accurately portray the "hard-headedness" that *we*, not Governor Carey, displayed in keeping Battery Park City afloat so that there was something later to be "rescued," it at least does acknowledge that the development did not rise spontaneously from the deep, like the resurfacing of some amazing Atlantis.

Frucher served until 1988, when David Emil replaced him. By the time Frucher left, the esplanade had opened and the World

Financial Center was completed, giving Battery Park City largely the appearance it has today.

What of that appearance? Early in 1989, Ellen Posner, in what struck me as a relatively even-handed and interesting piece in the *Wall Street Journal*, evaluated the development's fit into the look and feel of the rest of Manhattan. She described the consequences of the Cooper-Ekstut plan as a project "less idiosyncratic, more recognizable, and more understandable" than the one our architects had envisioned. In other words, as it was finally built, Battery Park City had added more of the same to Manhattan. (In fact, the American Institute of Architects' *Guide to New York* has dubbed Battery Park City's residential architecture, "instant past.")

Posner was referring not just to the way Battery Park City plugged into the island's street grid, but also to the look and feel of its buildings and streets. Where we had striven for boldness and a new departure in this new-town-in-town, she saw West End Avenue and Riverside Drive *redux*. Also, she noted, although the development seemed from a distance to offer something different, up close, parts of it suggested a suburban shopping mall. The promised diversity of style, on close inspection, appeared "fake."

One aspect of artificiality she did not dwell on but which still bothers me is the project's South Cove. Of the two coves that cut into Battery Park City's shoreline, there is ample justification for the one closer to the northern end. Besides offering docking facilities for the boats moored there, it serves also as a focal point for lounging in the sun, socializing after work and during the lunch hour, and dining alfresco. It's the front porch for the great public space, the Winter Garden, and the World Financial Center.

The South Cove is another story. What does the development gain from the carving out of this second, smaller inlet? Very little, especially considering that any such feature had to be created at the expense of whatever might have been built on the landfill that was lost at that highly desirable development location.

Mainly, the South Cove serves to collect refuse that the tides and prevailing westerly winds produce from the Hudson. In the summer of 2002, early on a bright Sunday morning, about sixty others and I competed in a swim along the mile and a quarter length of Battery Park City's shoreline. We began at the South Cove and we had hardly jumped in when someone yelled out, "There's a dead dog over here!"

But it could have been even worse. Phillip Johnson had pushed for six coves that would have cut seriously into the land left for us to develop. When Richard Weinstein took over from Dick Buford as our main contact with the city in the early '70s, I took him on a boat ride to give him a sense of the entirety of the project. I described to him the saw-toothed coastline—it would have made a fine crocodile's mouth—that Johnson's proposal would have bequeathed to us had I not fought it down, getting him to settle for just two coves, and at that, one too many. Weinstein listened and just shook his head at the waste of valuable land we had barely avoided. He said he would have dispensed with *all* of the coves.

In the '90s, Battery Park City would add the Museum of Jewish Heritage at the development's south end and buttress the northern boundary with the prestigious Stuyvesant High School. Recently the project dedicated a memorial, now known as the Irish Hunger Memorial, to the victims of the Irish Potato Famine, on its site, and currently on the planning boards is a museum of American women. Frankly, I believe that these institutions and memorials belong elsewhere, where there is more foot traffic and an opportunity for more visitors. And the land they occupy could have been devoted to structures more germane to Battery Park City and certainly more productive of income to help run the development. In fact, I believe that a more efficient use of Battery Park City's land and the potential one million square feet of air rights could be worth an additional one hundred million dollars to the city and state.

With the project in its fourth decade, the time has come to ask, who should control and run it? I don't think it could have been built without the cooperation of government and the private sector, and

I'm proud of the role I played in helping to facilitate this always delicate combination. But Battery Park City has long since become a going concern, so it's fair to ask, why is government still running it?

There are good arguments for privatizing the project. The first is the enormous sum—possibly as much as $2 billion—it would bring in to enhance state and city coffers just when the funds are so desperately needed. That could be achieved through increased cash flow resulting from privatizing, quicker development of the six—as of this writing—undeveloped sites on the landfill, the trimming of fat from Battery Park City's now expansive budget, and the sale of air rights.

Privatization would also serve to more greatly facilitate the building of new low- and middle-income housing and the renewal of the city's older housing stock. The reader will recall that Governor Rockefeller's vision of Battery Park City included a mix of housing by income. As a public benefit corporation, the Battery Park City Authority was created with that as one of its missions. But beginning with the real estate recession in the '70s and the need to sell market-rate apartments to make the project economically viable, Battery Park City evolved into a largely luxury-class residential area.

It's ironic that it was that very commitment to provide housing for those in the upper-, middle- and lower-income brackets that caused so much of our problems as to feasibility. Equally ironic was the jettisoning of that commitment by the very people who claim to be so concerned about it. When the *New York Times* early in 2001 featured a front page article proclaiming, "Battery Park City Is Success, Except for Pledges to the Poor," Avrum Hyman, by then twenty-two years away from Battery Park City, wrote, in a letter that the *Times* printed:

"We stereotypically tend to think of Republicans as favoring the rich and Democrats the poor. But in the 25 years since Battery Park City was, as you put it, 'a barren riverside landfill and a dream,' it has been under two Democratic governors, Hugh L. Carey and Mario M. Cuomo, and two Democratic mayors, Edward I. Koch and David N. Dinkins, that the plan to house low-income families in Battery Park City was abandoned. The original plan was developed by the Battery Park City's first chairman, Charles J. Urstadt, and Gov. Nelson A. Rockefeller, a Republican.

"So much for stereotypes."

In 1984, Sandy Frucher proposed to Governor Cuomo that the authority, the state, and New York City achieve the original goal by using surplus revenue from these market-rate units to subsidize lower-cost housing in other parts of the city. The upshot was a series of agreements in which state bond revenues backed by surplus funds generated by Battery Park City residential rents would be used to upgrade older housing in other neighborhoods. In addition, the authority would pay some of the surplus directly to the city for constructing new housing. By now, it had been anticipated, these measures would have resulted in the availability of sixty thousand units for low- and middle-income families.

It hasn't happened, and Frucher, now head of the Philadelphia Stock Exchange, was recently quoted by the *New York Times* as characterizing that failure to act as "a breach of faith." What went wrong? The Battery Park City Authority fulfilled its end by turning over the revenues—upward of $150 million this past year and about $1 billion in the last five years. But Mayors Koch, Dinkins, and Giuliani, facing the budget crunches familiar to their predecessors, managed to use technicalities in the agreements to divert the funds to general use. The result is that the city built and repaired some lower-income units, and a token 5 percent of the housing in Battery Park City currently is reserved for moderate-income families (under $28,000 yearly for a family of four). But Nelson Rockefeller's vision remains unfulfilled.

However, *if* Battery Park City remains under the control of the authority, I believe it should extend the northern boundary of the project and beyond that, the authority should be put to better use for the future prosperity of New York City. The value of an authority type of organization is that it's independent enough from any one political administration—those six-year terms help immeasurably—to be able to act in the face of political stalemate. Case in point: Governor's Island, just south of the tip of Manhattan, with its marvelous potential. Abandoned by the Coast Guard several years ago and offered to the city by the federal government, it sits unused while the politicians bicker. Place it under the Battery Park City Authority and make that valuable, strategic piece of land productive!

The building of Battery Park City should have taught us many things, and one of the most important is the efficacy of using landfill, whenever possible, in the planning and building of large projects. Obviously, this approach avoids having to displace anyone. But just as important, it is environmentally sound. The process is strictly regulated by numerous government agencies, thus guaranteeing compliance with sound environmental practice. And since the use of landfill reduces commuting, it is inherently desirable from the environmental perspective.

A Second Tour of Duty

They say "You can't go home again," but I did. At the end of 1998, Governor George Pataki appointed me to a six-year term as one of the three members of the Battery Park City Authority, which is how my name got on that construction barge tied to the project's bulkhead that I described at the beginning of my story. In fact, he had earlier offered me my old position as chairman. But at that point, I felt I had a responsibility to my family, staff, and stockholders of Urstadt Biddle Properties to devote my main energies to my business.

Yes, there are times when I wish I were still at the helm of Battery Park City. I felt that especially in recent years when politics once again rewrote history. Officially, it is now the "Hugh L. Carey Battery Park City Authority," while the man who conceived and initiated the building of the development was figuratively put out to pasture in the "Governor Nelson A. Rockefeller Park" at the project's north end. We wouldn't be pleased if an architect got it backward, and should be no more content when posterity slights a project's progenitor in this way. But I guess that's something with which Governor Rockefeller's other admirers and I will have to live.

What I don't have to abide, though, is credit misappropriated by private individuals. A few years ago, Sam LeFrak delivered a series of lectures at Columbia and Harvard in which he said his organization had "planned and implemented Battery Park City on Hudson River landfill . . . on landfill *we* created out of abandoned docks and piers that *we* recycled and developed into one of the gems of New York City." I added the emphasis, but I don't think I have to add a comment for anyone who has read this far.

No, I didn't dislike Sam LeFrak. In fact, I admired and respected him and often enjoyed his ebullient company. But he had his quirks, and he could be difficult.

It's not like the old days at Battery Park City, and it shouldn't be. I'm in a much different place in life than I was back then, and so is Battery Park City. But I'm still fighting the good fight to make this project live up to its potential. In that regard, I respectfully but strongly disagreed with my colleagues on the authority on a recent crucial vote on what should go up at the southernmost tip of the development. They opted for conventional structures, while I felt that we were missing a golden opportunity. Here, at the very entrance to New York City, at the nation's "front door," we could build something that, in the spirit of the Eiffel Tower, the Sydney Opera House, the TransAmerica Tower in San Francisco, or the arch that graces downtown St. Louis, boldly symbolized the majesty, power, and promise of a great city.

We voted on that question on September 10, 2001. The next day, just across the street from where we had been sitting, terrorists brought down the World Trade Center, leaving in New York's gateway only the Statue of Liberty, almost part of New Jersey, to mark Gotham's portal.

Today, the skywalk that linked the World Financial Center to the World Trade Center's Twin Towers is gone, destroyed by the terrorists of 9/11. Battery Park City stands alone, untethered. The attack on the twin towers, of course, left its emotional and physical mark on the city-sized project across the street. People fled for their lives, and many never came back, choosing to move elsewhere. But such was the appeal of Battery Park City that the apartment buildings refilled and the damage to the residential buildings and the World Financial Center, which has 7 million square feet of office space, 70 percent of that which was lost in the collapse of the Trade Center, was repaired, although it took a year to bring everything back. The restaurants that were closed for a year have reopened. The American Express building once again houses people administering one of the world's great financial services companies; it is no longer a temporary morgue. You can once again hail a cab on West Street and have pizza delivered to your door. We remember—who could ever forget?—but we go on.

James Gill, chairman of Battery Park City at this writing, and Timothy Carey, its president, are both able men, good friends, and I greatly admire them. We have had our minor disagreements, but I'm pleased that with their skill and dedication, Battery Park City has emerged from the trauma of 9/11 strong and vibrant. The project continues to grow and in a small way is even echoing the development's earlier, more innovative years with a "green," energy-efficient apartment building that will make use of solar-generated electric power for its public areas.

Buildings will continue to rise at Battery Park City. There are about forty thousand people working in the World Financial Center and just under ten thousand residents in the development. By the time residential construction is completed, fifteen thousand people will call Battery Park City their home.

And the project has been a rousing financial success. It has, after all, generated more than $1 billion net to the city.

The Judgment of History

People who participate in the making of history are acutely aware that they have no control over how the history of their time will be written, nor even much power to influence how current events are interpreted. Judgments since the 1970s about the course of developments at Battery Park City have run the gamut from carping to thoughtful critique. One of the first came from Jack Newfield and Paul Dubrue in their 1977 book, *The Abuse of*

Power: The Permanent Government and the Fall of New York. It was not favorable. In fact, they placed me in something of an old-fashioned real estate plutocracy. They wrote: "There can be little doubt that the David Rockefellers, the Urises and the Urstadts sincerely believe that they have done well for the people whose lives they dominate. Their problem is that the people are beginning to understand that in fact they have merely done well for themselves."

Well, it's at least flattering to be placed in such company. Fortunately, my professional life, both in public service and private enterprise, is a matter of public record. I have pointed out the relevant facts about Battery Park City in this book and have added information that only an insider could supply to flesh out the story. I will let those facts speak for me in response to Newfield, Dubrue, and others who think like them.

By 1984, even the *New York Post* was finally able to get it right. On June 4, reviewing progress on the Battery Park City project, the paper described my function as having "wet-nursed the Battery Park idea from 1966-78 through political squalls, design debates, and a years-long real estate market slump."

But the *New York Times*, when it came to Battery Park City, often continued to fall short of being "the newspaper of record." They kept writing about the problems of the project's early years as if they were happening in a vacuum. As I wearily reminded them in a letter to the editor in 1988: "Delays not due to the office and apartment glut were due to politically dictated bureaucratic foot dragging in the City Planning Commission, the Board of Estimate, the Emergency Financial Control Board, the City Council and the Federal Department of Housing and Urban Development—to mention a few." Five years later, Avrum Hyman had to write to the editor to correct their perpetual error of attributing the source of all of our landfill to the debris from construction of the World Trade Center.

Fortunately, a number of writers have offered a more informed perspective than did the *Times*. In fact, one of them was significantly associated with the *Times*. The late Roger Starr, an authority on urban affairs, who wrote on that subject as a member of the *New York Times* editorial board in the 1970s and '80s, took readers on a virtual "Stroll Through Battery Park City" in the magazine *City Journal* in 1993. Roger, who was beginning work on his own book on Battery Park City when he died in 2001, had some interesting things to say about the progress of the project after my years there. "No one can deny that the Battery Park City program benefited significantly from an immense stroke of luck. By 1979, the city was emerging from the acute phase of its fiscal crisis. At the same time, the boom of the 1980s was particularly beneficial for the financial industries," he wrote. Citing the revenues that were finally being turned over to New York City, ostensibly to be spent on social amelioration in other parts of town, Starr reminded his readers of the source of these funds. Our "filling in the 92 acres created very valuable land out of totally valueless water in a high-value neighborhood at a very low cost."

I appreciated Roger's measured appraisal of all that had happened since the late 1960s, and thanked him for it. "It reminded me that there are a lot of stories about the first 12 years of this project and, hopefully, some day I will get the time to put them on paper," I wrote to him. I finally got the time, and so I have.

Appendix A

March 22, 1967

Dear Mr. Harper:

I have been meaning to call you during the past few weeks to tell you how pleased we are that Charles Urstadt has accepted assignment as Deputy Commissioner of the State's Division of Housing and community Renewal.

He is, as you know, a brilliant young man and brings to public service the imagination and talent needed to cope with the difficult problems we face in government.

For example, one of the most serious problems in our large urban centers is the lack of job-producing industries located within reasonable distance from adequate housing. If we are to preserve the viability of our large urban centers, we must develop new methods for bringing jobs to where people live and to assist in providing decent housing within easy commuting distance of jobs. In this regard I have developed, in conjunction with private industry, a plan for a balanced community providing housing, industrial and commercial space and parks within the City of New York to be known as Battery Park City.

It is developments similar to this to which Mr. Urstadt can lend his talent and ability. We are deeply appreciative of the cooperation of your Company in making it possible for him to enter public service.

With appreciation and best wishes.

Sincerely,

Nelson A. Rockefeller

Mr. John D. Harper, President
Aluminum Company of America
1501 Alcoa Building
Pittsburgh 19, Pennsylvania

Appendix B

March 2, 1977

Governor Hugh L. Carey
Executive Chamber
Albany, New York 12224

Dear Governor Carey:

During the brief discussion which you and I had last Saturday, you made two comments with respect to Battery Park City which really require detailed answers and so I am taking the liberty of writing you in order to fully reply to your comments. You said that you felt a complete review should be made of our plans in respect to the location of buildings, roads, utilities and other facilities with an eye toward developing a new master plan. You said also that you thought it might be advisable to hold up the construction of our housing until an office building could be started, possibly one containing the American and/or the New York Stock Exchange.

With respect to the first comment, our Master Plan, which took three years and several million dollars to develop, has been adopted by the City Planning Commission as part of the Special Zoning District for Lower Manhattan. It was carefully reviewed by all parties which might be involved, especially the Office of Lower Manhattan Development, developers and the Authority and is, from all points of view, as fine a plan as can be prepared. (For your information I am attaching a copy of an article by Ada

Louise Huxtable which appeared in the New York Times which praised our exciting Master Plan.)

If we have to make changes in the Plan and start all over again the process to get such changes approved by the local Community Board, The City Planning Commission, the Mayor's Office of Development and the Board of Estimate, we would necessarily incur an extraordinary and costly delay which we can ill afford. Such a revision would include changes in a highly interdependent and very intricate network of roads, utilities, parks, esplanades, playgrounds, view corridors, light and shadow effects, height restrictions, building locations, building uses, etc. Because the Plan is incorporated into our Master Lease with the City of New York, any changes would also require us to undertake and obtain a new feasibility study for the entire project. From a practical point of view, any change which is more than minor would lead to debate and delay and probably kill the project, leaving the State with the moral obligation to pick up the entire debt service on our $200 million of outstanding bonds.

I agree with you that it is highly desirable for commercial facilities to be built and we would certainly welcome the opportunity to develop an office building for the use of either or both of the Stock Exchanges. For that purpose we have set aside ten (10) acres at the south end, which is the most desirable commercial location but there is also available any number of sites throughout our 100 acres which could be set aside for such purpose. In fact, we have already presented three different locations for the American Stock Exchange which they are now studying. I cannot agree, however that the development of housing, and particularly the housing for which we have already constructed the foundations, should be held up pending the erection of an office building. As you know, the foundations for the first 1642 units are completed at the foot of Liberty Street. This is a self-contained entity and its completion should be pursued now, without waiting for the Exchanges, or any other commercial tenant, to go through an extended period of planning and financing which, even at best, would take at least two or three years. Incidentally, we have already received close to 2,700 applications, together with $50 deposits, indicating a strong market for not only our first 1,642 units but for our second-phase housing as well. It will be a sore disappointment to these households to be told now that the State is holding up their plans for moving to better housing.

I hope the foregoing fully responds to your comments, if not, I would be glad to amplify these reasons to yourself and to Messrs. Heimann and Hennessy, who are in contact with us on a weekly, if not, daily basis.

I would also like to take this opportunity to stress our urgent desire to have your public support of this worthwhile project. It has been over thirteen months since the Emergency Financial Control Board received our application for the construction of the roads and utilities, during which time it has cost the Authority $23,000 per day in net interest and operating expenses, which, if we are not successful will ultimately be borne by the State, or if the "moral obligation" is not honored, then by the bondholders. The sooner we start, the less likelihood there is of failure. In addition, the costs of the roads and utilities alone have escalated during this time by 6, or about $220,000.

The Federal Department of Housing and Urban Development is making good progress in processing our mortgage insurance application. If they act soon we would be in a position to start the superstructure work on the first group of buildings within sixty days. This is important so that we can minimize the amount of winter work to be performed. I am sure that your support would help to expedite their decision which would result in over seventy million dollars worth of new investment in New York, about 3,000 jobs in the construction and related spin-off trades, and more importantly, an immediate visible contribution to the City which would help keep business here, as well as satisfy the need for housing. Lower Manhattan today shows signs of a weakening economic position which further or even continued delay of Battery Park City will only make worse. The most positive step which could be taken to reestablish in everyone's mind the future vitality and continuation of Lower Manhattan as a viable part of the City's tax base would be to show construction going on at Battery Park City. Fortuitously, this can be done without encumbering any State or City funds. I am convinced that if the State government would indicate a positive interest in Battery Park City, the Federal approval of Battery Park City's mortgage insurance would be swiftly forthcoming.

Thank you for spending a few moments with me and for taking time to read my expanded comments. I hope it was time well-spent for the benefit of the people of this City and this worthwhile project.

Respectfully,

Charles J. Urstadt

Appendix C

April 10, 1978

The Honorable Judah Gribetz
Counsel to Governor Hugh Carey
Executive Chamber
The Capitol
Albany, New York 12224

Dear Judah:

This will confirm my advice to you in our telephone conversation of April 6, 1978 that Mayor Koch has spoken with Secretary Harris in support of the Battery Park City Project and has asked her to issue the conditional commitment for the first housing units. The conversation with Secretary Harris and the Mayor's position has been confirmed to me with persons both in the business community and City Administration.

As a result we now have support of both Senators, our Congressman and of the Mayor. Therefore I strongly urge, as I have for the last two years, that the Governor make an affirmative plea to the Secretary of Housing so that the conditional commitment can be issued and we can proceed with further steps outlined in my memorandum to you of March 29, 1978. It is crucial that we sell our bonds and buy our construction contracts in this favorable market, otherwise, the opportunity may be lost and the project doomed.

As you know, we made our application to HUD in April of 1975 and they are aware of every facet of this project. I have been told informally on several occasions that they can issue a conditional commitment "within three days" but for some reason unknown to me, they are holding it up.

This delay grows more serious every day and at some point (which may have already passed) the delay is tantamount to denial.

As I have previously indicated to you we have an interest payment in the amount of $6,200,000 coming due on May 1, 1978 on our $200,000,000 Bond issue. Section 503 (2) (b) of our General Bond Resolution provides that in order to make this interest payment an authorized officer must sign a certificate stating that the requisition for the interest ". . . . is a proper charge upon such Project Construction Fund and constitutes a proper item of Project Cost." Both the Treasurer of the Authority and I have great concern about executing such an authorization without first having received a conditional commitment from HUD.

The crux of the matter is that with a HUD commitment the first section of housing can be built and it will follow that the other housing and office buildings can then be started and the project will succeed.

If however, HUD will not issue a commitment (or further delays the commitment which is really a denial) then, the first housing cannot be built nor will there be any subsequent housing, nor will any office developers agree to build. This must result in a failure of the entire undertaking which in turn means that we must be concerned about the erosion of the security of the bondholders.

To pay the May 1st interest from the Project Construction Fund rather than from the Debt Service Reserve Fund reduces the bondholder's security which gives rise to our concern about the payment being a "proper charge".

I intend to call a special meeting of the Members this week in order to discuss this crucial matter of the payment of interest. In the meantime I would urge that you do what you can as promptly as possible to help obtain the HUD commitment. A communication from the Governor, or from you on behalf of the Governor, to Secretary Patricia Harris or Assistant Secretary

Lawrence Simons would, I believe, produce the conditional commitment within a matter of hours and thereby avoid what might otherwise be a very difficult decision with obviously adverse results to both the Authority and the State.

Sincerely,

Charles J. Urstadt